Suppose there could be such a curious office as minister, as Professional Good Man; such a thing as learning Goodness just as one learned plumbing or dentistry. Even so, what training had he or his classmates, or his professors — whose D.D. degrees did not protect them from indigestion and bad tempers — in this trade of Professional Goodness?

Sinclair Lewis, *Elmer Gantry*

# PREACHER AND CROSS

*Person and Message*
*in Theology and Rhetoric*

ANDRÉ RESNER JR.

WILLIAM B. EERDMANS PUBLISHING COMPANY
GRAND RAPIDS, MICHIGAN / CAMBRIDGE, U.K.

© 1999 Wm. B. Eerdmans Publishing Co.
255 Jefferson Ave. S.E., Grand Rapids, Michigan 49503 /
P.O. Box 163, Cambridge CB3 9PU U.K.

Printed in the United States of America

04 03 02 01 00 99     7 6 5 4 3 2 1

**Library of Congress Cataloging-in-Publication Data**

Resner, André.
    Preacher and cross: person and message in theology and rhetoric /
André Resner, Jr.
        p.       cm.
    Includes bibliographical references.
    ISBN 0-8028-4640-8 (pbk.: alk. paper)
    1. Preaching.    2. Rhetoric.    3. Ēthos (The Greek word)    I. Title.
BV4211.2.R45    1999
251 — dc21                                      98-53604
                                                    CIP

*To Tripp and Genie*

# Contents

# Acknowledgments

I am indebted to more people than I can relate here, yet I must mention some who have encouraged this project. Several churches have lent warm and enthusiastic support: The Westwood Church of Christ in Woodbury, New Jersey, and, in Abilene, Texas, the Highland Church of Christ and the S. 11th & Willis Church of Christ.

Abilene Christian University has been more than generous in its support. First on the list in this regard is Ian A. Fair. As Dean of the College of Biblical Studies, Ian brought me to ACU and then supported my work in imaginative ways. Colleagues at ACU have read parts of this dissertation and generously provided wise counsel: Jack Reese, current Dean of the College of Biblical Studies, James Thompson, Chair of Graduate Bible, Charles Siburt, Director of the Doctor of Ministry Program, and fellow colleagues Doug Foster, Jeff Childers, and Leonard Allen. Several graduate students and Student Technology Consultants from ACU's Computer Assisted Teaching Lab have made my life easier: Johnny Miles, Jeff Scott, Brady Bryce, Reed Benedict, Paul Natale, Kim Seidman, Kris Natale, Carter Schulz, and Danny Mathews. Special thanks are due Paul and Kris Natale, who prepared the indexes. Several students have studied these matters with me in a more in-depth manner and deserve special mention for the help they gave me in clarifying my ideas: Brian Hughes, Chris Seidman, Mark LaValley, and Jeff Christian. Royce Money, President of Abilene Christian University, and Dwayne van Rheenan, Provost, have shown keen interest in this project reaching completion.

Donna Quick of Princeton Theological Seminary was always helpful as was my colleague Scott Black Johnston. During a year leave of absence from ACU, Tom Gillespie, President of Princeton Theological Seminary, Donna Klein, Wentzel and Hester van Huyssteen, and Jeff and Jill Shade were very gracious in helping my family in our year back in Princeton. Jeff and Jill, thanks for your ongoing hospitality. Thanks, too, to my colleague in the Ph.D. program at PTS, David A. Davis, for the use of some of his original research on Augustine.

Because of the many "moving parts" that this study had, it proved to be a very difficult project to advise. I thank my advisory committee, James F. Kay (chair), Thomas G. Long, Nora Tubbs Tisdale, and Charles Bartow, for their patience with me as I traversed ancient Greek and Roman rhetoric, homiletical history, New Testament studies, and contemporary homiletical theory. Dr. Kay, your guidance through the many theological and editorial conundrums that I faced was most helpful. Thank you.

Our "covenant group" in Abilene — Mike and Diane Cope, Adam and Donna Hester, David and Pam Lewis, Eddie and Judy Parish, and Darryl and Anne Tippens — surrounded us with continual support throughout this process. The "Heartbeat" crew has been a constant source of refreshment — thank you Landon Saunders, Doug Brown, and James Walters.

These acknowledgments would be incomplete without recognizing the encouraging support of J. McDonald Williams and Dub Orr. They have been gently persistent, while always sympathetic. Jim and Genie Roberts are as responsible as any for seeing that we came to Princeton and stayed in Princeton, even when everything seemed to be saying that we should leave. Danny and Amy DeWalt were pillars of strength for us during this difficult time. I thank my father, Andy Resner, and mother, Claudine Jones, for their unceasing belief in me. I thank also my father-in-law and mother-in-law, Ray and Patty Beindorf, for their willingness to let me take their daughter and grandchildren across the country. I thank the Bowmans and the Shipps, too, who collaborated with the Resners on the idea of going to Princeton in the first place. You all kept me going.

Lastly, and most importantly, I thank Mary, Danny Ray, and Anastasia. You have sacrificed the most for me to do this. Mary, you believed in me, and in this project — that it needed to be done — even when I could not. Thank you for your patience and your love.

# Introduction

In his helpful anthology of readings from homiletical theorists spanning the early church to the present, Richard Lischer states:

> The person of the preacher is a good example of a topic that was once of great importance to the medieval church but is now seldom discussed in homiletics. . . . Despite the wave of interest in spirituality in the church today, one discerns no revival of the classical concern for the holiness of the preacher. The book on the preacher's holiness . . . has not been written. The recent discovery of "my story" as a major element in what is sometimes called autobiographical preaching is not a substitute for Christian character, without which the sermon is only words.[1]

This study does not promise to fill the lacuna which Lischer has identified in contemporary homiletics. That would be an enormous undertaking, and certainly outside the humble scope of this book. Some preliminary work toward filling in the current gap can be accomplished here, however, namely the spade work of assessing the nature and history of the problem, suggesting methodological procedures that may prove fruitful, and offering some initial proposals for how the person of the preacher ought to be understood in both theological and rhetorical perspective.

One way of approaching the topic of ministerial character is from rhetoric's frame of reference. According to this frame of rationality (especially in its Aristotelian form), the preacher is appraised in terms of *ēthos*

---

1. Richard Lischer, *Theories of Preaching: Selected Readings in the Homiletical Tradition* (Durham, NC: The Labyrinth Press, 1987), 3.

1

(speaker character). One difficulty that is immediately confronted in a study of *ēthos* from the rhetorical frame of reference is the confusion that exists over the spelling, pronunciation, and meaning of this word. The macron over the *ē* of *ēthos* is the diacritical marking used to transliterate the Greek letter *ēta*. It is pronounced with a long "a" sound as in "eight." This macron differentiates *ēthos* from "ethos," a commonly used English word which has to do with "customs," "beliefs," or "standards." The confusion in the critical literature is due to the common practice of mistransliterating *ēthos* into English without diacritical marking, and, most often, without even the italics which would indicate that it is a foreign word and not the word "ethos" which has become a functional word in the English language.[2] As a technical category within classical rhetoric, *ēthos* was a debated concept. The most pertinent background for understanding its meaning and function in the history of homiletical theory, though, traces *ēthos* back to Augustine's retrieval of the category with explicit dependence on Cicero. Cicero's usage, in turn, can ultimately be traced back to Aristotle's groundbreaking work on rhetorical proofs in persuasive discourse.

Early church fathers, such as Jerome, eschewed rhetoric as a potentially contaminating influence on the proclamation of the gospel. Augustine, however, argued that rhetoric was a neutral tool which ought to be put to the service of the gospel's proclamation in the same way that other philosophies of the time employed it to vie for their audiences' allegiance. With the assumption of rhetoric's neutrality, Augustine treated the person of the preacher in a pragmatic way, while stopping short of making a donatistic move, one which would tie the preached word's efficacy to the preacher's persuasive *ēthos*. Due to Augustine's influence the classical understanding of *ēthos* dominated homiletical theory until Karl Barth — Martin Luther being a notable exception.

With the advent of the twentieth century, rhetoric suffered a "Barth attack."[3] Since the category of the preacher's person primarily had been

---

2. See in this regard Thomas E. Corts, "The Derivation of Ethos," *Speech Monographs* 35 (1968): 201-2. See also Jerry Harvill, *Aristotle's Concept of Ethos as Ground for a Modern Ethics of Communication* (Ph.D. diss., The University of Kentucky, 1990). Susan K. Hedahl perpetuates the confusion between terms in her recent article "Character," in *Concise Encyclopedia of Preaching*, ed. William H. Willimon and Richard Lischer (Louisville: Westminster John Knox Press, 1995), 66.

3. Thomas G. Long, "And How Shall They Hear? The Listener in Contemporary Preaching," in *Listening to the Word: Studies in Honor of Fred B. Craddock*, ed. Gail O'Day and Thomas G. Long (Nashville: Abingdon Press, 1993), 174.

treated in homiletical theory from the thought-frame of rhetorical theory, when Barth sent rhetoric into the intensive care unit, *ēthos* found itself part of the quarantine. Barth's reaction was a theological recoil caused by the overzealous claims made by rhetorical phenomenologists regarding the power (or impotence) of the person who speaks to win (or lose) the hearer. From a frame of reference which understands preaching to be God's very word — especially with reference to its God-empowered efficacy to save hearers — the rhetorically pragmatic claims for the person of the preacher were theologically blasphemous to Barth. They were idolatrous in that they purported the power of human personality and morality to make efficacious the preached word of God.

Since rhetoric's devaluation by theology early this century, a peculiar state of affairs has existed in homiletics with regard to the person of the preacher. Some, following Barth, have virtually omitted the category from their homiletical schemes because of the donatistic suspicions that attend any *ēthos* construct. These homiletical theorists bracket the human preacher out of preaching's equation, sometimes almost as a matter of homiletical theodicy — the defense of God's power and providence to alone provide preaching's efficacy.

Others have bypassed Barth's objections and continued the traditional rhetorical understanding of the preacher's role in hearer consciousness which began, for the homiletical tradition, with Augustine. These homileticians refuse to remain deaf to what the social scientists tell us "really goes on" in the rhetorical situation of preaching. The honest listener wants to know if the preacher practices what he preaches. Preacher hypocrisy or moral uprightness are factors in listener receptivity to the message spoken whether Barth likes it or not. If anything, the rhetorically minded homiletician who conscientiously follows rhetorical theory, tends to bracket God out of preaching's situation, relying instead on what can be known phenomenologically from the situation.

This study does not advocate the exclusionary choice of any one frame of reference to the dismissal of others in plotting the nature and function of ministerial character for homiletics. Such reduction to a single frame of reference has been the chief problem in the study of ministerial character. Rather, I propose a "bilingual" approach which self-consciously looks from the two diverse frames of reference described above — the rhetorical and the theological.[4] There is a certain validity to the conclusions

4. Bilingualism is a concept borrowed from Deborah van Deusen Hunsinger. See her

that each frame offers, when such assertions are understood within their proper realm of discourse, i.e., when they take into account the assumptions, the methodology, and the goals which pertain to that particular frame of reference. This does not eliminate conflicts between frames nor does it lessen the possibility that a genuine incommensurability of paradigms may emerge.[5]

An arbitrator in this discussion is the Apostle Paul. Paul's letters, especially 1 Cor. 1–4, are in large part a working out of an approach to the person of the preacher which is at once message-driven, yet not dismissive of the rhetorical realities which confronted Paul and his churches. Paul constructs a notion of ministerial *ēthos* in the midst of a culture thoroughly enmeshed in classical rhetorical ideals and assumptions. Moreover, he does so within the context of Christian community which has been created and is sustained by the apocalyptic word of the cross. Paul's strategy for orienting the Corinthians to a rightful view of ministers of the gospel consists of reorienting them to the proper grounds for discerning ministerial identity. These grounds center in a *kata stauron* ("according to the cross") orientation which acknowledges the Christian's placement at the juncture of the ages. Paul engages rhetorical concerns but subordinates such concerns in view of the claims of the cross-event-proclaimed. What is annulled at the cross, then, is not rhetoric as such but its *kata sarka* ("according to the flesh") enslavement. Without the theological insight that comes *kata stauron* ("according to the cross"), rhetoric cannot be used faithfully, i.e., in a way that accords with the nature of the message of preaching.

Paul uses what may be called a reverse-*ēthos*. Reverse-*ēthos* is a theologically-informed rhetorical category which describes the nature and function of the preacher's person in the rhetorical situation of Christian proclamation. It is designated "reverse" or "ironic" *ēthos* to differentiate it from an Aristotelian notion of *ēthos* which derives its meaning and function primarily from paying attention to audience expectation for how a speaker is to be deemed credible. Reverse or ironic *ēthos* highlights the turn first to the message of Christian proclamation and considers the demands that it exacts on the rhetorical situation.

---

discussion in describing the interdisciplinary approach she takes to pastoral counseling. See Hunsinger, *Theology and Pastoral Counseling: A New Interdisciplinary Approach* (Grand Rapids: William B. Eerdmans Publishing Co., 1995).

5. On the nature of paradigms and incommensurability see Thomas S. Kuhn, *The Structure of Scientific Revolutions*, 2nd rev. ed. (Chicago: University of Chicago Press, 1962, 1970), 198-204.

A study by Ronald E. Osborn illustrates the importance of this subject in our time. Osborn displays and explains twelve models for the Christian minister that dominated the American religious scene over the past three centuries. As a historian, he wishes to describe the social and cultural influences which contributed to the different expectations for ministers. But as a theologian he is not content to leave the matter simply to forces that exert their "from below" influences. Osborn writes:

> My thesis is this: Our history has imposed on us a burden of diverse, even contradictory, expectations, impossible for any mortal to fulfill. Only as we clearly formulate a guiding concept of ministry of our own, assimilate to it those features from other patterns that are essential to ministry, make it plain to those with whom we work, and decline any contract that does not consent to it as valid, can any of us who minister find integrity and freedom — or raise a legitimate set of standards by which to measure the effectiveness of our work.[6]

For Osborn, the confusing disarray in ministry that marks the history of ministry in America comes down to the issue of ministerial identity. Who is the minister? Who determines that, and why? All ministerial action proceeds from a sense of identity: who one is prompts what one does. Thus, the sources for one's identity become quite crucial for the nature of ministerial personhood:

> My thesis holds that our problem in ministry in America today is the problem of great expectations joined to hopeless confusion over basic definition. No clear consensus prevails in America as to what a minister is or ought to be. The question lies deeper than frustration over priorities: It arises from perplexity as to essential identity.[7]

How does one proceed in clearing the path and bringing clarity to ministerial identity? One significant problem has to do with our radical historical situatedness as human beings. Because we are products of our social and cultural situations, it is tempting to argue, as the social historian might, that precisely because we are human beings we are essentially the sum of our socially conditioned parts. This problem is true even in Christian community since various construals of Chris-

6. Ronald E. Osborn, *Creative Disarray: Models of Ministry in a Changing America* (St. Louis: Chalice Press, 1991), vii.
7. Osborn, *Creative Disarray*, 5.

tianity, scripture, and community life produce different construals of ministerial identity:

> Our crisis in ministry is conceptual, arising from our lack of a common understanding as to "goals, norms, and values." How can you and I agree as to my effectiveness in ministry when we measure it by different standards based on different conceptions of what a minister is? If a person's identity is a social creation (as maintained by the distinguished philosopher and sociologist George Herbert Mead), it is no wonder that many a young minister in America struggles with a serious identity crisis, for neither the church nor society at large agrees on what it means to be a minister.[8]

With *ēthos* defined as an audience construct (within its rhetorical frame of reference), what is to prevent the identity of the minister from becoming whatever the audience says that it is, from eighteenth-century saint, priest, master, and awakener, to nineteenth-century pulpiteer, revivalist, builder, and missionary, to twentieth-century manager, counselor, impresario, and teacher?[9] With "Jesus C.E.O." as a dominant christological orientation for our time, what is to prevent the capitalistic, consumer-driven, felt-needs-driven church from desiring and selecting a minister to function partly as buoyant master of ceremonies and entertainer (taking Cicero's and Augustine's stated purpose of the orator "to delight" seriously) and partly as a Wal-Mart-style manager and motivator, with the goal of happier, greater, bigger, and more?

Unfortunately, Osborn proves more historian than theologian, since the bulk of his book is a description of the forces which gave rise to each of the twelve models, a description of the mostly positive characteristics of each model (the lone exception being the "impresario" model), with an all-too-brief "reflection" on each. Missing in Osborn's analysis of these models is the very thing he calls for in the beginning: "a common understanding as to 'goals, norms, and values.'" To his credit he does wave a hand in a positive direction: "Our world waits for a demonstration of ministry that echoes the portrait of Jesus in the Gospels — a ministry concerned for the poor, the hungry, the outcast, the lonely, and the lost."[10] But that only hints at what might be called a ministry that is grounded in a theology of the cross.

---

8. Osborn, *Creative Disarray*, 5.

9. These are Osborn's categories. See ibid. for Osborn's descriptions of these various images.

10. Osborn, *Creative Disarray*, 184.

# Introduction

Paul's response to the Corinthian Christians' confusion over ministerial identity took the route of redirecting their consciousness via the cross-event-proclaimed. For Paul, this was the foundation for ecclesial reflection on ministerial identity. The cross-event-proclaimed was to function as the church's epistemological reorientation to value. For Paul, the minister's identity proceeds from ecclesiology and ecclesiology flows out of Christology. Such an identity, reoriented via the cross-event-proclaimed, has implications for both the "real" preacher (who is known ultimately only to God) and the "perceived" preacher (that social construct that is based on information available to hearers about the preacher). In addition, the fundamental identity claims for the preacher that Paul gives — "servant of Christ" and "steward of God's mysteries" — have implications for the preacher's use of self-disclosure in preaching.

This study will unfold as follows: chapter one surveys the classical rhetorical tradition as the backdrop to Augustine's appropriation of the concept of *ēthos* for the Christian preacher. Chapter two surveys the history of homiletical theory. The perusal reveals a basic conflict which exists between dominantly rhetorical approaches to homiletics (typified by Augustine in the early church and a league of hearer-driven homiletical theorists in our day) and dominantly theological approaches to homiletics (typified by the Latin fathers in the early church and Karl Barth in our day). Chapter three retrieves Paul's *ēthos* argument as a way beyond the impasse that exists in homiletical theory. Chapter four advances the theoretical and practical implications of reverse-*ēthos* for contemporary homiletics.

# 1. *Ēthos* in Classical Rhetoric

Virtue is above all things desirable, since honest, just, and conscientious industry is ennobled with honors, rewards, and distinctions; but the vices and frauds of mankind are punished by fines, ignominy, imprisonment, stripes, banishment, and death.

*Cicero*[1]

It seems to me that God has put us apostles at the end of his parade, with the men sentenced to death; it is true — we have been put on show in front of the whole universe, angels as well as men. Here we are, fools for the sake of Christ; while you are celebrities, we are nobodies. To this day, we go without food and drink and clothes; we are beaten and have no homes; we work for our living with our own hands. When we are cursed, we answer with a blessing; when we are hounded, we put up with it; we are insulted and we answer politely. We are treated as the offal of the world, still to this day, the scum of the earth.

*The Apostle Paul*[2]

1. Cicero, *De Oratore,* trans. H. Rackham and E. W. Sutton (Cambridge, MA: Harvard University Press, 1992), 1.43.
2. 1 Cor. 4:9-13, Jerusalem Bible.

9

## Introduction

Aristotle's *Rhetoric,* written in ca. 330 B.C., joined a conversation about the nature of rhetoric which had been going on for almost two hundred years. Such a lengthy discussion provided sufficient time for widely divergent schools of thought and practice to emerge.[3]

Rhetoric as an art and practice arose because of the need for means of argumentation in contexts of persuasive discourse. These contexts were situations in which "matters could be otherwise"; contexts such as the law court (forensic speech), the legislature (deliberative speech), and the state funeral (epideictic speech) are typical examples. In such situations, positions are advanced in as persuasive a manner as possible over against the weaknesses of alternative possibilities. Audiences hear the speech appropriate to the situation and decide on the basis of its merits.

## The Sophists

The Sophists mark the earliest period of classical rhetoric, their beginnings being traced to the early part of the fifth century B.C. Scant direct evidence remains of their written work, most of which is contained in polemical writings which are unfavorable to them. Names such as Tisias, Corax, Antiphon, Gorgias, and Isocrates frame the earliest beginnings, with some literary remains from Empedocles, who connected rhetoric to magic.[4]

From its inception rhetoric stood in close relationship with epistemology, for the way one envisions the nature of human knowing dictates the way one approaches the task of human communication. The "rhetorical circle" would insist that the inverse is also true: the activity of human communication reveals in part the nature of human knowing. Key concepts like "probability" and "opinion" form the epistemological backbone of the pre-Socratic rhetoricians. Working off Protagoras' (born c. 486 B.C.) dictum that "Man is the measure of all things," truth's purchase price went to the highest bidder, with rhetorical artistry serving as the negotiable

---

3. For surveys of the classical rhetorical tradition as a whole see especially George A. Kennedy, *Classical Rhetoric and its Christian and Secular Tradition from Ancient to Modern Times* (Chapel Hill, NC: The University of North Carolina Press, 1980), and Renato Barilli, *Rhetoric,* trans. Giuliana Menozzi, Theory and History of Literature, vol. 63 (Minneapolis: University of Minnesota Press, 1989).

4. Barilli, *Rhetoric,* 3.

coinage. This was because, as Gorgias (born c. 483 B.C.) writes, "Nothing exists; . . . even if it exists it is inapprehensible; . . . even if it is apprehensible, still it is without a doubt incapable of being expressed or explained."[5] With such a worldview the stakes in human argumentation rise to the highest level. In fact, in situations where "matters could be otherwise," truth becomes perception, as depicted by the disputants.

Some scholars suggest that Greeks came to distrust the Sophists for three primary reasons: (1) they were itinerant philosophers and, thus, often aliens; (2) they claimed that wisdom, a Greek virtue, could be taught, something that conflicted with traditional Greek convictions; and (3) they charged money for their services. This went against convention and also made their services exclusive.[6]

The Sophists were perhaps most criticized for the unethical among them. For these, winning was everything, and any means necessary to accomplish that end was justified. As Donald Clark comments, "In this narrow view the whole aim of rhetoric was to win cases, to win by hook or by crook, and if truth was trampled on in the process, so much the worse for truth."[7] Since truth for the Sophists was negotiable in terms of rhetorical skill, rather than some "stable mass" to which one's words pointed, it is not difficult to see why ethics became a critical matter within the history of rhetorical theory. Moreover, among many Sophists, the category of *ēthos* (speaker character) was generally not considered to be a crucial aspect of persuasion, except insofar as one could portray the kind of character that would "work" in persuading one's current audience. Whether or not one was of such character was secondary to the perception of the current audience, and to the pragmatic need to project an image of character which would be "effective" for persuasion in that particular time and place. As an old proverb says, "An ounce of image is worth a pound of reality."

Traces of a view contrary to this are found even among the Sophists, however. Isocrates speaks of a practical wisdom *(phronēsis)* which was considered particularly useful in one's rhetorical training and practice. It was a component of one's nature and consequently could not be taught, yet could be nurtured by good training. An important factor in having and using practical wisdom was moral character. His speech discussing all this, *Against the*

---

5. Barilli, *Rhetoric*, 5.

6. See Sonja K. Foss, Karen A. Foss, and Robert Trapp, *Contemporary Perspectives on Rhetoric*, 2d ed. (Prospect Heights, IL: Waveland Press, Inc., 1991), 2.

7. Donald Lemen Clark, *Rhetoric in Greco-Roman Education* (New York: Columbia University Press, 1957), 25.

*Sophists,* ends abruptly, however, and we are not able to hear from him fully how in fact this is so. Nevertheless, even for Isocrates, the real moral character *(ēthos)* which gives rise to a practical wisdom *(phronēsis)* was understood still in terms of how it functioned in the rhetorical activity of persuasion.[8]

Writing at the same time as Plato, and in many ways in response to some of Plato's criticism of the sophistic tradition, Isocrates focuses on the morality of the orator as a way around the criticism of the abuses of Sophism. As George Kennedy comments, for Isocrates

> rhetoric as a system is presumably neither good nor bad; only men are good or bad, and Isocrates would start with a young man who is good, developing that potential for goodness by the contemplation of great models. This view of the orator is a permanent feature of classical rhetoric, most developed in the ensuing centuries by Cicero and Quintilian, who claim that only a good man can be a good orator.[9]

Individual *ēthos* thus becomes the yardstick for determining the virtue or vice of the ostensibly neutral category of rhetoric. *Ēthos,* moreover, is a significant means of gaining the conviction of one's hearers. Isocrates stresses this in his *Antidosis:*

> Furthermore, mark you, the man who wishes to persuade people will not be negligent as to the matter of character; no, on the contrary, he will apply himself above all to establish a most honorable name among his fellow citizens; for who does not know that words carry greater conviction when spoken by men who live under a cloud, and that *the argument which is made by a man's life is of more weight than that which is furnished by words?* Therefore, *the stronger a man's desire to persuade his hearers, the more zealously will he strive to be honorable and to have the esteem of his fellow citizens.*[10]

## Plato

The Sophists, viewed as the initial "thesis" of rhetoric, were followed by their "antithesis," Plato (428-348 B.C.). "If the Sophists do away with truth

---

8. Kennedy, *Classical Rhetoric,* 32.

9. Kennedy, *Classical Rhetoric,* 33.

10. Isocrates, *Antidosis,* trans. George Norlin, Loeb Classical Library (New York: G. P. Putnam's Sons, 1928-45), 1.277-78. Emphasis is mine.

in favor of appearance, Plato does the opposite: he gave unmitigated pre-eminence to *epistemē* [knowledge] over *doxa* [opinion]."[11] Plato argues that there is a certainty of knowledge rather than a mere probability. From the brief sketch of the sophistic tradition above, one can see that, in the epistemology of the Sophists, truth becomes democratic: the majority determines what is true. Truth is thus construed on the basis of rhetorical depiction, or, as in Isocrates, trust in the *ēthos* of the individual rhetor. In this worldview, "common sense," defined as the cultural or situational consensus, prevails as truth. For the Sophists, words are tools used by skilled rhetors and as such have the power of magic or even of a drug *(pharmakon)*. For Plato, on the other hand, words have the function of pointing to a reality that the words themselves cannot adequately capture. The words themselves are not the unseen reality, but serve a kind of witnessing function to that which is beyond the realm of human sense. "This means the divorce between words and things, where the latter are considerably privileged."[12]

Truth for Plato is a reality, the knowledge of which becomes obfuscated by the trappings of rhetoric. This is why he prefers the discourse of dialectic to rhetorical persuasion. Dialectic involves the to and fro interchange of questions and answers in the pursuit of truth. Dialectic is the whittling knife carving away at a truth that is surely present somewhere in even the most misshapen chunks of wood. One participating in the dialectical dialogue cannot know in advance where the matter would end up. Rhetoric, on the other hand, starts with its destination known, and attempts to marshal evidence in convincing its hearers of this end. For Plato, dialectic is the only appropriate philosophical discourse, because it is the only way to tap the knowledge that human beings already possess within themselves. As Kennedy observes, for Plato, "new truth is not discovered, but rather old truth is recollected: we all existed before birth and we know much more than we can immediately remember."[13] Thus, Plato's epistemological predispositions set in motion his approach to human discourse and his negative evaluation of the rhetorical tradition that preceded him.

Plato developed his critique of the sophistic tradition primarily through his *Apology* and *Gorgias*. In each work Socrates plays the role of the dialectician in a world seemingly dominated by sophistic rhetoric. In

11. Barilli, *Rhetoric,* 6.
12. Barilli, *Rhetoric,* 5-7.
13. Kennedy, *Classical Rhetoric,* 46.

the *Apology*, rather than capitulate to flattery and sham, Socrates, while on trial for atheism and corrupting youth, receives an unjust verdict of guilty, and is sentenced to death. It would appear that his only crime is disdain for the conventional political life of the *polis*. His contempt for orators seems to have disposed his audience against him. His choice of "the bald truth" over forms of discourse which would have pleased his audience, or at the least met the customary expectations of the day, sealed a fate that, if he had used sophistic means of discourse, would likely have meant his acquittal. Socrates becomes, however, a martyr for something greater. His final speech in Plato's *Apology* illustrates this:

> Perhaps, gentlemen of the jury, you think that I have been convicted because of a lack of the kind of words by which I would have persuaded you if I had thought it right to do and say everything so as to escape the charge. Far from it. I have been convicted by a lack of daring and shamelessness and of wanting to say to you the kinds of things which you most like to hear: you would have liked me to wail and carry on and do and say lots of things unworthy of me in my own judgment. This is what others have accustomed you to hear. But during the trial I didn't think I should do anything slavish and I have no regrets now at the nature of my defense; indeed, I much prefer to die after a defense like this than to live after another kind of defense. Neither in court nor in battle should I, nor anyone else, fight in order to avoid death at any cost. . . . Avoiding death, gentlemen, is probably not very difficult; it is much more difficult to avoid doing wrong. . . . Now having been condemned to death I leave you, but my opponents leave having been convicted by the Truth of wickedness and injustice. I stick with my punishment and they can have theirs.[14]

Integrity of character is more important for Socrates than the appeasing of the social context — even if it means death.

Plato's *Gorgias* is perhaps his most important work concerning his views on rhetoric. It is an imaginary discussion between Callicus, Socrates, Chaerephon, Gorgias, and Polus. For our purposes the first third of the dialogue, which focuses on Socrates and Gorgias, is the most significant. Socrates' chief question of the Sophist Gorgias is, "Answer me about rhetoric: with what particular thing is its skill con-

---

14. Plato, *Apology*, trans. W. Heinemann, Loeb Classical Library (Cambridge, MA: Harvard University Press, 1917), 38d-39b. Cited in Kennedy, *Classical Rhetoric*, 44-55.

cerned?"[15] Socrates is attempting to show that rhetoric has no particular subject matter about which it is expert. In contrast to physicians, physical trainers, and financial specialists, each of whom deals with a particular knowledge, the rhetorician deals with no particular knowledge of things. Gorgias's retort is to say,

> The skill in those other arts is almost wholly concerned with manual work and similar activities, whereas in rhetoric there is no such manual working, but its whole activity and efficacy is by means of speech. For this reason I claim for the rhetorical art that it is concerned with speech, and it is a correct description, I maintain.

At this point in the dialogue we reach an impasse. For Socrates the art of rhetoric must be attached to something of substance. It cannot simply glide over many different areas of knowledge, without a true knowledge of that which it purports to speak. Thus Socrates asks in exasperation, "Then tell me what they deal with: what subject is it, of all in the world, that is dealt with by this speech employed by rhetoric?" The Sophist Gorgias appears to see rhetoric as a neutral commodity which can be applied to any arena, even those about which it is ignorant. And, when pressed by Socrates, Gorgias can even praise rhetoric in ethereal terms. Gorgias responds: "The greatest of human affairs, Socrates, and the best." To which Socrates replies, "But that also, Gorgias, is ambiguous, and still by no means clear." This forces Gorgias to become explicit:

Socrates: Well, and what do you call [the greatest good]?

Gorgias: I call it the ability to persuade with speeches either judges in the law courts or statesmen in the council-chamber or the commons in the Assembly or an audience at any other meeting that may be held on public affairs. And I tell you that by virtue of this power you will have the doctor as your slave, and the trainer as your slave; your money-getter will turn out to be making money not for himself, but for another, — in fact for you, who are able to speak and persuade the multitude.

Socrates: I think now, Gorgias, you have come very near to showing us the art of rhetoric as you conceive it, and if I at all take your meaning, you say that rhetoric is a producer of persuasion, and has therein its whole

15. Plato, *Gorgias,* trans. W. Heinemann, Loeb Classical Library (Cambridge, MA: Harvard University Press, 1917), 449.D. The following excerpts are from passages 450.B-460.A.

business and main consummation. Or can you tell us of any other function it can have beyond that of effecting persuasion in the minds of an audience?

Gorgias: None at all, Socrates; your definition seems to me satisfactory; that is the main substance of the art.

Socrates thus reveals Gorgias' version of rhetoric, which represents Plato's view of the sophistic tradition. The subject matter of rhetoric is persuasion, and persuasion here smacks of manipulation.

Two other criticisms emerge from the dialogue. The first has to do with epistemology. Rhetoric as persuasion leads to belief but not to knowledge. Socrates says:

> Thus rhetoric, it seems, is a producer of persuasion for belief, not for instruction in the matter of right and wrong. . . . And so the rhetorician's business is not to instruct a law court or a public meeting in matters of right or wrong, but only to make them believe; since, I take it, he could not in a short while instruct such a mass of people in matters so important.

The second has to do with power and appearances. Several short passages illustrate this. Gorgias says: "So great, so strange is the power of this art [of rhetoric]" that a rhetorician could supplant even the experts in their fields of expertise, whether they be physicians, skilled workmen or whatever. "It is the power of rhetoric which bends people to a certain disposition more than it is the raw truth of the matter." Gorgias again speaks, recognizing that some abuse the art, but those abuses are not to be blamed on the teacher: "The abuses of rhetoric are not the teacher's fault. They are the fault of the student who has misused the power. He must use his rhetoric fairly. . . . it is the man who does not use it [rhetoric] aright who deserves to be hated and expelled and put to death, and not his teacher."

Socrates, however, shows that Gorgias' persuasiveness depends upon appearances. For though Gorgias could persuade that he should be the physician rather than the one trained to be so, he could convince only a crowd of ignorant hearers. Those who knew medicine would not be so persuaded. Socrates says:

> So he who does not know will be more convincing to those who do not know than he who knows, supposing the orator to be more convincing than the doctor . . . there is no need to know the truth of the actual matters, but one merely needs to have discovered some device of persuasion

which will make one appear to those who do not know better than those who know. . . . [H]e [the rhetorician] does not know what is really good or bad, noble or base, just or unjust, but he has devised a persuasion to deal with these matters so as to appear to those who, like himself, do not know to know better than he who knows. Or is it necessary to know, and must anyone who intends to learn rhetoric have a previous knowledge of these things when he comes to you? Or if not, are you, as the teacher of rhetoric, to teach the person who comes to you nothing about them — for it is not your business — but only to make him appear [*dokein*] in the eyes of the multitude to know things of this sort when he does not know, and to appear to be good when he is not? Or will you be utterly unable to teach him rhetoric unless he previously knows the truth about these matters? Or what is the real state of the case, Gorgias? For Heaven's sake, as you proposed just now, draw aside the veil and tell us what really is the function of rhetoric?

For Plato, orators must not merely communicate in a persuasive manner, they must truly know the matters of which they speak. For truth is not merely in the argument. As Kennedy points out, Plato's main thrust in the *Gorgias* is that the rhetor must be a good person. Kennedy writes that the Sophists'

> separation of the rhetorical function from other qualities in an individual, logical as it is, did run the risk of tolerating evil. Plato's integration of the intellectual, moral, and rhetorical qualities of the orator into the whole man avoids that risk, but at the cost of practical effectiveness.[16]

## Aristotle

In *On Rhetoric*, Aristotle presents his most comprehensive treatment of rhetoric.[17] As was his custom, he defines rhetoric by comparing and con-

---

16. Kennedy, *Classical Rhetoric*, 52.

17. Though there is much discussion concerning the nature of the composition of *On Rhetoric*, Jakob Wisse, *Ethos and Pathos: From Aristotle to Cicero* (Amsterdam: Adolf M. Hakkert Publisher, 1989), 13, comments that "fortunately, most problems presented by the parts on ethos and pathos depend much less on the view adopted with respect to the unity of the work than do the problems about rational arguments (the status of the *topoi*, the theory of enthymeme and example, etc.)." See also Jerry Harvill, *Aristotle's Concept of Ethos as Ground for a Modern Ethics of Communication* (Ph.D. dissertation, University of Kentucky, 1990), 155-99.

trasting it with something else. "Rhetoric is an *antistrophos* to dialectic; for both are concerned with such things as are, to a certain extent, within the knowledge of all people and belong to no separately defined science."[18] Kennedy chooses not to translate *antistrophos* here but has an extensive note on the word. He offers "counterpart," "correlative," "coordinate," and "converse" as possible translations. Kennedy suspects that behind Aristotle's use of the word lies a critique of Plato:

> Aristotle is . . . probably thinking of, and rejecting, the analogy of the true and false arts elaborated by Socrates in the *Gorgias,* where justice is said to be an *antistrophos* to medicine (464b8) and rhetoric, the false form of justice, is compared to cookery, the false form of medicine (465c1-3). . . . Aristotle thus avoids the fallacy of Plato's *Gorgias* where Socrates is obsessed with finding some kind of knowledge specific to rhetoric.[19]

Rather than polarize rhetoric and dialectic, as Plato did, Aristotle sees them as "correlatives."

Kennedy defines dialectic as "the art of logical argument on general issues of political or ethical nature; practiced as an exercise for students of philosophy in the form of question and answer dialogue."[20] In discourse, it is the ability to "see" syllogisms or apparent syllogisms. Rhetoric is an art, not confined to any particular genus of subject, which has the function of discovering "the available means of persuasion in each case."[21] The visual metaphor of "seeing" is important to Aristotle, since he uses it each time he defines his terms. As Kennedy comments, "*to see* translates *theoresai*, 'to be an observer of and to grasp the meaning or utility of.'"[22] Rhetoric's utility in various subjects makes it unique among the arts, "for each of the others is instructive and persuasive about its own subject." Examples of these "others" are medicine, geometry, and arithmetic. These all require technical knowledge of some particular subject matter, and thus the persuasive element within each has to do primarily with such intramural ex-

18. Aristotle, *On Rhetoric,* trans. George A. Kennedy (New York: Oxford University Press, 1991), 1.1.1. Kennedy uses brackets, [], in order to indicate words and phrases implied in the Greek text which help clarify the meaning in English. Parentheses ( ) indicate remarks that Kennedy felt Aristotle intended to be parenthetical.

19. Aristotle, *On Rhetoric,* 28-29, n. 2.

20. Aristotle, *On Rhetoric,* 314. (The words are Kennedy's.)

21. Aristotle, *On Rhetoric,* 1.1.14.

22. Kennedy, in Aristotle, *On Rhetoric,* 37, n. 34.

pertise. Rhetoric is persuasive, on the other hand, about "the given." "That is why it does not include technical knowledge of any particular, defined genus [of subjects]."[23]

For Aristotle, in rhetoric there are *pisteis,* "proofs," some being "atechnic ['nonartistic'], some entechnic ['embodied in art, artistic']." Atechnic proofs are those that exist apart from the rhetor, such as witnesses, testimony exacted from torture, and contracts. Entechnic proofs are those invented by the rhetor. They "can be prepared by method and by 'us.'"[24] There are three artistic *pisteis: ēthos, logos,* and *pathos. Ēthos* has to do with the perceived moral character of the speaker. *Logos* has to do with the logical argumentation of the speech itself. *Pathos* has to do with the way in which the hearers are moved to emotion in the speech.[25] Of these three, "moral character *(ēthos)* may almost be called the most potent means of persuasion." Kennedy's translation reads: "Character is almost, so to speak, the controlling factor in persuasion." Aristotle elaborates:

> [There is persuasion] through character whenever the speech is spoken in such a way as to make the speaker worthy of credence; for we believe fair-minded people to a greater extent and more quickly [than we do others] on all subjects in general and completely so in cases where there is not exact knowledge but room for doubt. And this should result from the speech, not from a previous opinion that the speaker is a certain kind of person.[26]

We can see more clearly now that dialectic itself is a part of rhetoric, that part which has to do with *logos* as a persuasive element, i.e., the reasoned argumentation of a discourse. *Pathos* has to do with a knowledge of how the emotions are aroused and the qualities and characteristics of such. *Ēthos* has to do with the nature of character and virtue in the speaker.[27]

---

23. Aristotle, *On Rhetoric,* 1.2.1.

24. Aristotle, *On Rhetoric,* 1.2.2.

25. A literature has arisen concerning the relationship of *ēthos* and *pathos* to the enthymeme, which for Aristotle is the quintessential rational *(logos)* appeal. Kennedy, in his edited volume of Aristotle's *On Rhetoric,* 315, defines enthymeme: "a rhetorical syllogism, i.e., a statement with a supporting reason introduced by *for, because,* or *since* or an *if . . . then* statement. In contrast to a logical syllogism, the premises and conclusion are ordinarily probable, not necessarily logically valid. A premise may be omitted if it will be easily assumed by the audience." On the enthymeme, see Aristotle, *On Rhetoric,* 1.2.8-22, 2.22.

26. Aristotle, *On Rhetoric,* 1.2.4.

27. Aristotle, *On Rhetoric,* 1.2.7.

A knowledge of each of these components of persuasion is important for the would-be rhetor since rhetoric is essential to those realms of public life in which judgments must be made. The three specific situations of judgment in which rhetoric must operate are: (1) epideictic (situations of praise or blame, such as public holidays or funerals; see 1.3.1-6, 1.9, 3.12); (2) deliberative (situations about which some action in the future must be decided; see 1.3-8, 3.12, 3.17); and (3) judicial (situations of prosecution or defense in a court of law to resolve conflicts of the past; see 1.3, 1.10-15, 3.12, 3.14.5, 3.16.4).

The rhetorical moment, the rhetor, and the ordered argumentation are of utmost importance even in situations where "hard" evidence is available for the audience to hear and see. Stronger proofs are provided by rhetors in their person, argument, and "working" of the hearers than in any other evidence that could be marshaled. Kennedy explains why the "soft" evidence of the rhetor was more important in persuading hearers in ancient times than "hard" evidence:

> The [rhetorical] handbooks concentrated on what was called 'argument from probability' to the neglect of using direct evidence. Greek juries distrusted direct evidence such as witnesses or documents because they thought these might be bribed or faked. They put more confidence in what those involved would have been likely to do in terms of the circumstances or their character.[28]

Thus, Aristotle's *On Rhetoric* answers the need to understand the way in which one could be most persuasive in situations requiring judgment, i.e., situations in which matters could be otherwise.

One critical point of debate in the literature on Aristotle is whether Aristotle is concerned for the "real" character of the rhetor or only about the "perceived" character of the rhetor in the estimation of the hearers. More often than not, scholars dwell on the perceived aspect of speaker character as Aristotle's burden. Typical of these commentators on Aristotle is William E. Arnold: "Aristotle stated that the speaker should be thought credible. He did not say ethical."[29] For Arnold, *ēthos* is essentially about image projection. Alan Brinton is another rhetorical theorist who understands Aristotle's notion of *ēthos* in terms of audience-perceived credibility. Brinton concludes that for Aristotle "what *works* in persuasion . . . [is] a

---

28. Kennedy, *Classical Rhetoric*, 9.
29. William E. Arnold, "Ethos — A View," *Pennsylvania Speech Review* 22 (1966): 77.

focus on the effectiveness of appeal to *ēthos* and never any attention to the question of its legitimacy." It is "the *appearance* of good character rather than good character itself" which is of primary importance.[30]

Jerry Harvill, on the other hand, represents perhaps the strongest voice for Aristotle's insistence on "real" character. Harvill executes a thorough philological analysis of *ēthos* in Aristotle's *Nicomachean Ethics, Politics,* and *Rhetoric.* Working first from Aristotle's *Nicomachean Ethics,* then the *Politics,* and only lastly from the *Rhetoric,* Harvill argues for an inherent or "real" moral character as the backbone to Aristotle's notion of *ēthos.* Harvill is disturbed with the reductionistic readings of Aristotle which relegate *ēthos* to a pragmatic category that has to do with persuasion. From the depiction of *ēthos* in the *Ethics,* Harvill concludes that

> Ethics for Aristotle turns out to be character showing itself. What this means is that *ēthos* for Aristotle is neither an image nor an impression, but is rather that crucial decisional zone within the human personality where excellence of proportion in passion and reason harnessed together in the service of truth generates what ethics is all about. . . . For Aristotle *ēthos* is no more detachable from the individual than the soul, of which *ēthos* is a vital part.[31]

From the *Politics* Harvill concludes that "for Aristotle *ēthos* is speaker centered, for moderns ethos is receiver centered; for Aristotle rhetorical *ēthos* has to do with *praxis,* for moderns rhetorical ethos has to do with effects. . . . Ethos has turned into an audience variable, no longer a speaker's character."[32] For Aristotle *ēthos* is an embodiment, for moderns it is a mere polish. Having established this foundation for *ēthos,* Harvill turns to the *Rhetoric.* He claims that the *Rhetoric* ought to be considered as being "embedded" in the contextual moral philosophy of Aristotle's work at large, and implies as well that the *Ethics* and *Politics* provide the appropriate philological context for understanding the way *ēthos* is to be understood in the *Rhetoric.* This is, of course, Harvill's own suggestion, since Aristotle himself nowhere subordinates his treatment of rhetoric in this way.

Harvill's consternation is due to the fact that whereas Aristotle labored in the *Ethics* and the *Politics* to establish the criteria for "real" moral char-

---

30. Alan Brinton, "Ethotic Argument," *History of Philosophy Quarterly* 3 (1986): 246. Emphasis is Brinton's.

31. Harvill, *Aristotle's Concept of Ethos,* 129.

32. Harvill, *Aristotle's Concept of Ethos,* 143.

acter in the supreme ethical person *(ho phronimos),* when modern critics turn to the *Rhetoric* they focus on what Harvill calls "Problem Passages in Aristotle's *Rhetoric*" and slide down a slippery slope into Sophism.

In spite of Harvill's insistence, there is good reason why Aristotle has been read as a pragmatist on *ēthos* when it comes to rhetoric. This is because he was an astute phenomenologist and even though he would not support Protagoras (and in fact inveighs against him in the *Rhetoric* 2.24.11.1402a), he nevertheless recognizes that every audience constructs a character portrait of the speaker which may or may not correspond to the speaker's real character. Several texts bear this out:

> For when speaking of these [virtue and vice], we shall incidentally bring to light the means of *making us appear* of such and such a character, which as we have said, is a second method of proof.[33]

> Wherefore, since all men are willing to listen to speeches which harmonize with their own character and to speakers who resemble them, it is easy to see what language we must employ *so that both ourselves and our speeches may appear* to be of such and such a character.[34]

> Maxims should also be used even when contrary to the most popular sayings . . . either *when one's character is thereby likely to appear better,* or if they are expressed in the language of passion.[35]

> And *one's character would appear better,* if one were to say that it is not right, as men say, to love as if one were bound to hate, but rather to hate as if one were bound to love.[36]

All of these represent Aristotle's attempt to instruct the rhetor in pragmatic ways in order that he may prove persuasive to the hearers. They are means by which the wise speaker may "put on" character masks which convince of credibility. All of Book II of the *Rhetoric* concerns the different characters, prejudices, and presuppositions of different target audiences so that the rhetor may know which masks of character to wear when so as to be most persuasive. Harvill is more correct when he states: "Aristotle, too, represents a tension between the ideal and the actual, be-

---

33. Aristotle, *On Rhetoric,* 1.9.1.1366a26. Emphasis is mine.
34. Aristotle, *On Rhetoric,* 2.13.16–14.1.1390a24ff. Emphasis is mine.
35. Aristotle, *On Rhetoric,* 2.21.13.1395a22. Emphasis is mine.
36. Aristotle, *On Rhetoric,* 2.21.13.1395a26. Emphasis is mine.

tween truth and appearances, nevertheless he does not relinquish either."[37]

For Aristotle, then, it can be concluded that from the perspective of moral philosophy and ethics he urges the real formation of genuine character within community, that the wise practitioner *(phronimos)* might be formed, the perfect person. But when Aristotle considers the role of *ēthos* in rhetoric he recognizes that the real is subject to viewer perception. He may wish that the genuine internal character of the speaker would be manifest in the speech, but he knows that this may not happen.[38]

For Plato, character necessarily entails one's real moral stature, even if no human being could perceive the difference. Aristotle recognizes, contra Plato, that whether one is virtuous or not, what counts in a persuasive speech is the perception of the speaker's virtue on the part of the human hearers. When speaking from his rhetorical frame of reference, Aristotle comes to prescription by way of description. He writes:

> Since rhetoric is concerned with making a judgment (people judge what is said in deliberation, and judicial proceedings are also a judgment), it is necessary not only to look to the argument, that it may be demonstrative and persuasive but also [for the speaker] *to construct a view of himself as a certain kind of person* . . . for it makes much difference in regard to persuasion (especially in deliberations but also in trials) that *the speaker seem to be a certain kind of person* and that his hearers *suppose him* to be disposed toward them in a certain way . . . for *the speaker to seem to have certain qualities is more useful.*[39]

Harvill's reading of Aristotle conflates "real" and "perceived" *ēthos* in his attempt to read the *Ethics,* the *Politics,* and the *Rhetoric* all from the same frame of reference. Aristotle, however, claims different things for *ēthos* depending on his frame of reference. Therefore, when analyzing *ēthos* in a rhetorical situation, it is only appropriate to talk in pragmatic terms about the audience's "perceived" nature of *ēthos.* When analyzing *ēthos* from the perspective of ethics or moral philosophy, one necessarily has to deal with the nature of "real" *ēthos* and its formation within communities. Harvill actually appears to be imposing Quintilian's ideal orator upon Ar-

---

37. Harvill, *Aristotle's Concept of Ethos,* 218.

38. See Aristotle, *Rhetoric,* 3.14.8.1415b, 1416a, where he describes listeners who do not perceive aright what the speaker attempts to communicate.

39. Aristotle, *On Rhetoric,* 2.1.2-4. Emphasis is mine.

istotle's discussion of *ēthos*. He attests to that verdict by citing Quintilian in an attempt to sum up Aristotle in the last paragraph of his dissertation: "Aristotle's concept of *ēthos* . . . confirms that the classical vision of rhetoric as 'the good man speaking well' is much more than a slogan."[40]

Nan Johnson advances our understanding of Aristotle's use of *ēthos*. She identifies three issues of difference in Aristotle and Plato that set in motion conflicting conceptions of the nature and role of the orator in public speaking. The three issues are:

> 1) what constitutes truth or knowledge: ideal principles or received opinion; 2) the nature of the Good: absolute perfection or excellence in final form; and 3) rhetoric's role in the discovery of truth and presentation of the Good: dialectical activity of edification in the ideal or strategic skill in the communication of human values and opinion.

Thus, for Aristotle, "'ethos' is defined as a pragmatic strategy which serves practical wisdom in human affairs. The rhetorician need not be virtuous in a Platonic or objective sense, only wise about human values, opinions, and motivations." For Plato, on the other hand, the orator is a philosopher whose oratory is nothing less than revelatory of Truth and Goodness, both with capital letters. As Johnson says, "the orator bears witness to the ideal Good by being an incarnation of truth."[41]

Aristotle elaborates on the nature of the perceived character of the rhetor in two ways. First, he gives three reasons why a speaker is persuasive in his or her person. With specific regard to the speaker's personal *ēthos*, the most important of factors in persuading hearers in situations of judgment, Aristotle writes,

> There are three things we trust. . . . These are practical wisdom [*phronēsis*] and virtue [*aretē*] and good will [*eunoia*]; for speakers make mistakes in what they say or advise through [failure to exhibit] either all or one of these; for either through lack of practical sense they do not form opinions rightly; or though forming opinions rightly they do not say what they think because of a bad character; or they are prudent and fair-minded but lack good will, so that it is possible for people not to give the best advice although they know [what] it [is]. These are the only

40. Harvill, *Aristotle's Concept of Ethos*, 302.

41. Nan Johnson, "Ethos and the Aims of Rhetoric," in *Essays on Classical Rhetoric and Modern Discourse*, ed. Robert J. Connors, Lisa S. Ede, and Andrea A. Lunsford (Carbondale: Southern Illinois University Press, 1984), 103.

possibilities. Therefore, a person seeming to have all these qualities is necessarily persuasive to the hearers.[42]

Practical wisdom, virtue, and good will are the components of persuasive *ēthos*. They could be characterized as the attributes of the successful rhetor. And, it should be remembered, they serve their persuasive function, according to Aristotle, by their artful deployment in the speech itself. Antecedent *ēthos,* such as reputation, seems to be an unimportant factor to this ancient philosopher, or at least inconsequential once the speech begins. Whatever may have preceded a particular rhetorical situation is put aside, or at least must be established anew, in the new situation.

Harvill's chart entitled, "Aristotle's theory of rhetorical character" helpfully depicts the nature of rhetorical *ēthos* for Aristotle.

### Rhetor's Character as Rhetor

| *phronēsis* | *aretē* | *euonia* |
|---|---|---|
| [practical wisdom] | [virtue] | [good will] |

*ēthikē aretē*
[ethical virtues]

1. Liberality
2. Justice
3. Courage
4. Temperance
5. Magnanimity

6. Magnificence
7. Prudence
8. Gentleness
9. Wisdom

Manifested in Choices of

| Invention | Style/Delivery | Arrangement |
|---|---|---|

**Fig. 1. Aristotle's Theory of Rhetorical Character**[43]

One can see from this figure that, for Aristotle, the rhetor's character consists fundamentally in practical wisdom, virtue, and good will. These root metaphors of character consequently express themselves in nine virtuous

---

42. Aristotle, *On Rhetoric,* 2.1.5-6.
43. Harvill, *Aristotle's Concept of Ethos,* 182.

aspects. These then influence the way that one's actual speech will be invented, constructed, and delivered.

The second matter in understanding *ēthos* is the way in which the rhetor adapts his or her own character to that of the audience. As foreshadowed in our analysis of Harvill, in chapters 12-17 of Book 2, Aristotle turns to a matter which Kennedy traces back to Plato in the *Phaedrus*. Plato's Socrates "argues that there cannot be a true art of speech without a knowledge of the soul, enabling a speaker to fit the appropriate argument to the soul of the hearer."[44] Aristotle has in mind rhetorical target groups which could be categorized in terms of age, good birth, wealth, power, and fortune:

> Since *pisteis* not only come from logical demonstration but from speech that reveals character (for we believe the speaker through his being a certain kind of person, and this is the case if he seems to be good or well disposed to us or both), we should be acquainted with the kinds of character distinctive of each form of constitution; *for the character distinctive of each is necessarily most persuasive to each.*[45]

In order to address various groups successfully, the speaker needs to take into account the various characteristics of his or her audience and, in the speech, match his or her own character to those.[46] As Aristotle himself explains, "since all people receive favorably speeches spoken in their own character and by persons like themselves, it is not unclear how both speakers and speeches may seem to be of this sort through use of words."[47] It would seem that Aristotle assumes a strong audience homogeneity in rhetorical situations. He does not comment on an audience that is quite mixed in its ethnic, social, economic, and age — a group such as Paul envisioned meeting together in Christian *ekklēsia*.

Aristotle's chief contribution to the rhetorical discussion is his organized division of *ēthos*, *pathos*, and *logos* as the means of persuasion in rhetorical situations. In summary, his introduction to the three aspects of *ēthos* (good sense, goodness, goodwill) pinpoints its importance in oratory: *ēthos* is to function in one's speech by presenting the speaker as reli-

---

44. Kennedy, in *Aristotle, On Rhetoric*, 163.
45. Aristotle, *On Rhetoric*, 1.8.6. Emphasis is mine.
46. In this regard, see William M. A. Grimaldi, *Aristotle, Rhetoric, A Commentary* (New York: Fordham University Press, 1988), 2.186.
47. Aristotle, *On Rhetoric*, 2.13.16.

able, "or from the point of view of the hearer, as the element that makes the audience regard the speaker as trustworthy."[48] *Ēthos* is a proof *(pistis)* within the speech which is ideally based upon the speaker's real moral character. Nevertheless, in the rhetorical situation, *ēthos* is a projected character, in view of the target audience's character which attempts to show that the speaker "has the socially approved *aretai* or excellences, that he makes decisions and performs actions a good man should. . . . [I]ndeed, such a presentation is crucial to winning the audience's goodwill and so influencing their feelings."[49]

## Cicero

*De Oratore,* "The Making of an Orator," is the work of Cicero's maturity, composed in 56/55 B.C. when he was fifty or fifty-one years old. It is commonly considered his greatest work and is the most explicit regarding the function of *ēthos* in oratory. Renato Barilli places Cicero in relationship to Plato and Aristotle:

> If the Platonic moment is one of negation, and the Aristotelian one of Olympian acceptance and systematization, Cicero's model marks the triumph of rhetoric, which with him is privileged and raised to the rank of art of the arts.[50]

As James M. May points out, after Aristotle the concept of *ēthos* fell into virtual disuse in theorizing about rhetoric. This neglect also included Cicero's early work and the influential *Rhetorica ad Herennium,* another Roman work which has often been ascribed to Cicero, yet surely was the work of another. But with *De Oratore, ēthos* and *pathos* "would be restored on a par with *logos*."[51] Cicero recognizes his own indebtedness to Aristotle, remarking in 2.152 and 2.160 how his treatise itself is written in Aristotelian style. Both Kennedy and May point to 2.115 where Cicero divides the persuasive aspect of rhetoric's task in the same way that Aristotle did in *On Rhetoric:*

---

48. Wisse, *Ethos and Pathos*, 33.
49. Christopher Gill, "The Ethos/Pathos Distinction in Rhetorical and Literary Criticism," *Classical Quarterly* 34 (1984): 153.
50. Barilli, *Rhetoric*, 26.
51. James M. May, *Trials of Character: The Eloquence of Ciceronian Ethos* (Chapel Hill, NC: The University of North Carolina Press, 1988), 3.

Thus for purposes of persuasion the art of speaking relies wholly upon three things: the proof of our allegations, the winning of our hearers' favor, and the rousing of their feelings to whatever impulse our case may require.[52]

"The proof of our allegations" corresponds to *logos;* "the winning of our hearers' favor," to *ēthos;* "and the rousing of their feelings to whatever impulse our case may require," to *pathos.* May thus discerns Cicero's "Aristotelianism" at work in the heart of his rhetorical theory:

> Cicero's concurrence with Aristotle in this matter demonstrates his belief in a rhetoric based broadly on the three major sources of demonstration and persuasion (logos, ethos, and pathos) and on his conviction that such foundations of proof cannot rightly be subordinated to any one structural element of the speech but must permeate the whole, as blood does the body (see 2.310 and 2.80-82, 322).[53]

Cicero has Antonius describe *ēthos* in 2.182-185. Like Aristotle, the discussion has to do with the *ēthos* which the speaker reveals in the speech itself. Both the perceived nature of the speaker's character and that of the audience come into focus. Unlike Aristotle, however, Cicero connects *ēthos* closely with *pathos,* does not give *ēthos* a superior position to *logos* and *pathos,* but does speak of the importance of "antecedent *ēthos*" (i.e., "a reputable life"):

> A potent factor in success, then, is for the characters, principles, conduct and course of life, both of those who are to plead cases and of their clients, to be approved, and conversely those of their opponents to be condemned. . . . Now feelings are won over by a man's merit, achievements or reputable life, qualifications easier to embellish, if only they are real, than to fabricate where non-existent. But attributes useful in an advocate are a mild tone, a countenance expressive of modesty, gentle language, and the faculty of seeming to be dealing reluctantly and under compulsion with something you are really anxious to prove. It is very helpful to display the tokens of good-nature, kindness, calmness, loyalty and a disposition that is pleasing and not grasping or covetous, and all the qualities belonging to men who are upright, unassuming and not given to haste, stubbornness, strife or harshness, are powerful in win-

52. Cicero, *De Oratore,* 2.1.15.
53. May, *Trials of Character,* 4, 172.

ning goodwill, while the want of them estranges it from such as do not possess them; accordingly the very opposites of these qualities must be ascribed to our opponents. . . . And so to paint their [the speaker again, not opponents] characters in words, as being upright, stainless, conscientious, modest and long-suffering under injustice, has a really wonderful effect; and this topic, whether in opening, or in stating the case, or in winding-up, is so compelling, when agreeably and feelingly handled, as often to be worth more than the merits of the case. Moreover so much is done by good taste and style in speaking, that the speech seems to depict the speaker's character. For by means of particular types of thought and diction, and the employment besides of a delivery that is unruffled and eloquent of good-nature, the speakers are made to appear upright, well-bred and virtuous men.[54]

One notices here that Cicero dwells on the character traits that need to be displayed, those that ought to appear to be the case, whether they are in fact the case or not. This distances him from Plato, of course, and seems to put him nearer the Sophists and Aristotle. However, like Aristotle and distancing himself from Sophism, he does not advocate here or elsewhere being deceitful in order simply to win one's case. There is an ethical dimension for him, which, combined with his phenomenological approach, makes him resemble Aristotle all the more. This ethical dimension is to be seen in Cicero's expansion of the *ēthos* category to include reputation. As May comments, to confine the effect of *ēthos* only to the impression made in the speech at hand

> would have been incomprehensible to a Roman steeped in the tradition of the *mos mairorum* (noble will), surrounded by a nobility of rank, and influenced by the culture's general assumptions concerning human nature and character. . . . Aristotle's conception of an ethos portrayed only through the medium of a speech was, for the Roman orator, neither acceptable nor adequate.[55]

In his *Orator* Cicero identifies three primary duties of the orator: *probare* (to teach), *delectare* (to delight), and *flectere* (to persuade). Three styles attend these duties: the plain style in order to teach; the middle style in order to delight; and the grand style in order to persuade. Both

---

54. Cicero, *De Oratore*, 2.182-84.
55. May, *Trials of Character*, 9, 173, n. 42.

Quintilian and Augustine show the influence of these categories, while also revealing a knowledge of the traditional Aristotelian triad of *ēthos, pathos,* and *logos* which exceeds Cicero's treatment of those categories.

## Quintilian

> The orator, then, whom I am concerned to form, shall be the orator as defined by Marcus Cato, 'a good man, skilled in speaking.' But above all he must possess the quality which Cato places first and which is in the very nature of things the greatest and most important, that is, he must be a good man.[56]

Quintilian (c. 35-95 A.D.) is the last major rhetorical theorist before Augustine. His most important work is the massive — twelve books fill four volumes in the Loeb Classical Library — *Institutio Oratoria,* or *Education of the Orator.* As the title indicates, it is a treatise which deals with the training of the ideal orator.

Quintilian is famous for the definition of rhetoric as "the good man speaking well," though he is quoting Marcus Cato. Quintilian elevates eloquence over all other factors in the rhetorical equation. For him, persuasion may fail to occur among the hearers even though the orator may succeed in being eloquent. Because of this, persuasion is not the aim of rhetoric, as it was for the Sophists. Reflecting the truth is not the aim, as it was in Plato. Discovering the available means for persuasion in the given situation is not his goal, as it was for Aristotle. Rather, eloquence itself becomes a virtue, independent of the pragmatics of persuasion. His is a rhetorical aesthetics of sorts, though ethics remained a critical component. Quintilian writes concerning the relationship of eloquence and ethics:

> My aim, then, is the education of the perfect orator. The first essential for such an one is that he should be a good man, and consequently we demand of him not merely the possession of exceptional gifts of speech, but of all the excellences of character as well.[57]

Quintilian goes on to lament the split that occurred between philosophy and rhetoric, thus effecting the divide between ethics and speech. The split

---

56. Quintilian, *Institutio Oratoria* (London: Bell, 1875-76), 12.1.1.
57. Quintilian, *Institutio Oratoria,* 9.

sent philosophy one direction, down the road of moral inquiry, while rhetoric went the other, down a path wherein speaking publicly could become a means of livelihood. The results of the divide are that rhetoric becomes amoral, while philosophy becomes "the prey of weaker intellects."[58] For Quintilian, the ideal is philosophy and oratory coinhabiting a single person. Education ought to be aimed to train such:

> If it were proved that schools, while advantageous to study, are prejudicial to morality, I should give my vote for virtuous living in preference to even supreme excellence of speaking. But in my opinion the two are inseparable. I hold that no one can be a true orator unless he is also a good man and, even if he could be, I would not have it so.[59]

After sweeping aside an impressive array of rhetorical theorists, most of whom "have as a rule held that the task of oratory lies in persuasion or speaking in a persuasive manner," Quintilian concludes that "we are now in a position to see clearly what is the end, the highest aim, the ultimate goal of rhetoric, that *telos* in fact which every art must possess. For if rhetoric is the science of speaking well, its end and highest aim is to speak well."[60]

Book VI is the centerpiece of Quintilian's discussion of *ēthos*. He, in fact, uses the Greek terms of *ēthos* and *pathos,* commenting about the former, "a word for which in my opinion Latin has no equivalent: it is however rendered by *mores* (morals) and consequently the branch of philosophy known as *ethics* is styled *moral* philosophy by us."[61]

Quintilian describes *ēthos* in two ways: first, as an emotion, one both calmer and more comedic than the violent and tragic *pathos;* second, and more traditionally, as related to the ethical character of the speaker.

In this latter understanding of the term, Quintilian avers back to the suasive:

> If *ēthos* denotes moral character, our speech must necessarily be based on *ēthos* when it is engaged in portraying such character. Finally *ēthos* in all its forms requires the speaker to be a man of good character and

58. Quintilian, *Institutio Oratoria,* 14.
59. Quintilian, *Institutio Oratoria,* 1.2.3.
60. Quintilian, *Institutio Oratoria,* 2.14.3; 2.15.38.
61. Quintilian, *Institutio Oratoria,* 6.2.8.

courtesy. For it is most important that he should himself possess *or be thought to possess* those virtues for the possession of which it is his duty, if possible, to commend his client as well, while the excellence of his own character will make his pleading all the more convincing and will be of the utmost service to the cases which he undertakes. For the orator who gives the impression of being a bad man while he is speaking, is actually speaking badly, since his words seem to be insincere owing to the absence of *ēthos* which would otherwise have revealed itself.[62]

Maribeth Impson sums up Quintilian's view of rhetoric:

Quintilian rejects the definition of rhetoric as 'the art of persuasion' on the basis that such a definition requires the rhetor to be successful in order to be considered eloquent. Eloquence, he asserts, lies in the art, not in its end, since persuasion might not be effected for reasons other than lack of eloquence on the rhetor's part. Instead, he defines rhetoric as 'the art of speaking well' — which he reminds us, 'embraces all the virtues of oratory at once, and includes also the character of the true orator, as he cannot speak well unless he is a good man.'[63]

Thus, *ēthos* for Quintilian has to do with the indispensable ethical aspect of oratory, the aspect which prevents it from degenerating into the ills associated with Sophistry.

The orator whom Quintilian envisions is nothing less than something dropped from above, from the gods:

It is no hack-advocate, no hireling pleader, nor yet, to use no harsher term, a serviceable attorney of the class generally known as *causidici*, that I am seeking to form, but rather a man who to extraordinary natural gifts has added a thorough mastery of all the fairest branches of knowledge, a man sent by heaven to be the blessing of mankind, one to whom all history can find no parallel, uniquely perfect in every detail and utterly noble alike in thought and speech.[64]

Commenting on this text, Alan Brinton suggests that Quintilian's vision of the perfect orator is in fact "an abstraction, a Platonic Ideal," yet he speaks

---

62. Quintilian, *Institutio Oratoria*, VI.ii.17-18. Emphasis is mine.

63. Maribeth Impson, *The Concept of Ethos in Classical and Modern Rhetoric* (Ph.D. diss., University of Kentucky, 1988), 38.

64. Quintilian, *Institutio Oratoria*, 12.1.1.

of this abstraction, this Ideal, "as one which could possibly be fulfilled in some actual orator."[65]

Even in view of this, there is some inconsistency in Quintilian's discussion of *ēthos*. For as we observed in discussing VI.ii.17-18, one aspect of *ēthos* for Quintilian is its ability to convince others of one's position, despite Quintilian's understanding of an *ēthos* freed from the constraints imposed by the pragmatics of persuasion. The eloquent orator might in fact be good as well, yet not persuade the hearers. Yet one also notes (esp. VI.ii.17-18) that if the orator is indeed the "one sent from heaven," then persuasiveness is almost assured.

## Conclusion

This survey of the classical rhetorical tradition reveals that the person of the speaker is a prominent matter of discussion. What is it that we have learned about *ēthos* from the classical rhetorical tradition?

Because of the Sophists' epistemology ("Man is the measure of all things"), truth was understood to be a matter of perception. "Truth" was a matter to be depicted or constructed by disputants in a particular case. But even though "image was everything," astute Sophists knew that their hearers are more strongly persuaded by the speech that is a good person's life than by the speech that a person speaks. For this reason the Sophist worked to project the kind of character mask that would most likely persuade the hearer at hand. Sophists were not generally trusted since they were itinerant, and thus not "truly" known to their hearers; they taught wisdom, which the Greeks believed could not be acquired by verbal pedagogy, and they charged money for their services.

Plato represents a reactionary swing to the other side of the epistemological pendulum. Plato prized knowledge over opinion. Truth for Plato is reality, not a rhetorical construction. Words bear witness, if only in a shadowy way, to the unseen Truth. In view of this, Plato had no tolerance for rhetoric as advanced by the Sophists. For Plato, the rhetor is a witness to the Truth and as such must be a truly good person, even if such witness to and instantiation of the Truth demands martyrdom, as it did for Socrates.

---

65. Alan Brinton, "Quintilian, Plato, and the *Vir Bonus*," *Philosophy and Rhetoric* 16 (1983): 181.

For Aristotle, rhetoric is an art which has the function of seeing the available means of persuasion in any given situation. Certain stock proofs exist, both atechnic (such as witnesses) and entechnic, the artistic proofs invented by the rhetor. The three fundamental entechnic proofs are *logos* (the reasoned argumentation of the speech itself), *pathos* (the way in which the hearers are affected in a speech), and *ēthos* (the perceived moral character of the speaker). Of these three Aristotle gives priority of potency to persuade to *ēthos*. Unlike the Sophists or Plato, Aristotle does not take sides in the "perceived" or "real" character argument. Rather, he deals with the nature of "real" *ēthos* in his discussions of ethics and moral philosophy and "perceived" *ēthos* in dealing with the phenomenological realm of rhetoric. Given the nature of the rhetorical situation as one in which the speaker projects a certain *ēthos* and the hearers "read" that *ēthos* projection in certain ways, Aristotle urges the rhetor who would seek to be persuasive to study well one's target audience in order to wear the *ēthos* mask that would most appropriately play to their predispositions and prejudices.

Cicero takes up Aristotle's mantle, especially in his depiction of the three proofs in the speech. Like Aristotle, *ēthos* for Cicero is the chief proof in "the winning of our hearers' favor." And, like Aristotle, *ēthos* in the rhetorical situation has primarily to do with the perception of the hearers. However, Cicero does introduce the notion of "antecedent" *ēthos*, the reputation of the speaker in the minds of the hearers. The fact that Cicero deals with *ēthos* as a perceived phenomenon constructed by the hearers does not imply that he is a Sophist. Neither Aristotle nor Cicero advocated deceitful pragmatics. Each shows awareness of the limitations of the rhetorical event to deal only on the level of speaker projections and audience perceptions.

Quintilian is, at least on the topic of the person of the speaker, Plato redivivus. Goodness and eloquence coalesce for Quintilian in "the good man speaking well." The speaker becomes a kind of art form for Quintilian. Hence, he seems only remotely concerned about persuasion. For Quintilian, eloquence and goodness are oratorical ends in themselves, not pragmatic means of persuasion. Thus, it is possible in Quintilian's understanding of rhetoric for a person to be truly good and artistically eloquent but not necessarily persuasive. Quintilian disdains rhetoric as persuasion since that requires the rhetor to be successful in order to be considered eloquent. The rhetor, rather, is to be truly good and really eloquent — a Platonic abstraction perhaps impossible to instantiate — yet, a condition that Quintilian cannot imagine not being ultimately persuasive.

The four major rhetorical theorists that we have surveyed here can be grouped into two pairs based on the way in which they define rhetoric's aim, and the role *ēthos* plays in each system. Cicero and Quintilian mirror the differences we noted in Plato and Aristotle, particularly on the matter of whether moral character in the rhetorical situation is a matter of reality or perception. Nan Johnson notes that rhetorical theory to the present day mirrors these ancient dichotomies:

> The overall shape of the discipline of rhetoric can be understood as a composite of neo-Platonic and neo-Aristotelian views which incorporates the moral obligation of rhetoric to objective truth on the one hand and the strategic role of rhetoric in pragmatic communication on the other. The status of ethos in the hierarchy of rhetorical principles has fluctuated as rhetoricians in different eras have tended to define rhetoric in terms of either idealistic aims or pragmatic skills.[66]

Borrowing a heuristic device from Reader-Response criticism, it might prove useful to plot our findings to this point. In Wayne Booth and Wolfgang Iser's literary theory it is more accurate to speak of "the implied author" of a text since "the real author" is shrouded in mysterious hiddenness behind the text.[67] The implied author is that author that the reader constructs from the text itself. In turn, it is more accurate to speak of "the implied reader" of a text that emerges from the text itself rather than a "real reader" that exists outside the text, since there is really no way to identify an entity such as a "real reader" apart from the text itself. With this in view, observe the following chart which attempts to plot the nature of the speaker and hearer in the rhetorical situation according to the guidelines offered by Reader-Response criticism.

| Real Author | Implied Author | Text | Implied Reader | Real Reader |
|---|---|---|---|---|
| Real Spkr | Prcvd Spkr | Speech | Prcvd Hearer | Real Hearer |

**Fig. 2. Reader-Response Chart Applied to Speech Situation**

66. Nan Johnson, "Ethos and the Aims of Rhetoric," 105.
67. Cf. Wolfgang Iser, *From Reader Response to Literary Anthropology* (Baltimore: Johns Hopkins University Press, 1989); and, Wayne C. Booth, *The Rhetoric of Fiction* (Chicago: University of Chicago Press, 1961).

This chart shows the nature of *ēthos* from the rhetorical frame of reference. The nature of the rhetorical situation of the speech is more complex than that of reading, however, since both speaker and hearer are present physically to one another in ways that they are not in the rhetorical situation of reading a text.

Cicero's insight into the nature of antecedent *ēthos* further nuances our chart:

| Real Spkr | Prcvd Spkr | Antcdnt *Ēthos* of the Spkr | *Ēthos* of the Speech | Antcdnt *Ēthos* of the Hearers | Prcvd Hearer | Real Hearer |
|-----------|------------|------------------------------|------------------------|---------------------------------|--------------|-------------|
| → | → | → | X | ← | ← | ← |

**Fig. 3. Nuanced Reader-Response Chart
Applied to Speech Situation**

The hearer perceives the character of the speaker first through antecedent *ēthos* (reputation), and then through the *ēthos* which the speaker projects in the speech event itself. The speaker, in mirror-image fashion, perceives the character of the hearers first through antecedent *ēthos* (reputation) and then through their state, demeanor, reactions, etc., during the delivery of the speech itself.

These charts underscore Aristotle's insight into the phenomenological nature of the rhetorical situations of oral discourse. Access to the "real" person of the speaker and his or her "real" character is always mediated by the perception of the hearers. It is never immediately available to their consciousness without their interpretation of the rhetorical situation. Though Aristotle does not describe the perspective of the speaker regarding the hearer in mirror terms, the nature of the situation allows such, and the matter is further clarified in doing so. For in the process of "invention," speakers see an audience in their mind's eye, a projected audience of their imaginations based upon perception. It is a constructed image of the audience's character. This is crucial for speakers to do as they attempt to "connect" with their target group of hearers. But again, there is no pure immediacy to the "real" audience character, only a mediated construct. Even Aristotle's advice about adapting oneself to various audiences is an abstraction based upon imagined perception of their attitudes. Each rhetor must construct a perceived *ēthos* for himself or herself as speaker for the particular rhetorical situation, one which is governed by the implied or perceived audience which the rhetor imaginatively anticipates. Plato and Quintilian may accede to the fact that there is such a thing as "implied rhetor" and "implied hearer" but they would not likely agree to dirty their hands with such matters since that might smack of manipulation, or a compromise of the Truth in some way. The Sophists — at least the unscrupulous among them — would rejoice in the fact that the real rhetor is shrouded in mysterious hiddenness. For their goal of winning might be hampered if people knew who they "really" were in their essence. This chart will be taken up again in chapter four's discussion of the "real" and "perceived" preacher.

This backdrop of the classical rhetorical tradition will prove heuristic as we now turn to the homiletical tradition's portrayal of the preacher's person. Chapter two will survey representatives from the early and contemporary church regarding the intertwined issues of rhetoric's relationship to theology and the preacher's person in the rhetorical situation of Christian proclamation.

# 2. *Ēthos* in the Homiletical Tradition

Lord, how can man preach thy eternal word?
   He is a brittle crazy glass:
Yet in thy temple thou dost him afford
   This glorious and transcendent place,
   To be a window, through thy grace.
But when thou dost anneal in glass thy story,
   Making thy life to shine within
The holy preacher's; then the light and glory
   More rev'rend grows, and more doth win:
   Which else shows wat'rish, bleak, and thin.
Doctrine and life, colours and light, in one
   When they combine and mingle, bring
A strong regard and awe: but speech alone
   Doth vanish like a flaring thing,
And in the ear, not conscience ring.

*George Herbert*[1]

---

1. George Herbert, "The Windows," *George Herbert and Henry Vaughan*, ed. Louis L. Martz (London: Oxford University Press, 1986), 58.

## Introduction

The nature and role of the person of the preacher, preacher-*ēthos*, has been an important topic throughout the history of homiletical theory. Even so, it is a topic that straddles the fence, precariously positioned between two "logically diverse" frameworks of rationality, namely, rhetoric and theology.[2] That very phrase, "preacher-*ēthos*," highlights the fundamental tension that exists between the theological and the rhetorical. "Preacher" is a theological category, referring to one who proclaims the gospel of Jesus Christ crucified and risen. "*Ēthos*" is a rhetorical category, referring to the role that a speaker's character has in any given rhetorical situation. Preacher-*ēthos* has been construed differently throughout homiletical history largely based upon which of the two terms is considered primary, the theological or the rhetorical. Those who start with "*ēthos*" often begin from the standpoint of the hearer and from the nature of the rhetorical situation. Rhetorically oriented homiletics are predominately hearer-driven. Those who begin with "preacher" often begin with the message he or she conveys in the theological conviction that the preaching event is prompted and empowered by God. Theologically oriented homiletics are in the main message-driven.

Historically, the earliest pertinent discussion for our purposes concerns those pre-Augustinian Christian writers who saw no way to reconcile the conflict that exists between rhetoric and theology. Before Augustine there was a great fear of classical rhetoric among Christian theologians. In large part, they assumed that rhetoric would have a contaminating effect on the gospel. However, some, especially among the Greek fathers, disagreed, paving the way for Augustine.

## Rhetoric and Preaching in Conflict: The Latin Fathers

Until Augustine, the earliest centuries of the Christian era contained no systematized discussion of the relationship between rhetoric and preaching. What we have, rather, are sketchy comments that generally indicate al-

---

2. "Logically diverse" is a phrase borrowed from Hans Frei via Deborah van Deusen Hunsinger. Even though theology and rhetoric are each human sciences in a sense, they proceed with different operating assumptions and goals. These matters will be clarified in chapter four.

most total disdain for anything deemed extra-Christian. This is especially true for the Latin church fathers. The Greek fathers show some tolerance, anticipating Augustine's claim that truth, wherever it be found, is God's truth.

According to Gerard L. Ellspermann, "Christian humanism" is purported to have been born among the Greek fathers Justin Martyr, Clement of Alexandria, and Origen. In fact, Clement cited the writings of the ancient Greek poets in excess of seven hundred times. Though Origen initially sought to jettison non-Christian sources he later recognized their necessity, especially those of rhetoric. His reasons are apologetic: he sought a way to defend Christianity on the playing field of its despisers. Ellspermann says that Origen is "one who had resolutely accepted the study of rhetoric and philosophy by young Christian students without fear of their being corrupted." Other Greek fathers, such as Aristides and Tatian, are more critical of extra-Christian sources. Theophilus of Antioch is moderately critical.[3]

The Latin fathers' scorn for rhetoric was due to the perception that classical rhetoric was tainted by extra-Christian use. It was primarily used in the service of matters that had to do with heathen political, religious, and social matters. Partly because this new era of Christian authorship took place in Latin, it was easier to be critical of the Greek philosophical legacy.

These Latin Christian writers did not operate with the earlier sophistic, and later Augustinian, view that rhetoric was merely a neutral phenomenon which could be employed with any subject matter. Rather, seeing rhetoric functioning throughout the various human arenas of the judicial, demonstrative, and epideictic kinds, they deemed rhetoric guilty by association. In the early apocalyptically oriented Christian framework of discourse, such "this-worldly" arenas were viewed as antithetical to the Kingdom of God and its gospel.[4] Peter Brown comments:

3. Gerard L. Ellspermann, "The Attitude of the Early Christian Latin Writers Toward Pagan Literature and Learning," *The Catholic University of America Patristic Studies* 82 (1949): 11-13.

4. Of course, this was based on Christians' perceptions. In reality, the early purveyors of Christian discourse "were both less and more distinctive than they themselves supposed. Indeed, the prominence of the notion of the *difference* between Christian and pagan expression in the work of the Christian writers themselves is to be read as a rhetorical device and a symptom of adjustment rather than as a description of a real situation." Cf. Averil Cameron, *Christianity and the Rhetoric of Empire: The Development of Christian Discourse*, Sather Classical Lectures, vol. 55 (Berkeley: University of California Press, 1991), 7.

Christian rejection of the classics was met by a pagan "fundamental-ism"; the conservatives crudely "divinized" their traditional literature; the classics were treated as a gift of the gods to men. Christians for their part, would play in with this reaction by "diabolizing" the same litera-ture. Many, indeed, wanted to end this tension by denying culture alto-gether.[5]

Some key Latin writers from the pre-Augustine period illustrate Brown's point.

Tertullian (160-225 A.D.) sardonically asked, "What indeed has Ath-ens to do with Jerusalem? What concord is there between the Academy and the church? What between heretics and Christians?"[6] Tertullian drew a sharp line between Christianity and anything deemed outside the faith. All things were to proceed from and return to the "rule of faith," for "every-thing worth knowing must proceed from the revelation of God." If, how-ever, one looks not only at Tertullian's critique, but his manner of critique, one sees that "he shows, on the whole, a secret, kindly attraction for rheto-ric, its refinements, and its tricks of style."[7]

Cyprian (d. 258 A.D.) encourages a spare use of rhetoric for Christian speakers:

> In courts of justice, in the public meetings, in political discussions, a full eloquence may be the pride of vocal ambition, but in speaking of the Lord God, a pure simplicity of expression which is convincing, depends upon the substance of the argument rather than upon the forcefulness of eloquence.[8]

It is apparent that, for Cyprian, the argument of the speech takes complete precedence over other aspects of the event. Cyprian thus relegates all spo-ken matters to *logos,* brushing aside the importance of *pathos* or *ēthos* in Christian discourse.

Jerome (342-420 A.D.) advises preachers to abandon rhetoric. He ar-gues that it is, in fact, antithetical to Christian proclamation. He punctu-ates this conviction with an authoritative experience analogous to Paul's Damascus road revelation. In a letter to Eustochium in 384 A.D., entitled

---

5. Peter Brown, *Augustine of Hippo* (Berkeley: University of California Press, 1967), 265.

6. Tertullian, *De Praescriptione,* PL II co. 20a-b.

7. Ellspermann, "The Attitude of Early Christian Latin Writers," 41-42.

8. *Ad Donatus,* CSEL 3, 4, 10-13. Cited in Ellspermann, "The Attitude of Early Chris-tian Latin Writers," 51.

"The Virgin's Profession," Jerome urges the woman to stay clear of all manner of secular matters since they would endanger her Christian commitment. Because of their remarkable nature, I quote Jerome's words at length:

> Do not appear over-eloquent. . . . So much do they like adultery even of the tongue. 'What communion hath light with darkness? What concord hath Christ with Belial?' What has Horace to do with the Psalter, Virgil with the Gospels and Cicero with Paul? Is not a brother made to stumble if he sees you sitting at table in an idol's temple? Although unto the pure all things are pure and nothing is to be refused if it be received with thanksgiving, still we ought not to drink the cup of Christ and the cup of devils at the same time. I will tell you the story of my own unhappiness.
>
> Many years ago for the sake of the Kingdom of heaven I cut myself off from home, parents, sister, relations, and, what was harder, from the dainty food to which I had been used. But even when I was on my way to Jerusalem to fight the good fight there, I would not bring myself to forgo the library which with great care and labour I had got together at Rome. And so, miserable man that I was, I would fast, only to read Cicero afterwards. I would spend long nights in vigil, I would shed bitter tears called from my inmost heart by the remembrance of my past sins; and then I would take up Plautus again. Whenever I returned to my right senses and began to read the prophets, their language seemed harsh and barbarous. . . . While the old serpent was thus mocking me, about the middle of Lent a fever attacked my weakened body . . . the ravages it wrought on my unhappy frame were so persistent that at last my bones scarcely held together.
>
> Meantime preparations were made for my funeral: my whole body grew gradually cold, and life's vital warmth only lingered faintly in my poor throbbing breast. Suddenly I was caught up in the spirit and dragged before the Judge's judgment seat: and here the light was so dazzling, and the brightness shining from those who stood around so radiant, that I flung myself upon the ground and did not dare to look up. I was asked to state my condition and replied that I was a Christian. But He who presided said: "Thou liest; thou art a Ciceronian, not a Christian. 'For where thy treasure is there will thy heart be also.'"

Jerome was subsequently tortured by a whip, but even more so by his conscience, he tells us. After intercession by those watching, the Judge allowed Jerome to repent "on the understanding that the extreme torture should be inflicted on me if ever I read again the works of Gentile authors." He insists that it was no mere dream, for upon waking his shoulders were black and blue, and he felt the pain of the bruises for quite some time. "And I acknowledge that henceforth I read the books of God with a greater zeal than I had ever given before to the books of men."[9]

That the Latin fathers were reticent as to how classical rhetoric and philosophy could be reconciled to Christianity is especially interesting given the personal background and training that they had in this area. As Kennedy indicates,

> it is a remarkable fact that of the eight greatest Latin Fathers of the Church, five (Tertullian, Cyprian, Arnobius, Lactantius, and Augustine) were professional rhetoricians before they became Christians, while the other three (Ambrose, Hilary, and Jerome) were thoroughly trained in the rhetorical schools.[10]

Each struggled with this question: What from my pre-Christian life may be brought into my Christian life without compromising the purity of the faith?

A basic and persistent irony exists between what Christian writers say about the dangers of rhetoric and how they still use it in their writing and speaking. They are critical of rhetoric in rhetorically impressive ways. Indeed, it could be argued that even Jerome's dream/revelation functions as a powerful *ēthos* argument as he uses the vision to repudiate rhetoric.

As the time of Augustine's synthetic analysis neared, Kennedy observes a growing tolerance toward classical rhetoric among the church's preachers, a tolerance that he ascribes to pragmatic forces:

> We need not charge such thoughtful Christians as Gregory or Chrysostom with pandering to the mob, but they were concerned with moving the hearts of their audience and inspiring their lives, and the devices of sophistic rhetoric had become the cues to which their audiences responded and by which their purposes could be best accomplished. This trend is in many ways a victory for classical rhetoric. Ambitious young Christians now did not hesitate to study in the schools of rheto-

9. Jerome, Letter XXII.29-30, *Selected Letters of Jerome*, trans. F. A. Wright, The Loeb Classical Library (London: William Heinemann, Ltd., 1933), 127.

10. George Kennedy, *Classical Rhetoric and Its Christian and Secular Tradition from Ancient to Modern Times* (Chapel Hill, NC: The University of North Carolina Press, 1980), 146.

ric, and as the fourth century advanced, the Christian communities were less and less a simple company of simple folk content with the message of the gospel.[11]

Chrysostom argues that rhetoric is necessary for the preacher to use because of human weakness. It is theologically justifiable as a matter of accommodation. The gospel, as received, is not enough by itself. The people need more than "the simple gospel." This "more" is provided by rhetorical embellishment.[12]

A major shift occurred in the fourth century under the leadership of Constantine and Theodosius I. With Constantine's conversion to Christianity and the subsequent Christianization of the Roman Empire, many things which were formally pagan and political were "baptized into Christ." Augustine uses the image of smuggled goods from Egypt to describe the act of smuggling rhetoric into the Christian camp. The task was to make such goods useful for God's people. What remained for Christianity now that it had conquered the world was to make Christian, without succumbing to potential idolatry, those elements taken captive that seemed "useful" for Christianity's ends. This was Augustine's triumph in *On Christian Doctrine*.

## The Church's First Homiletic:
## Augustine's *On Christian Doctrine*

Possidius indicates that once Augustine became a Christian he made a choice to forgo teaching rhetoric in order to carry out his resolve to be God's servant. That these two pursuits, teaching rhetoric and being God's servant, demanded a choice for Augustine says something important about his new convictions as a Christian. But though he stopped teaching rhetoric, he did not totally abandon his classical past, as Tertullian claims to have done. In Book 4 of *On Christian Doctrine* (hereafter *OCD*) we hear Augustine explain his understanding of the relationship of rhetoric to Christian preaching.

For Augustine, the relationship of preaching to rhetoric comes at the end of a larger discussion on the proper exegetical method to be applied to

11. Kennedy, *Classical Rhetoric*, 145-46.
12. See Kennedy, *Classical Rhetoric*.

scripture. In other words, eloquence in preaching is understood as essentially the ability to articulate what one has interpreted in scripture. Book 4 of *OCD* clearly shows Augustine's continuing debt to rhetoric, especially to the one he calls "the author of Roman eloquence," never mentioning Cicero by name.

Because of Christianity's continuing use of scripture, Augustine divides the preacher's task into fundamentally two movements: interpretation and articulation. Augustine's *OCD* can be helpfully structured according to these two movements. As Augustine himself states: "There are two things necessary to the treatment of the Scriptures: a way of discovering those things which are to be understood, and a way of teaching what we have learned. We shall speak first of discovery [Books 1-3] and second of teaching [Book 4]."[13]

Just as Quintilian attempts to portray the mythical "Ideal Orator," in Book 4 Augustine portrays the Christian counterpart to this classical ideal. It concerns six particular matters in the development of the ideal Christian orator: (1) the neutrality of rhetoric/eloquence; (2) speaking with both wisdom and eloquence; (3) clarity; (4) the tests of oratory and their styles; (5) the role of God in Christian oratory; and, (6) the role of the preacher's person in preaching.

## (1) The Neutrality of Rhetoric/Eloquence

Augustine makes clear that this will not be a rulebook of rhetorical principles. Rather, he offers a "theology of rhetoric." Rhetoric, to Augustine, is a

13. Augustine, *On Christian Doctrine* (New York: Macmillan Publishers, 1958), 1.1. No consensus exists as to what the primary subject matter of *OCD* is. Eugene Kevane organizes the discussion into four main views: (1) it is a treatise of biblical hermeneutics; (2) it is a textbook of rhetoric; (3) Marrou's influential view that it presents a comprehensive Christian culture; and (4) it is a treatise on education. In spite of this disparity, Gerald Press argues that these four viewpoints are not necessarily irreconcilable: "Augustine's DDC [*De Doctrina Christiana*] is about all of these things. It is a rhetoric in which exegesis plays a large part; like other ancient rhetorics (esp. Isocrates and Cicero) it purports to be or provide a comprehensive paideia; and as such it defines the cultural ideals of the new community. But since it defines them substantially in terms borrowed from the old culture, the work at the same time addresses the members of the old community and relates old to new by offering a new and special content for what is nevertheless affirmed as a common value." See Gerald A. Press, "The Subject and Structure of Augustine's De Doctrina Christiana," *Augustinian Studies* 11 (1980): 101, 123. Kevane's points are summarized by Press.

neutral tool of human expression. It carries no baggage. It creates no knowledge. As Augustine expresses it:

> By means of the art of rhetoric both truth and falsehood are urged; who would dare to say that truth should stand in the person of its defenders unarmed against lying, so that they who wish to urge falsehoods may know how to make their listeners benevolent, or attentive, or docile in their presentation, while the defenders of truth are ignorant of that art? . . . While the faculty of eloquence, which is of great value in urging either evil or justice, is in itself indifferent, why should it not be obtained for the uses of the good in the service of truth if the evil usurp it for the winning of perverse and vain causes in defense of iniquity and error?[14]

Augustine wants this book to be about the nature of preaching the Christian message, not rhetoric. However, he believes that rhetoric will make the Christian message competitive in the marketplace of ideas. How, then, is the Christian orator to learn this matter of eloquence? In two ways: (1) by observing the eloquence of scripture and the church's consequently eloquent spokespersons; and (2) by learning from Augustine here in Book 4 of *OCD*. Much of Book 4, then, is devoted to the development of a theory of Christian eloquence.

For Augustine the primary role of the preacher is to be "the defender of right faith and the enemy of error."[15] Preaching is fundamentally a labor of words in which the Christian orator is to: (1) conciliate opponents; (2) arouse those who are remiss; and (3) teach the ignorant.

## (2) Speaking with Wisdom and Eloquence Together

For Augustine, the Christian orator is set apart from classical orators in that the Christian orator is not simply eloquent, but also wise. Ironically, his rationale for this comes from Cicero.[16] Reflecting Cicero's *De Inventione* 1.1.1, he writes: "Wisdom without eloquence is of small benefit to states; but eloquence without wisdom is often extremely injurious and

14. Augustine, *OCD*, 4.2.3.
15. Augustine, *OCD*, 4.4.6. On this see Brown, *Augustine of Hippo*, 266.
16. In this regard, see esp., James Burnette Eskridge, *The Influence of Cicero upon Augustine in the Development of His Oratorical Training for the Training of the Ecclesiastical Orator* (Menasha, WI: The Collegiate Press, George Banta Publishing, 1912).

profits no one."[17] Baptizing Cicero into Christ, Augustine defines wise speech as expertise in the interpretation of holy scripture. Speaking wisely, i.e., interpreting scripture with understanding and bringing out its proper "sense," is the Christian orator's primary goal. But speaking wisely with eloquence is the ultimate achievement: "He can be of more worth if he can do both." They who speak eloquently delight their hearer so that they are heard with pleasure, while "he who speaks wisely is heard with profit."[18] The goal is twofold: (1) to hold the attention of one's hearers with a pleasing style, while (2) profiting their souls with wise content. He underscores this with an illustration from Paul, for "his wisdom was accompanied by eloquence." Indeed, Paul is a "companion to wisdom and a leader of eloquence, following the first and not scorning the second."

Augustine quotes Paul's description of the nature of his ministry from 2 Cor. 2:16-30 and comments at length on it. "Those who are awake will see how much wisdom lies in these words. With what a river of eloquence they flow that even he who snores must notice." But one quickly sees that Augustine is not commenting on the content of this text which likens the apostolic ministry to that of prisoners in a shameful parade of defeat, but rather on the stylistic character of Paul's argument, i.e., the way in which it is organized and presented via *caesa, kommata, membra,* and *circuitus.* Paul's argument in its content does not concern Augustine here, nor the way in which that content might inform the way it is articulated. Rather, for Augustine, the wisdom here lies in the style, as Paul "makes his hearer rest also with a charm and delight which I cannot sufficiently describe."[19] Augustine misses an ironic twist in Paul's argument, though, by assuming that Paul quotes his Corinthian critics approvingly.


## (3) Clarity

There are two aspects to clarity: (1) the clarity of the speech itself, i.e., the formal characteristics which the classical rhetoricians stress; and (2) the clarity of the interpretation of a difficult text.

Regarding the first aspect, Augustine goes counter to many of his predecessors in rhetoric in advising the speaker to use common ways of

17. Augustine, *OCD,* 4.5.7.
18. Augustine, *OCD,* 4.5.8.
19. Augustine, *OCD,* 4.7.11-13.

speech so that even the untrained listener could receive and understand the message. In this the classical rhetorician has been influenced by the gospel.

Clarity of speech, style, and vocabulary is important for Augustine so that people do not misunderstand the message on account of mere mechanics. If they are to misunderstand, it should be because of the nature of the message itself. However, according to Augustine, misunderstanding should rarely, if ever, occur. This is because difficult texts, which may cause sermons that are difficult to understand, should rarely be used as sermon texts. Instead, they should be written about so that the time of oral communication is reserved for the greater number of texts that speak not only truth, but with clarity themselves. Moreover, in 4.1-13, Augustine argues that difficult texts, when preached upon, should be explained with clarity even when one's study of the text reveals ambiguity. The sermon should be clear even if the text is not. This places the virtue of clarity, a virtue of classical rhetoric, above the concern to reduplicate the text's message. Allegory was a key hermeneutical tool in homiletically clarifying exegetical conundrums.

If one has to choose between being either eloquent or clear, there is no real choice: "The speaker should not consider the eloquence of his teaching but the clarity of it." What Augustine means by this is that "he who teaches should thus avoid all words which do not teach," i.e., one should waste no words merely for aesthetic or methodological ends.[20] In fact, if one fulfills the dictum of clarity one will be eloquent. His concern is that the truth be loved more than the words which bear them. He wants a balance between biblical truth and rhetoric. The burden of Book 4 of *OCD* is to effect a happy marriage between two potentially volatile entities, "the Gospel, spoken well." Thus, the ideal Christian orator will exposit scripture in a way that is faithful to scripture's center (love), while being pleasing to hear. "Even that food without which life is impossible must be seasoned."[21]

## (4) Tests of Oratory and Their Styles

Turning again to Cicero as if citing scripture, Augustine writes, "Therefore a certain eloquent man said, and said truly, that he who is eloquent should

20. Augustine, *OCD*, 4.9.23-24.
21. Augustine, *OCD*, 4.11.26.

speak in such a way that he teaches, delights, and moves. Then he added, "To teach is a necessity, to please is a sweetness, to persuade is a victory.'"[22] It can be said that Augustine takes these classical rhetorical virtues of eloquence and "puts them to Christian use."[23] For Augustine, teaching has to do with the content of what is taught, while delighting and persuading pertain to "the manner in which we say it." There is a progression to these as well of which the orator should be conscious. One teaches and delights while moving toward persuasion. "And of what use are the first two if the third does not follow?"[24] He is quick to point out, however, that delighting and persuading are not essential. Indeed, there is a delight and a persuasiveness to the truth itself that is beyond mere adornment and manipulation. He does not make clear, however, how truth's raw power to persuade is to be distinguished from the speaker's use of rhetoric to make the truth attractive. What would "the Truth" without rhetorical framing look like? Ultimately for Augustine, the use of rhetorical categories is a matter of accommodation to the post-Fall condition of human hearing and knowing:

> It is necessary therefore for the ecclesiastical orator, when he urges that something be done, not only to teach that he may instruct and to please that he may hold attention, but also to persuade that he may be victorious. For it now remains for that man [the hearer], in whom the demonstration of truth, even when suavity of diction was added, did not move to consent, to be persuaded by the heights of eloquence.[25]

There is, however, always the possibility that one will become too ornate in communicating the message of scripture. When this happens, the gift wrapping often becomes more loved than the present itself. "Trivial and fragile truths are ornamented with a frothy nexus of words of a kind which could not properly be used to ornament even weighty and important matters."[26]

Providing a nice balance to the three tests of oratory ("Does it teach, delight, persuade?"), Augustine couples each with an appropriate style. He derives this, too, from Cicero. Echoes of Quintilian also reverberate as Augustine claims almost in passing that success in eloquence is not to be

22. Augustine, *OCD*, 4.12.27.
23. G. W. Doyle, "Augustine's Sermonic Method," *Westminster Theological Journal* 39 (1976-77): 213.
24. Augustine, *OCD*, 4.12.28.
25. Augustine, *OCD*, 4.13.29.
26. Augustine, *OCD*, 4.14.31.

gauged by whether one persuades his or her hearers to agree with his or her position. Rather, the test for success is whether one has taught, delighted, and persuaded in the appropriate styles of each mode, that is, the subdued, the temperate, and the grand.

There seems to be a bit of an inconsistency here in his combining of Cicero and Quintilian. How can one fulfill at the same time the demand that the speech be persuasive in order to be successful (test #3), while claiming one's success is not dependent on actually persuading listeners, but rather on simply delivering the persuasive aspect of the speech in the grand style? Persuasiveness defined this way becomes a matter of style rather than result. Is the test for success aesthetic or pragmatic? Elsewhere in the *OCD*, however, Augustine insists that persuasion is not simply a matter of style, but of action and effect:

> For it is the universal office of eloquence, in any of these three styles, to speak in a manner leading to persuasion; and the end of eloquence is to persuade of that which you are speaking. In any of these three styles an eloquent man speaks in a manner suitable to persuasion, but if he does not persuade, he has not attained the end of eloquence.[27]

Every style, as every aspect of the orator's duty (including teaching and delighting), is trained upon the one end of persuasion. Indeed, Augustine even claims that when one speaks in the subdued or temperate styles that God may provide the "grand" boost to our subdued discourse and move the hearer to action.[28] This leads us to his fifth emphasis. One concern that remains, however, is whether the aesthetic or pragmatic goals coincide with goals inherent to the gospel.

## (5) God's Role in Christian Oratory

Where is God in all of this? Is preaching nothing more than the mastery of exegetical method and rhetorical artistry so that our subject is cogent, interesting, and convincing? Does God play any role in proclamation?

> Thus this orator of ours, when he speaks of the just and holy and good — nor should he speak of anything else — so acts when he speaks that

27. Augustine, *OCD*, 4.25.55.
28. Augustine, *OCD*, 4.18.37.

he may be understood and that he may be willingly and obediently heard. And he should not doubt that he is able to do these things, if he is at all able and to the extent that he is able, more through the piety of his prayers than through the skill of his oratory, so that praying for himself and for those whom he is to address, he is a petitioner before he is a speaker. When the hour in which he is to speak approaches, before he begins to preach, he should raise his thirsty soul to God in order that he may give forth what he shall drink, or pour out what shall fill him.[29]

Above all, Augustine's ideal Christian orator is dependent upon God. God is the source of the preacher's "ability" to teach, delight, and persuade. "He is a petitioner before he is a speaker." There are many things that the preacher must say to the people, and there are many ways in which these things can be said, but

> who knows better how we should say them or how they should be heard through us at the present time than He who sees "the hearts of all men"? ... And for this reason, he who would both know and teach should learn everything which should be taught and acquire a skill in speaking appropriate to an ecclesiastic, but at the time of the speech itself he should think that which the Lord says more suitable to good thought: "Take no thought how or what to speak: for it shall be given you in that hour what to speak. For it is not you that speak, but the Spirit of your Father that speaketh in you." If the Holy Spirit speaks in those who are given over to persecutors for the sake of Christ, why should it not also in those who give over Christ to learners?[30]

Augustine expresses a "both/and" argument here. One should *both* do all one can in interpretation and articulation *and* should be expectant that God will bring the message God chooses. Preachers fret over how best to understand scripture and then how best to express that which they have discovered, and that is as it should be. But when all is said and done, Augustine urges the preacher to allow God to fulfill his promise to say and do what needs saying and doing in that given situation.

For Augustine, prayer is the most crucial aspect of the preacher's ministry. As Augustine concludes Book 4 he returns to this topic to stress

---

29. Augustine, *OCD*, 4.15.32.
30. Augustine, *OCD*, 4.15.32.

the preacher's ultimate dependence on God for a good word to preach. The ideal Christian orator

> should pray that God may place a good speech in his mouth. For if Queen Esther prayed . . . that God would place "a well ordered speech" in her mouth, how much more ought he to pray for such a reward who labors in word and teaching for the eternal salvation of men. . . . And for the profitable result of their speech they should give thanks to Him from whom they should not doubt they have received it, so that he who glories may glory in Him whose 'hand are both we and our words.'[31]

Augustine does not elaborate on how exactly God's work in preaching is related to the preacher's work. He simply urges preachers to do their work and assures them that God will do God's.

## (6) The Role of the Preacher's Person in Preaching

Augustine's description of the preacher's life shows his dependence on the classical rhetorical understanding of *ēthos,* one that goes back through Quintilian and Cicero to Aristotle.

Augustine describes the ideal Christian orator's task as one of speaking with the wisdom of scripture in an eloquence which instructs, pleases, and persuades. In terms of Aristotle's "available means of persuasion," namely *ēthos, pathos,* and *logos,* Augustine develops only the latter two. As Book 4 nears its conclusion he takes up the category of *ēthos.* Augustine writes:

> However, the life of the speaker has greater weight in determining whether he is obediently heard than any grandness of eloquence.[32]

Aristotle's echo is not difficult to hear: "Moral character *(ēthos)* may almost be called the most potent means of persuasion."[33]

Augustine notes one explicit rebuttal to the traditional *ēthos* argument when it is applied to preaching. He recognizes it in Paul with regard to his enemies. They preached the gospel while Paul was in prison, hoping

---

31. Augustine, *OCD,* 4.30.63.
32. Augustine, *OCD,* 4.27.59.
33. Aristotle, *On Rhetoric,* 1.2.4.

that it would make matters worse for him. Thus, some were preaching the gospel out of jealousy or hatred toward Paul. They preached the gospel only as a pretense, their actual goal being malevolent toward the apostle. Augustine addresses this:

> For he who speaks wisely and eloquently, but lives wickedly, may benefit many students, although, as it is written, he "is unprofitable to his own soul." Whence the Apostle also said, "Whether as a pretext, or in truth [let] Christ be preached." For Christ is the Truth, and, moreover, the truth may be announced but not in truth, that is, evil and fallacious hearts may preach what is right and true. Thus indeed is Jesus Christ announced by those who "seek the things that are their own, not the things that are Jesus Christ's." . . . "All things whatsoever they shall say to you, observe and do: but according to their works do ye not," thus they may hear usefully those who do not act usefully.[34]

Augustine argues that there is "benefit" to hearers even from a preacher possessing poor character. What is "right and true" may even be proclaimed by the immoral.

Yet, what Augustine means concerning "benefit" is unclear. For he argues that it is possible to teach wisely *(logos)* and even delight eloquently *(pathos)*, but without personal moral character *(ēthos)* persuasion is unlikely:

> And thus they benefit many by preaching what they do not practice; but many more would be benefitted if they were to do what they say. For there are many who seek a defense of their evil lives in those of their superiors and teachers, responding in their hearts or, if it breaks forth so far, with their lips, and saying, "Why do you not do what you preach that I do?" Thus it happens that they do not obediently hear one who does not hear himself, and they condemn the word of God which is preached to them along with the preacher himself.[35]

"Practice what you preach" is an imperative that has achieved proverbial status.

For Augustine, though, there is a pragmatic reason to fulfill this imperatival proverb: if one does not practice what one preaches it impairs the persuasive capacity of that which is preached. *"They do not obediently*

---

34. Augustine, *OCD*, 4.27.59.
35. Augustine, *OCD*, 4.28.60.

*hear one who does not hear himself, and they condemn the word of God which is preached to them along with the preacher himself."* Augustine cites Paul approvingly in this vein when he instructed Timothy to be "an example of the faithful in word, in conduct, in charity, in faith, in chastity."[36] Augustine applies Paul's words to rhetorical ends:

> A teacher with these virtues, in order that he may be obediently heard, speaks without shame not only in the subdued and moderate style but also in the grand style because he does not live contemptibly.[37]

One who lives out the Christian virtues becomes more persuasive in every style of oratory.

Augustine recognizes as well that there will be Christian orators who do not live up to his ideal of speaking with wisdom and eloquence. If this is the case, all is not lost. For the preacher in his or her way of life also has a certain rhetorical impact:

> However, if he cannot do this [be orally eloquent in a classical manner], let him so order his life that he not only prepares a reward for himself, but also so that he offers an example to others, and his way of living may be, as it were, an eloquent speech.[38]

This survey of *OCD* reveals Augustine's argument for the adaptation of methods from classical rhetoric for pragmatic purposes. Several assumptions undergird this: (1) rhetoric is a neutral phenomenon; (2) the situation of Christian preaching is essentially rhetorical, i.e., a version of classical rhetorical situations; and (3) given these two assumptions, Cicero's rhetorical theory can be adopted by the ideal Christian orator uncritically.

Though Augustine started with the message, as is evident in his extended discussion of the interpretation of scripture in Books 1-3, when he turns to the articulation of the message he drops the use of the message as a means of assessing how one might legitimately appropriate classical rhetoric for preaching. He can do this because of his assumption that rhetoric is ideologically neutral and therefore needs no theological discrimination in its appropriation. However, what is becoming more clear is the fact that

---

36. Cf. 1 Tim. 4:12 and *OCD*, 4.27.60.

37. Augustine, *OCD*, 4.28.61.

38. Augustine, *OCD*, 4.29.61.

rhetoric subtly shifts the starting point for reflecting on all categories pertaining to the preaching situation from the message to the hearer. With rhetoric as preaching's guide, the hearers and their situation are becoming the primary determinant for how the message ought to be framed and articulated.

Augustine's treatment of the preacher's person proceeds from a rhetorical vantage point. He assumes the "neutral" advice of classical rhetoric on the matter, tying the preacher's person to one's effectiveness in persuasion. And it is at this point that he ties the person back to the message. But the message is largely abstract and one which reflects his presupposition that charity is preaching's central message. Quoting 1 Tim. 4:12, he writes: "Be thou an example of the faithful in word, in conduct, in charity, in faith, in chastity."[39] To what does Augustine's "ideal preacher," as a person, bear witness? Augustine's ideal preacher is similar to Quintilian's ideal orator, embodying the classical ideals, yet all in a frame of love of God and neighbor. The preacher's life should be one that embodies the threefold goal of delighting, teaching, and moving to persuasion.[40] Augustine often quotes at length Paul's self-description from 1 Cor. 1–4, but always in terms of its stylistic arrangement and effect on the hearer, rather than in terms of its claim on the life of the preacher whose own life is claimed by the cross.

Rarely in the homiletical tradition which follows Augustine does anyone question his key assumption about the neutrality of rhetoric. Yet one's position on this issue determines in large measure how one understands the nature and function of ministerial *ēthos*. Is rhetoric without ideological baggage? Are there no consequences for its use with any subject matter? Without an awareness of rhetoric's own powerful presuppositions and assumptions about discourse, situations, and outcomes, and without appropriate theological discretion, rhetoric can mean the subversion of the message itself.

In a related matter, Philip D. Kenneson has pinpointed one of the hidden presuppositions of the church growth theorists as the belief "that management and marketing techniques are themselves neutral, and so appropriating them poses no problem in principle for the church." Kenneson points out that such a position fails to recognize that "all technique is value-laden." Indeed, "by framing certain issues in particular ways these activities help *constitute* the very problems and conditions about which

39. Augustine, *OCD*, 4.27.60.
40. Augustine, *OCD*, 4.28.61.

they purport to be neutral."[41] The lens through which one looks alters what is seen. The lens determines what is seen in some sense. If rhetoric is understood in the Aristotelian sense of discovering the available means of persuasion in any given situation, and if the preaching of the gospel is viewed through this lens, one is led to ask, "How can I speak this gospel in such a way that hearers will believe it?" "What are the ways in which people are moved to belief, and how can I marshal those in this particular situation (worship of the faith community), with this particular subject matter (the gospel of Christ crucified and risen)?"

Technique is not neutral. Kenneson illustrates his point:

> Asserting that a hammer can be used both for construction or destruction does not establish its neutrality, for such an assertion fails to acknowledge the power a hammer has to shape the way one views and acts in the world. In short, having a hammer in your hand, whether for construction or destruction, encourages you to see every target as a nail. Ascribing neutrality to technique is supported by several assumptions, but three are especially important here: first, that a clear distinction can and should be made between form and content; second, that an equally clear distinction can and should be made between means and ends; and third, that within the above two distinctions, form and means are variable while content and ends remain constant.[42]

Augustine's second assumption, the situations of Christian oratory are essentially rhetorical, i.e., analogous to classically rhetorical situations, is only partially accurate. It will be argued more fully in chapters three and four that the Christian situation of worship can be construed to be a competitive situation, but what ought to be persuasive to the church at worship in this situation? In what sense does the Christian gospel of Jesus Christ crucified judge criteria for assessment that are derived outside the faith community, i.e., standards for speaker credibility?

Finally, Augustine's assumption about the neutrality of rhetoric permitted him to treat the person of the preacher primarily within the frame provided by the classical tradition. His construal of preaching's message, love of God and neighbor, exacted no critique of rhetoric's categories regarding the person of the preacher.

---

41. Philip D. Kenneson, "Selling [Out] the Church in the Marketplace of Desire," *Modern Theology* 9 (1993): 325-26.

42. Kenneson, "Selling [Out]," 327.

Augustine's *OCD* is a homiletic in tension between the message-driven demands of the gospel and the hearer-driven demands of the rhetorical situation that is preaching. As one well-trained rhetorically, Augustine frequently shifts uncritically into that frame of reference for evaluating the nature of preaching. This is especially the case when he treats the person of the preacher. In his theological treatment, Augustine asserts that the preacher truly ought to be a certain kind of person — the "real" preacher as authentic Christian. Moreover, he does avoid donatistic tendencies by indicating that the word can be rightly and efficaciously preached by evil people. In his rhetorical treatment, Augustine functionally rubber-stamps Aristotle's and Cicero's insights that the person of the preacher is the most persuasive aspect in the rhetorical situation of Christian proclamation.

## Rhetoric Suffers a "Barth Attack"

Homiletical theory largely followed Augustine's lead until Karl Barth.[43] As James J. Murphy comments, "no second Augustine appeared to propose a rhetoric of preaching."[44] Neither did anyone stand in the way of Augustine's assumptions concerning rhetoric.

Barth was a Swiss Reformed theologian whose theology of the Word of God challenged nineteenth-century liberalism and created the movement known as neoorthodoxy. His years spent as a preaching pastor in Safenwil (1911-1921) cannot be underestimated in the influence they wielded in Barth's theological shift. The implications of Barth's theology of the Word would have significant ramifications for understanding the person of the preacher.

Barth's homiletical starting point is God: "Preaching is the Word of

---

43. For representative voices along the way to the twentieth century, see Gregory the Great, Alan of Lille, Humbert of Romans, Robert of Basevorn, St. Francis of Sales, Alexander Vinet, John Broadus, and Phillips Brooks. Even theorists who have a strong theological emphasis, e.g., Gregory and Alan, show by their treatment of the preacher's person that they blur the lines between the rhetorical and theological frames of reference. This causes them to cloud the distinction between efficacy and persuasion in such a way as to be open to the charge of homiletical Donatism. Although he authored no systematic homiletic, Martin Luther stands as an exception to the predominant view of preaching as "sacred rhetoric."

44. James J. Murphy, *Rhetoric in the Middle Ages: A History of Rhetorical Theory from St. Augustine to the Renaissance* (Berkeley: University of California Press, 1974), 297.

God which he himself has spoken."[45] God chooses to use human words but is never bound by human words. God remains ever free and in that freedom gracefully chooses to use preaching as an avenue for revelation. The preacher must not, however, become arrogant, for preaching depends always on God and is possible only by God's power. "Revelation is a closed system in which God is the subject, the object, and the middle term." In preaching, "God alone must speak."[46] Preaching is not a forum for human thoughts, ideas, reflections, or the propagation of ideologies.

Preaching is hoisted between a "whence" and a "whither."[47] The "whence" is preaching's point of departure, namely the incarnation of Jesus Christ. The "whither" is preaching's point of return, namely the Parousia of Jesus Christ. Thus, the first coming and the second coming of Christ set the limits and content for preaching. Incarnation is paradigmatic for God's revelatory activity among human beings. God's Word descends vertically from above. The Word cannot begin below and be a Word of God. The Word must come from above, meet humanity below, and point to the fulfillment of God's revelation in the eschaton. The church preaches because God chooses this venue for God's self-revelation. We preach for no other reason. "Revelation is the only legitimate ground for preaching." It is clear that in designating preaching as God's work first and last, Barth radically redefines the preacher's role: "Take note of what is said, for it is unique: it is the Word of God and it owes nothing to man's ingenuity; he can only bear witness to it."[48]

Barth sums up the preacher's role as a "duty" or "task." The preacher is primarily a "herald," a "*kēryx*." The Word must be served and the preacher's task is to bear witness to that Word as scripture bears definitive witness to it. God reveals, the preacher sees, and tells. The preacher does not invent. Rather, the preacher obediently repeats the Word which he or she is shown.

Interestingly, Barth does list four qualities or "criteria on which, humanly speaking, authenticity [in a preacher] is usually made dependent." (1) The preacher must be aware of an interior call to the office of minister. Even this call, however, rests on it being *God's* call, not what the preacher knows or feels. (2) The preacher must be above reproach. "Ministers

45. Karl Barth, *The Preaching of the Gospel*, trans. B. E. Hooke (Philadelphia: The Westminster Press, 1963), 9.

46. Barth, *Preaching of the Gospel,* 12, 15.

47. Karl Barth, *Homiletics*, trans. Geoffrey W. Bromiley and Donald E. Daniels (Louisville: Westminster/John Knox Press, 1991), 51-55.

48. Barth, *Preaching of the Gospel,* 22, 82.

should be blameless in the sense of not doing what is contrary to prevailing morality." Barth is afraid of the preacher becoming the center of attention rather than the message to which he or she is to bear witness. Preachers, therefore, should abstain from "overenthusiastic and abnormal participation in the all too human things of this world."[49] (3) The preacher must have a systematic training in theology. "The preacher has no right to rely on the Holy Spirit in matters for which he is responsible, without making any effort himself."[50] Keeping the dialectic live on this matter, Barth comments elsewhere: "Since, however, the true *didaskalos* (teacher) has to be taught by the Holy Spirit, theological education is only a *conditio sine qua non*." (4) "Ministry is entrusted to the *ecclesia;* hence there is ministry only *from* the congregation and *to* the congregation." God is not bound by the church's choices, however. "Being called by the congregation does not mean being called by God."[51] Moreover, God may call someone to a ministry outside the normal bounds of Christian ministry and thus beyond the bounds of its ordination requirements. This "para-church" phenomenon Barth calls a *vocatio extraordinaria.*

Barth also issues three warnings to the preacher. (1) The preacher must not become puffed up. "There is no antidote to this disease except the strength which springs from a true understanding of Scripture." (2) The preacher must not be a visionary. "Faithful preaching is not visionary, for Holy Scripture was shaped in a very real world."[52] (3) The preacher must not be tedious. Barth is mortified that the words "sermon" and "boring" have become practically synonymous. This tragedy is heightened for Barth because he perceives scripture to be exciting. Faithful preaching of the Bible cannot help but be interesting.

It is in Barth's critique of the homileticians who immediately preceded him in Germany that we see him take dead aim at homiletical Donatism. Commenting on Christian Palmer, Barth writes:

> We have to ask . . . whether the preacher's offer [in the act of preaching] is anything more than the offer of his own pious personality. Furthermore, if we were to take the idea of offering salvation strictly, we might say that overmuch is really ascribed here to the preacher.[53]

---

49. Barth, *Homiletics,* 68.
50. Barth, *Preaching of the Gospel,* 35.
51. Barth, *Homiletics,* 68-69.
52. Barth, *Preaching of the Gospel,* 47.
53. Barth, *Homiletics,* 27.

Again, Barth notes C. I. Nitzsch's claim that "the true point of preaching is . . . the mediation of the spiritual life." The preacher is up to this enormous task by virtue of being a "cleansed, believing, born-again personality." Barth is doubtful that Nitzsch's approach can answer the nagging questions of how one can preach, and who can preach. Barth comments:

> We have to ask whether the foundation, i.e., the preacher as a cleansed and believing personality, can carry the structure that is to be built upon it, from correct explication and application to an edifying of the congregation that is equivalent to assimilation to Christ. Or do we have here the assurance with which the people of the late-eighteenth and nineteenth centuries sought to intervene in what takes place between God and us, thus making an illegitimate claim? . . . The concept of a Christian personality which can know the Word of God and know and edify humanity, and the concept of a proclamation whose goal in us is a new human attitude, give rise to problems which warn us not to be content with the answer that Nitzsch offers to the question of preaching but to inquire further.[54]

Barth's patience runs out quickly with Johannes Bauer. For Bauer preaching is the "free, individual, living confession of faith in personal proclamation of saving faith." Preaching's effectiveness depends upon "the personal conviction of the preacher concerning the truth of what he espouses, the gospel." Barth sums up Bauer's criteria for preaching: "Does it promote a devout Christian life, winning as many as possible, and if possible not repelling any? Above all, does it correspond to the individuality of the preacher, thus being authentic?" In Bauer's view, the preacher takes center stage in preaching. "Is this not an incredible claim? . . . The most concrete point in Bauer's doctrine of preaching is also the most questionable." The focus of preaching upon the preacher's life, devoutness, experiences, individuality, and enthusiasm signals to Barth the bankrupt condition of the church's current self-understanding:

> The fact that such a gross consideration should be the climax of a doctrine of preaching is the sign of a sick and sorry situation with a very serious background: the plight of the church that has totally forgotten its task, the plight of ministers who are put in congregations with this meager understanding, and the plight of their defrauded congregations.

54. Barth, *Homiletics*, 28, 31, 32-34.

Barth approaches Karl Fezer's work on preaching with greater appreciation. He approvingly cites Fezer's definition of preaching in the second edition of *Die Religion in Geschichte und Gegenwart,* in his article "Predigt" (1930):

> Preaching is the ministry, commanded to the church, of passing on to contemporaries the witness to revelation that is entrusted to it in scripture, in obedience to the God who acts with us in this word of scripture and in faith that this God in his grace and faithfulness, in, with, and under its poor human word, will himself be present among us as the living God, and will use our human word to speak his own Word.[55]

Barth approves because God is brought back as the subject and prime actor in the preaching process. The preacher recedes into the background. "It is not just that an enlightened witness is now talking; instead, someone is at work." Barth does notice, however, that Fezer omits a discussion of the person of the preacher:

> There is in some sense a gap there. Since, however, the person is not constitutive for the concept of preaching, there are good reasons for Fezer's omission. *Materially the lacuna is of no significance.*[56]

After Barth, homileticians had to make a conscious choice between envisioning preaching, and the preacher's role in preaching, in terms consonant with Barth's theology of the Word or in a pre-Barthian sense. Those who followed Barth's theology tended toward a homiletical Docetism, i.e., a discussion of the Word of proclamation apart from its physical embodiment in the preacher. Those who ignored Barth tended toward a homiletical Donatism, i.e., a position wherein the efficacy of the preached word is dependent in some way on the person of the preacher. Another group of homileticians can only be described as "dissonant," in that they uncritically and unsystematically correlate both Barth's strong theology of the Word with phenomenological insights, insights which conflict with this very theology!

Perhaps the most consistent homiletical Barthian is Dietrich Ritschl, who wrote *A Theology of Proclamation* while a professor of theology at Austin Presbyterian Theological Seminary in Austin, Texas. Ritschl explic-

---

55. Barth, *Homiletics,* 35-37.
56. Barth, *Homiletics,* 41. Emphasis is mine.

itly follows Barth's theology of the Word. In so doing, the first and last word about the preacher is that no human does it:

> Jesus Christ is the Preacher who proclaims Himself. . . . He places the preacher in the service of His Word. The authority of the preaching man is not a derivation or reflection, not an experience or a "status"; it is the gift of the presence of Jesus Christ in the Holy Spirit. This given authority is not smaller or less important than Christ's authority, *for He is the Preacher Himself.*

Ritschl's strong conviction that Jesus Christ is the preacher, who in preaching proclaims himself, creates a problem: how can the human element in preaching, the person who stands in the pulpit, be characterized? For Ritschl, only "infinite obedience" qualifies one to stand in the pulpit to preach God's gospel. And since no human being is capable of this, Jesus Christ alone qualifies. "So He is the only real Preacher."[57] Human beings only enter the role by virtue of their being "in Christ."

For Ritschl, the only way to remain theologically pure on this issue is by appeal to Karl Barth's depiction of the threefold form of the Word of God. The Word of God is revealed in: (1) the Word of God preached, (2) the Word of God written, and (3) the Word of God revealed.[58] Our words cannot be separated from God's Word in the sermon any more than human words can be separated from God's Word in scripture. Three false conceptions of the authority of the Word arise when we are not guided by Barth's theological guidelines: (1) Scripture is construed as the "objective Word of God," while our words are "subjective." (2) The ordination of the minister is understood to guarantee the objectivity and validity of the spoken Word. (3) The "indwelling Spirit" is understood to enable the preacher to preach God's Word and Will objectively. These three false positions are represented in "sacramentalism," "Roman Catholicism," and "theologia regenitorum," or the "spiritualism of the sects." We are, rather, to understand the relationship of human and divine words in preaching via the "christological analogy":

> That is: if it is true that the witness of the Bible is, according to the gracious will of the triune God, witness toward Jesus Christ (in the Old Tes-

---

57. Dietrich Ritschl, *A Theology of Proclamation* (Richmond, VA: John Knox Press, 1960), 33. Emphasis is mine.

58. See Karl Barth's discussion in *Church Dogmatics,* Vol. I, Part I (Edinburgh: T. & T. Clark, 1936), 89ff.

tament), and witness from Jesus Christ (in the New Testament), it must follow that Scripture also shares the humiliation and the form of the servant of the Lord, and not just his glorification. . . . This is true for the Biblical witnesses, and it is also true for us [preachers].[59]

Two heretical possibilities arise when we fail to remember the christological analogy: (1) "docetic christology" and (2) "ebionitic christology." Ritschl defines "docetic christology" as that position which believes the Bible is a heavenly word which the sermon attempts to convey in human words. This attitude creates the difficulty of trying to make the biblical word relevant "because we do not trust the Word of God in its very humanness and worldliness to make itself known." Ritschl defines the "ebionitic christology" as "the merely historical approach" to preaching. By this he means a kind of hagiographical preaching which culls from the biblical accounts larger-than-life characters for the hearers to emulate:

> In our sermons we will refer to "great Christians" or to "saints" in the history of the Church, in order to stimulate our people's desire to make a new effort to imitate those "spiritual leaders" of the Church. We will even create the desire in our people's hearts to have a "great preacher" in their pulpit; and we ourselves will appreciate being recognized as one of them.[60]

Ritschl, however, leaves no way of talking about the human preacher at all. Whenever the category of "preacher" comes up, he speaks only of Jesus Christ, fearing that any acknowledgment of a human presence in the pulpit might send his homiletic down some donatistic slippery slope. The two heretical tendencies, Docetism and Ebionitism, are problematic in the very sense that some rhetorically minded homileticians believe preaching can only be successful. What is a problem theologically for Ritschl is promising for Robin Meyers. Listen to Ritschl's condemnation of the very thing Meyers hopes will happen in preaching:

> Either of these errors will not escape a type of ecclesiology that is an end in itself: the word which comes *to* the Church, actually comes *from* the Church. The Church is in conversation with herself; the sermon says what the Church already believes.

59. Ritschl, *A Theology of Proclamation*, 35-38.
60. Ritschl, *A Theology of Proclamation*, 38-39.

Ritschl's concern is that with such an ecclesiology,

> No longer is Jesus Christ the Preacher who proclaims Himself through the mouth of His ignorant and sinful servants; but the clergyman becomes the preacher who must strive to a maximum of faith, sinlessness, Christian example, and eloquence as the necessary prerequisites for an authoritative preacher.[61]

Ironically, Ritschl himself fails to avoid the error of homiletical Docetism because he sees no way to treat the role of the person of the preacher; in fact, to do so would be a violation of the nature of preaching, as he sees it. Is it possible to remain theologically pure and still account for the rhetorical character of preaching's situation in which the preacher as person does play a significant role? Another way to frame the issue is to reckon with Richard Lischer's indictment: "There are *no* Barthians in pulpits today."[62] Is this claim lamentable or praiseworthy? Does Lischer mean that "true" preachers, in a neoorthodox sense, cannot get preaching jobs in an American Christianity which has sold out to pragmatics? Or, does it mean that Barth's attempt to enlarge preaching's vision is actually a reductionistic understanding of the preaching situation?

## Baumann, Fant, and Meyers: The Rebirth of Hearer-Driven Homiletics

Daniel J. Baumann, Clyde Fant, and Robin R. Meyers are chosen as representatives of the rhetorical approach to homiletics chiefly because each treats the topic of the person of the preacher in an extended way and as a central aspect of their homiletic.

Baumann was pastor of the College Avenue Baptist Church in San Diego, California. He also chaired the Pastoral Ministries Department at Bethel Seminary in St. Paul, Minnesota. In his popular introductory preaching manual Baumann defines preaching as follows: "*Preaching is the communication of biblical truth by man to men with the explicit purpose of*

61. Ritschl, *A Theology of Proclamation*, 39-40. On Meyers, see below.
62. Richard Lischer, "Before Technique: Preaching and Personal Formation," *Dialog* 29 (1990): 178.

*eliciting behavioral change."*[63] Following his definition carefully, Baumann divides his homiletic into three parts: (1) "Communication," wherein the aspects of the preaching situation (preacher, audience, setting, and "means," i.e., forms and structures for sermons) are each developed in a chapter of their own; (2) "Biblical Truth," which deals with matters along the path from biblical text to sermon; and (3) "Behavioral Change," which seeks to implement change theory for preaching's primary goal of persuasion.

Baumann consciously attempts to mesh his concern for preaching with the insights and procedures operative in the varied field of communication theory. Communication theory is the grandchild of classical rhetoric and continues to have a branch devoted to the ancients, particularly Aristotle. Baumann shows a particular affinity for Aristotle and contemporary change theorists. He stresses that these theories and practices from rhetoric and communication theory are important for preaching since theorists from the rhetorically minded frame of reference build their systems based upon principles of human behavior which are "essentially valid." For Baumann, preaching, insofar as it is similar to all public speaking, is "a selective application of the knowledge and skill" discovered in all areas of science, including behavioral science.[64]

Given this point of departure, Baumann is keenly interested in how communication in preaching fails. Using the image of a game of catch between a pitcher and a catcher, communication failure is either due to pitcher error or catcher error. The preacher errs when he or she throws poorly in some way. This is often a matter of ministerial *ēthos*. This "breakdown is in integrity, where the preacher has not been nearly convincing enough because of the low correlation between his words and his deeds."[65] One envisions the catcher walking away from the game, even while the ball is in the air, because of the preacher's poor credibility.

Baumann frames chapter two on the person of the preacher with two key quotes, the first from Karl Barth, the other from John Knox:

> What are you doing, you man, with the word of God on your lips? Upon what grounds do you assume the role of mediator between heaven and earth? Who has authorized you to take your place there and to generate

63. Daniel J. Baumann, *An Introduction to Contemporary Preaching* (Grand Rapids: Baker Book House, 1972, 1988), 13.

64. Baumann, *Introduction to Contemporary Preaching*, 21.

65. Baumann, *Introduction to Contemporary Preaching*, 28.

religious feeling? And, to crown all, to do so with results, with success? Did one ever hear of such overweening presumption, such Titanism, or — to speak less classically but more clearly — such brazenness! . . . Who dares, who can, preach, knowing what preaching is?

And,

How good we are as preachers depends — not altogether but (make no mistake!) primarily — on how good we are as men.

These two quotes illustrate the extent to which Baumann wishes to be eclectic. He recognizes the polar opposite character of these two assertions, but fails to recognize that they each have a certain validity when understood within their given frames of reference. They are theologically and rhetorically irreconcilable, if one chooses to operate with only one frame of reference. Yet, with his primary frame of reference, namely rhetoric, Baumann very quickly leaves Barth. His commentary on Barth lasts all of one paragraph after which he comments: "And yet it must, in the final analysis, be humbly acknowledged that God's sovereign purpose in the world is to be accomplished through men."[66] With this bold stroke, Baumann subsumes theology under rhetoric. In doing so he follows a queue of homiletical thinking that reaches back to John A. Broadus' influential homiletic of the nineteenth century. David James Randolph places much blame for contemporary preaching's sellout to rhetoric at Broadus' feet:

It was a fateful day when the venerable John A. Broadus asserted, in the work that was to become the standard in the field for generations, that homiletics was a branch of rhetoric. American homiletics has not yet been completely reconstituted after this stroke which severed the head of preaching from theology and dropped it in the basket of rhetoric held by Aristotle.[67]

In his attempt to understand the essential nature of the preacher's *ēthos*, Baumann proceeds to list his six qualifications for the preacher followed by their "implications." The preacher must be: (1) called (to sonship, to discipleship, and to apostleship); (2) healthy (in spirit, body, and mind); (3) disciplined (particularly in time/scheduling and in appropriate

---

66. Baumann, *Introduction to Contemporary Preaching*, 33, 43.

67. David J. Randolph, *The Renewal of Preaching* (Philadelphia: Fortress Press, 1969), 21.

separation from the things of this world); (4) compassionate (in love with the people); (5) humble (not prideful, but cognizant of his or her limitations); and (6) courageous (having convictions and the courage to speak them).

The implications of these qualifications are that they "combine to make up what the rhetoricians have traditionally called *ethos*." Baumann paraphrases Aristotle's famous passage from *On Rhetoric* in support:

> Persuasion is achieved by the speaker's personal character when the speech is spoken as to make us think him credible. We believe good men more fully and more readily than others: this is true generally whatever the question is, and absolutely true where exact certainty is impossible and opinions are divided. This kind of persuasion, like the others, should be achieved by what the speaker says, not by what people think of his character before he begins to speak. It is not true, as some writers assume in their treatises on rhetoric, that the personal goodness revealed by the speaker contributes nothing to his power of persuasion; on the contrary, his character may almost be called the most effective means of persuasion he possesses.

Baumann comments: "Twenty-five centuries of history have not seriously altered this conclusion." Gathering together a bushel basket full of contemporary communication theorists' opinions on *ēthos*, Baumann approvingly cites Gary Cronkhite:

> It seems safe to conclude that a speaker who is "agreeable" in Norman's sense, "trustworthy" in Berlo's sense, "safe" in Lemert's, or possessed of good "character" as McCroskey puts it, is likely to be more persuasive. Further, if he has "culture" and "conscientiousness" (Norman), "competence" (Berlo), "qualification" (Lemert), or "authoritativeness" (McCroskey), he will enhance that persuasiveness.

Baumann himself develops a twofold notion of *ēthos:* an "*antecedent ethos*, which is the role, title, position that a man brings into a situation; and *manifest ethos*, which is what the man actually projects in the speaking situation." Citing Thomas M. Schneidal's *Persuasive Speaking*, Baumann states that studies now indicate that three elements define the nature of *ēthos* operationally: (1) expertness; (2) trustworthiness; and (3) personal dynamism. Baumann is persuaded by the results of this scientific, empirical research. Baumann concludes his chapter on the preacher by stating: "Effectiveness in the pulpit is indeed tied to the life, the integrity, the

Christian character of the man who declares the gospel. Good men are full of their message and will be heard."[68]

Showing his dependence on rhetorical theory, Baumann believes that persuasion is the ultimate goal of preaching. He also perceives that preaching, as a form of communication, breaks down primarily because of pitcher error. *Ēthos* is the key to "effective" preaching, as it is to all effective communication, "effectiveness" here understood as the ability to persuade one's hearers of one's position — the classical rhetorical ideal, in the tradition of Aristotle, Cicero, and Augustine. Efficacy for Baumann has become effectiveness of persuasion. As one might expect given his rhetorical frame of reference, Baumann leans heavily on culturally construed standards for determining the kind of components that lend credibility to the preacher/speaker.

Clyde Fant was formerly Professor of Preaching at Southwestern Baptist Theological Seminary, Fort Worth, Texas, and pastor of First Baptist Church in Richardson, Texas. He recognizes the need to link the theological concerns of preaching with its rhetorical concerns. Fant describes the problem as follows:

> The practical aspects of speaking the sermon *must be united theologically* with the theoretical aspects of preaching. If we do not do so, then preaching as a practical act within the church will be hopelessly schizoid. One half of its personality will be Hebrew-Christian, and the other half will be Greek-pagan.[69]

In this vein, Fant goes on to grapple with practical theology's question of how cognate disciplines from theology and the human sciences will work together, i.e., converse with one another with the common goal of a joint venture in practical ministry, in this case with its eye trained upon homiletics.

Fant's discussion points to the "generative problematic" of homiletics as a discipline.[70] Most homiletical theorists conclude that they must

68. Baumann, *Introduction to Contemporary Preaching*, 42-43.

69. Clyde E. Fant, *Preaching for Today*, rev. ed. (New York: Harper and Row, Publishers, 1987), xiii.

70. "Generative problematic" is James Loder's helpful phrase. He uses it to describe the fundamental impasse which persistently emerges within the analytical study of any subdiscipline in practical theology. This concept will be explored more fully in chapter four. Cf. James E. Loder, "Normativity and Context in Practical Theology: The Interdisciplinary Issue," unpublished paper presented to the annual conference on practical theology, November, 1995.

choose between frames of reference and that this choice imposes an either/ or situation: Either we have a rhetorical homiletic which is theologically suspect or a theological homiletic which bypasses the otherwise necessary rhetorical scaffolding. Fant, however, recognizes that one cannot simply choose one frame of reference to the exclusion of the other. Some relationship between theology and rhetoric/communication theory necessarily pertains in critically conceiving homiletics as a discipline. The difficulty consists in how the relationship is conceived, and how it proceeds concretely. Utilizing the metaphor of marriage, Fant struggles to come to grips with the nature of the relationship between theology and rhetoric in preaching:

> Shall the Jew marry the Greek? Shall Judeo-Christian proclamation cohabit with Greco-pagan rhetoric? If so, it will never become one flesh. There has never been, and there will never be, more than one possible result from this uneasy union. Preaching will go on being praised in theory and damned in practice.[71]

It will be "praised in theory," presumably as its theological virtues are cited, but "damned in practice," presumably because of disdain for its necessary rhetorical features.

Thomas G. Long asserts that the "either/or" cannot stand: "Preachers cannot avoid rhetorical concerns. There is a scandalous fleshiness to preaching, and while sermons may be 'pure' theology all the way through Saturday night, on Sunday morning they are inescapably embodied and, thus, rhetorical."[72] Long's comments bring to the surface one of the major difficulties in contemporary discussion, namely, what is meant by the term "rhetoric"? In this context, Long seems to understand rhetoric to mean nothing more than "form." Sermons as linguistic discourse must have some form, and if "rhetoric" is taken to be a functional synonym for "form," then all sermons must be rhetorical.[73] By contrast, Aristotelian-inspired rhetoric, as discussed in chapter one, is a phenomenological pur-

---

71. Fant, *Preaching for Today*, xiv.

72. Thomas G. Long, "And How Shall They Hear? The Listener in Contemporary Preaching," in *Listening to the Word: Studies in Honor of Fred Craddock*, ed. Gail R. O'Day and Thomas G. Long (Nashville: Abingdon, 1993), 178.

73. Long fails to account for the fact that even theology is not "pure" in the sense he implies, since it too is an exercise of human discourse and as such has an essential linguistic and logical form or structure revealed in its articulation.

suit of all the factors in a rhetorical situation that aid the speaker's goal to win the hearer to his or her position, i.e., "seeking the available means of persuasion" in a situation in which matters could be otherwise. Fant does not use the term rhetoric generically as Long does, but rather understands it in its classical sense. Nevertheless, Fant also uses the terms "form," "methodology," and "delivery" as virtual synonyms, or perhaps better, as aspects of "rhetoric." Unfortunately, this threatens to confuse more than clarify.[74]

Fant's solution to the dilemma posed by preaching's hybrid character comes from the doctrine of the Incarnation. He writes:

> Theology itself provides us with the decisive clue. The divine-human nature of its concerns are precisely those of preaching: "The Word became flesh and dwelt among us (John 1:14, RSV)." *Form, methodology, and delivery are nothing more, and nothing less, than the word of God taking on flesh and dwelling among us.*[75]

With the metaphor of Incarnation, Fant hopes to bring together both the human and divine dimensions of preaching. Fant calls the Incarnation "the truest theological model for preaching because it was God's ultimate act of communication." Because Jesus Christ himself took on flesh that was appropriate for a particular situation, preaching cannot do otherwise.

Fant recognizes, however, that preaching's great possibility to be God's ongoing incarnation of the Word is potentially threatened by two heretical tendencies: "the leaven of the Pharisees," a phrase which Fant uses to describe an undue focus on the historical aspects of the gospel, and "the leaven of the Sadducees," a phrase which Fant uses to designate an undue accommodation to the new situation of the hearer. Fant names the first a form of "homiletical Docetism" which emphasizes the divine side of preaching's equation to the neglect of the human. He calls the second a form of "homiletical Montanism" wherein the preacher makes the event of proclamation happen. In homiletical Montanism the human factor is not feared (as in homiletical Docetism); rather, it is exalted and celebrated.[76]

Fant's goal is to offer a theological and rhetorical solution to these heretical tendencies. Theologically, Fant looks to H. Richard Niebuhr in his classic, *Christ and Culture*. Rhetorically, Fant looks to several

74. See ibid., xii-xiv, and passim.
75. Fant, *Preaching for Today*, xiv. Emphasis is Fant's.
76. Fant, *Preaching for Today*, 76-79.

homiletical theorists, namely Sleeth, Wingren, Farmer, as well as theologians Tillich, Bonhoeffer, and Cox. As one can see, Fant's attempt at uniting theology with communication has a lopsided beginning on the side of theology since no "purely" social or human science theorist is allowed full or even significant voice. Nevertheless, he estimates the value of communication theory in nearly messianic terms. For Fant "communication" has *the* critical role in the task of uniting past (historic faith) and present (contemporary situation):

> *The preacher must understand that the historic word and the contemporary situation are not mutually exclusive and that preaching unites the two in the act of communication.*[77]

The "act of communication" comes to particular focus in the "speech" of the preacher. For it is here that preaching either fulfills its high calling as God's own embodiment anew or that it fails by giving in to one of the aforementioned heretical tendencies:

> *Proper speech is essential to overcome the wrong stumbling block to the gospel, our inability to communicate.* But it is at this point that theology begins to raise its red flags of warning. Eberhard Bethge says that Dietrich Bonhoeffer never asked, "How can we better communicate to modern man the message we possess? That question would turn the interpreter into a salesman to the have-nots." This suspicion of any studied approach to the oral communication of the gospel is widespread in theology.[78]

Fant enlists the help of Ronald Sleeth to help sort out the relationship between rhetoric and theology. In his "Theology vs. Communication Theories," Sleeth voices six criticisms of theology against communication theory: (1) theology shows its disdain of communication theories by ignoring them; (2) this inattention is due to the belief that since preaching is ultimately God's work any theorizing or tinkering on the human side is at best theologically reductive and at worst idolatry; (3) communication, as a God-given reality, is theological in its essence; (4) as per (3), communication must not be made instrumental or pragmatic; (5) nor should it be reduced to manipulable technique; and (6) theology fears that a focus on behavioral and social sciences will create a nontheological anthropology

---

77. Fant, *Preaching for Today,* 82. Emphasis is Fant's.
78. Fant, *Preaching for Today,* 48. Emphasis is Fant's.

which dictates to theology, and ultimately to God, how preaching ought to take place. Thus, the theologian "contends communicators are consorting with strange new gods, holding views which border on the heretical."[79]

Fant returns to his dialectic by calling on Tillich's discussion of the two kinds of stumbling blocks which the preacher may lay before his hearers. The first *skandalon* is legitimate since it is inherent to the message proclaimed, Jesus Christ crucified. The second *skandalon* is of the preacher's own device. It occurs when the preacher's inability to communicate effectively renders opaque the gospel.[80] Following Tillich, Fant asserts that preaching the gospel is not a matter of persuasion. It is rather a matter of faithful and fitting presentation — faithful in terms of historic faith and fitting in terms of contemporary situation.[81]

It is in this context that Fant treats the person of the preacher. In chapter four, "We Are Men Like Yourselves," Fant suggests that if the greatest confession of the early church was Peter's Caesarean one, "Thou art the Christ," the second great confession was Paul's Lyconian one, "We are men. . . ." Honest confession of our humanity is the first qualification for preaching. Such confession allows for witness to God and away from one's self. "But what does it mean to be human?" Fant shies away from moralistic "character traits" which usually end up implying that the best place to find a preacher would be in the Eagle Scout ranks. He stresses rather that no force of personality or morality qualifies the preacher. He cites P. T. Forsyth from the classic Beecher Lectures of 1906-1907:

> No man has any right in the pulpit in virtue of his personality or manhood itself. . . . To be ready to accept any kind of message from a magnetic man is to lose the Gospel in mere impressionism. . . . And it is fatal to the authority either of the pulpit or of the Gospel. The church does not live by its preachers, but by its Word.[82]

79. Ronald L. Sleeth, "Theology and Communication Theories," *Religion in Life* 32 (1964): 549-51.

80. Fant, *Preaching for Today*, 89-90.

81. This anticipates two of Charles Wood's three tests for Christian witness. See Wood, *Vision and Discernment* (Chico, CA: Scholars Press, 1985).

82. Fant, *Preaching for Today*, 58, 103-4. Cf. P. T. Forsyth, *Positive Preaching and the Modern Mind* (Grand Rapids: Eerdmans Publishing Co., 1964, reprint). Batsall Barrett Baxter comments in his chapter on the person of the preacher in the Yale Lectures that Forsyth was a lone dissenting voice with regard to the potentially donatistic effect of the preacher's personality: "Only one, P. T. Forsyth, mentioned the preacher's personal power in a negative way." Cf. Baxter, *The Heart of the Yale Lectures* (New York: The Macmillan Company, 1947), 25.

Nevertheless, in Fant's next chapter, "Credibility and Charisma," he commits the error he is trying to avoid. Though he does not cite Thomas Schneidal's *Persuasive Speaking* as Daniel Baumann does, Fant implicitly follows him.[83] Fant focuses on the two necessary traits of a preacher which give him or her credibility and charisma. These are trustworthiness and expertness:

> *Expertness* is the extent to which a communicator is perceived to be capable of being a source of valid assertions; *trustworthiness* is the degree of confidence which the listeners have in the intent of the speaker to communicate valid assertions.

These two factors are important because they sum up for Fant the essential nature of *ēthos* for homiletics:

> The importance of these credibility factors for the minister is obvious. Unless he is perceived as both trustworthy and expert by the people with whom he ministers, *his influence will be seriously impaired.*[84]

The personal factors of hearer-perceived trustworthiness and expertness in the minister determine to large measure whether or not the message is accepted. Preacher "influence," hearer persuasion, and divine efficacy become blurred at this point in Fant's analysis.

Expertness for Fant is tied to the preacher's theological education and ability to know and get along with people. Trustworthiness has to do with the preacher's personal motivation, avoidance of manipulative method, and capacity to practice what he or she preaches. The capacity of the preacher to embody these values and properties renders him or her "charismatic." Indeed, Fant now is able to list the character traits of the charismatic leader which earlier he refused, on theological grounds, to specify. Two presuppositions preface the preacher's essential character traits: (1) the preacher must be possessed of a purpose greater than himself or herself; and (2) the preacher must be surrounded by a community which believes in his or her leadership. With these two factors in place, eight specific traits characterize the ideal preacher/charismatic leader:

83. Fant shows a progression in the three factors that Schneidal claims define *ēthos* operationally in the present time. For Fant, trustworthiness and expertness lead naturally, are the building blocks, to charisma.

84. Fant, *Preaching for Today,* 112. Emphasis is mine.

(1) exposure to varied environments and norms; (2) the ability to identify with, have empathy toward, and communicate with the plurality within the group they serve; (3) a high energy level, or an extraordinary degree of vitality; (4) presence of mind or composure under conditions of stress or challenge; (5) unswerving dedication toward one's goals; (6) the ability to project the impression of a powerful mind and range of knowledge; (7) a capacity for innovation and originality; (8) identification with the continuity of tradition, and the proclamation of the vision of a new and different order to come.[85]

Within the history of homiletical theory, Fant is perhaps the most astute at naming the tension which exists between the rhetorical and theological frames of reference when attempting to analyze the nature of preaching. Unfortunately, he is unable to achieve his goal of clarifying the relationship that pertains between these often conflicting visions. Fant ends up choosing the rhetorical over the theological and confusing key issues, such as efficacy, persuasion, and preacher "influence." Moreover, given this move to the rhetorical, he saddles up beside the cultural credibility standards for preacher-*ēthos* rather than inquiring as to what the gospel message's criteria might be especially vis-à-vis the culture's criteria.

Our last figure, Robin Meyers, is professor of speech and rhetoric at Oklahoma City University and senior minister at the Mayflower Congregational Church in Oklahoma City, Oklahoma. It is appropriate to begin our inquiry into Meyers' homiletic by examining Fred Craddock's position on the person of the preacher in preaching, for the seeds that Craddock planted produced Meyers' approach to preaching.

Craddock, the longtime professor of New Testament and Preaching at the Candler School of Theology of Emory University, Atlanta, sweeps aside concerns for the debate concerning homiletical Donatism. Craddock candidly treats the preacher's person from a communication theory perspective. From such a perspective — a study of the "way things are" (phenomenologically) in the preaching/speech-giving situation — "the separation of character from performance is impossible." For Craddock, preaching involves a relationship between the preacher and the hearers that is primarily characterized by trust, intimacy, and self-disclosure. Preaching as an act of self-disclosure is not a matter unique to preaching but states "a truth about communication" per se. So, for Craddock, the

85. Fant, *Preaching for Today,* 123.

preacher is to be a person of faith because "*faith* makes one believable, and if the messenger is not believable, neither is the message." The preacher is to be passionate because "*passion* makes one persuasive." The preacher is to have an *authority* which is at the same time ecclesiastical, charismatic, personalized by means of talent and education, and "democratic by reason of the willingness of the listeners to give their attention." And, finally, the preacher is to have *grace* "which keeps the speaker a listener."[86]

Craddock chooses to make the topic of the preacher's person primarily a matter for the rhetorical frame of reference to analyze and prescribe. Persuasiveness, as the goal of preaching the gospel, is achievable only by a speaker who has faith, passion, authority, and grace. Otherwise the message *will not be heard.* The nature of the relationship between efficacy and persuasion is thus blurred and rendered problematic theologically.

Meyers expands Craddock's last point about the "grace of the preacher which keeps the speaker a listener" into a full-blown approach to preaching. Whereas Craddock developed this briefly as a matter of the preacher's "identification" with the hearers, Meyers makes this aspect of preaching the solution for preaching's fundamental problem: persuasion of the hearer.[87]

Meyers assumes, operating consciously from the rhetorical frame of reference, that preaching's number one goal is persuasion. With this assumption the preacher proceeds as a neo-Aristotelian, "seeking the available means of persuasion." The basic clue to the potency of preaching's persuasiveness is, as Meyers puts it, "a simple idea from the real world."[88] Meyers' "real world" is the empiricist's world wherein reality is determined by scientific procedures which are able to verify results sensorially and quantitatively. He points out that merely espousing good theology doesn't guarantee persuasiveness, nor does it make a preacher great. Preaching's problem, which he names as the failure of preachers to be persuasive and great, is not a matter of *what* is said but *how* it is said.[89]

The basic ingredient that makes the preacher both great and persuasive is passion. "There is no persuasion without passion. Passion makes us

86. Fred B. Craddock, *Preaching* (Nashville: Abingdon, 1985), 23-25.

87. See Craddock, *Preaching,* 162-65.

88. Robin R. Meyers, *With Ears to Hear: Preaching as Self-Persuasion* (Cleveland: The Pilgrim Press, 1993), 1.

89. Craddock's shadow again falls over Meyers' work. See Craddock's classic *As One Without Authority* (Nashville: Abingdon, 1978), where he argues a case similar to Meyers'.

persuasive." Moreover, passion can be cultivated, actually must be cultivated, by acts of self-persuasion. Meyers approvingly cites Herbert W. Simmons from his article "Persuasion and Attitude Change": "In a real sense we do not persuade others at all; we only provide the stimulus with which they persuade themselves." The preacher must be persuaded to create the conditions wherein the ball is handed off to the hearers in such a way that they persuade themselves of the message. Meyers contends that this is true because "homiletic intuition and experimental social psychology have unwittingly merged common sense with laboratory results in the name of a new and compelling metaphor for human communication." The preacher becomes "the model self-persuader. In other words, the best way to persuade the people is to persuade the toughest customer the Gospel has: the preacher."[90]

Like Craddock, Meyers recognizes that he is treading on sensitive theological turf. But, again like Craddock, he bypasses Barth's theological objections in deference to the tried and true insights of rhetoric:

> All of this raises ancient debates within the church about the relationship between the Gospel and the faith of the preacher. Nobody wants to make a case that the tale is completely dependent on the teller, but honesty demands that we admit the inseparability of message and messenger — at least as far as effective communication is concerned.[91]

Shifting to a metaphor from music, Meyers likens the sermon to the preacher singing a song that is either contagious in its ability to attract others to join in or repulsive to the point where the hearers want to change the channel. In Meyers' construal, the hearers are completely dependent on the preacher's ability to carry a tune.

Meyers' authority for his theory of preaching as self-persuasion comes from one basic premise: "The messages we generate for ourselves are more authoritative than those from an outside source." Thus, persuasion is located not at the mouth of the preacher but at the ear of the hearer. "And there exists a substantial body of research to back up the claim that when it comes to authority, *the holiest of trinities is Me, Myself, and I*." "Again, the operating principle is that *the self is the highest seat of authority. . . .*"[92]

Preaching as self-persuasion is like Tevya in "Fiddler on the Roof"

90. Meyers, *With Ears to Hear*, 2, 6.
91. Meyers, *With Ears to Hear*, 19.
92. Meyers, *With Ears to Hear*, 49, 51. Emphasis is mine.

arguing with himself and answering his own questions. "It was in listening to himself ask the questions that answers came. And it was in listening to himself speak the answers that resolution came." For Meyers, this is as good as preaching gets. For, "the purpose of the sermon is to plead everyone's pleading, to exalt everyone's exaltation, and to talk so honestly about the life of faith that everyone's tongue is loosed."[93]

Ironically, since he wants to recognize preaching to be a hearer-driven phenomenon, Meyers' homiletic is the most preacher-centered version of preaching yet developed in homiletical history. This is because of his self-conscious choice to operate exclusively from a rhetorical frame of reference in setting preaching's agenda. In Chapter 6, "Self-Persuasion and the Person of the Preacher," Meyers addresses the issues of *ēthos* directly. He asks, "Is the efficacy of preaching contingent upon the faith and morals of the preacher?" Meyers answers in the affirmative. He then approvingly cites Aristotle, Quintilian, and Marcus Cato's ideal for oratory: "a good man, skilled in speaking."[94] For Meyers, this is preaching's ideal, too.

The goal in a homiletic of self-persuasion is that the preacher get the hearers talking to themselves so that true persuasion can take place. This happens most effectively when the preacher models such acts of self-persuasion. This is because of the classical principle of *ēthos*: the hearers will be most likely to do whatever the speaker models or requests if they perceive the speaker as credible. Meyers optimistically anticipates that preaching as self-persuasion could even effect a new Pentecost:

> Who knows, if all this lip-syncing got out of hand, and grew from a whisper to a murmur, and from a murmur to a song, someone might write about it some day. They might describe it as the "rush of a mighty wind," as if the whole church was caught up in a contagious self-persuasion. They might even call it Pentecost.[95]

There are a number of problems with Meyers' approach to preaching: (1) Meyers' "gospel," which the preacher is to embody, is never well-described. If preachers are to stand close to the gospel so that when people are persuaded by the preacher they are persuaded of the gospel, to what exactly are preachers standing close? Meyers counsels the preacher to be like the actor, donning the appropriate mask for the role at hand:

93. Meyers, *With Ears to Hear*, 55, 59.
94. Meyers, *With Ears to Hear*, 61.
95. Meyers, *With Ears to Hear*, 137.

> To act the part, one must become the part. If an actor fails to self-persuade, the lines she delivers will have a distinctly hollow sound. . . .
> Listen to yourself deliver the lines until it is not yourself that you hear but the character you have become.[96]

However, after a performance, actors revert to their true identity. At first it appears that Meyers is referring to "perceived" character, but in the end it seems that he refers to "real" character. From which frame of reference is he really operating? The rhetorical frame of reference must work chiefly with perceptions, whereas the theological frame deals primarily with the "real." Which is it that Meyers is urging? A conflation of frames of reference renders confusion at this point.

Moreover, does the gospel itself, by God's working, constrain human character in any way? And, what is the nature of the community created and shaped by the ongoing proclamation of the gospel? Can the church become a community wherein gospel-shaped *ethos* is prized over against cultural expectation? Meyers' character description of the preacher is, following the assumptions of the rhetorical frame of reference, culture- and situation-driven rather than message-driven.

(2) Meyers unashamedly commits the sin of homiletical Donatism. Even though he recognizes that the homiletical tradition has identified theological potholes in a preacher-centered and preacher-dependent homiletic, he accelerates right over them. For Meyers, preaching's goal, persuasion, is ultimately dependent on the preacher. It is thus a thoroughly human activity, and one is hard-pressed to find any room for God, Jesus Christ, or the Holy Spirit in his approach to preaching. Even his neo-Pentecost is a thoroughly human feat. This fails to recognize one key aspect of the first Pentecost: it was the act of God in the outpouring of the Holy Spirit. Meyers imagines a contemporary Pentecost "from below" in stark contrast to the one Luke depicts that is forcefully presented as a "from above" act of God.

(3) Meyers' homiletic depends upon an assumption that the preacher can easily identify with his or her hearers. He says that "the self-persuading preacher has a simple but profoundly important tool at her disposal: her own ear. . . . It is the same ear as that belonging to her listeners." His assumption is that there is a remarkable commonality to everyone's hearing experience. He goes so far as to claim that

96. Meyers, *With Ears to Hear,* 50.

Preaching as self-persuasion takes *identical human nature* as much for granted that it proceeds almost like a *rhetorical mime* — where movements have meaning because so many are universal. . . . The preacher strikes the chord not by announcing it but by using *the pitch pipe of human commonality*.[97]

Thomas G. Long's critique of David Buttrick's homiletical approach is also applicable here to Meyers: "He builds his practical homiletic on a . . . sterile base, the idea of people in the pews as a loosely hooked up collection of computer clones, all processing information in the same predictable ways."[98]

(4) Meyers' preacher-centered homiletic produces a two-pronged idol. The speaker and hearer are in collusion with the Christian faith, while jettisoning any role for God.[99] In this move, God is reduced to an internal human conversation. Preaching is preachers talking to themselves, answering themselves, with a view to hearers joining a similar self-focused conversation. "God's word" for us erupts within the conversation in the form of answers we come up with to our own questions. It is a closed internal loop. Personal experience and human reasoning are constitutive, thus creating a thoroughly humanistic, anthropocentric homiletic.

Working from rhetoric's frame of rationality, Meyers understands *ēthos* to be the chief mode for the preacher to "get the hearer talking to herself." No homiletic in the preaching tradition has been so preacher-centered, nor so blatantly ties the efficacy of preaching to the preacher's *ēthos*.[100]

97. Meyers, *With Ears to Hear*, 42, 58. Emphasis is mine.

98. Long, "And How Shall They Hear?" 184.

99. See Meyers, *With Ears to Hear*, esp. 52, where he discusses "Appropriation, Authentication, Ownership."

100. Numerous other contemporary approaches to preaching commit the same error, though not perhaps to the same degree as Meyers. In this regard, see Ronald E. Sleeth's books, *Persuasive Preaching* (New York: Harper & Brothers, Publishers, 1956) and *God's Word & Our Words: Basic Homiletics* (Atlanta: John Knox Press, 1986); Willard F. Jabusch, *The Person in the Pulpit: Preaching as Caring* (Nashville: Abingdon, 1980); Hans van der Geest, *Presence in the Pulpit: The Impact of Personality in Preaching* (Atlanta: John Knox Press, 1981); Rodney Kennedy, *The Creative Power of Metaphor: A Rhetorical Homiletic* (New York: University Press of America, 1993); Errol Hulse, R. C. Sproul, and Lester De Koster, *The Preacher and Preaching: Reviving the Art in the Twentieth Century* (Phillipsburg, NJ: Presbyterian and Reformed Publishing Company, 1986); Ralph L. Lewis, *Speech for Persuasive Preaching* (Berne, IN: Economy Printing, 1968); and John Killinger, *The Centrality of Preaching in the Total Task of Ministry* (Waco, TX: Word Books, 1969. See also Baxter, *The*

## Conclusion

The history of homiletical theory on the topic of the preacher's person has been the story of a swing of the pendulum between two dominant frames of reference, the rhetorical and the theological.

The early Latin fathers exhibited a fear and disdain for anything deemed extra-Christian. At the top of their list of contaminating influences was classical rhetoric. As Jerome illustrates, however, they were not able to recognize their own use of rhetoric, both overtly in their reasoned argumentation *(logos)* and covertly in their self-depictions *(ēthos,* especially as in Jerome's revelatory dream), and in the effect these arguments and personal testimonies had on their hearers and readers *(pathos).*

Augustine attempts to "come clean" by asserting the essential neutrality of rhetoric and the need for Christian witnesses to make use of whatever will make them more persuasive in the battle for allegiance to the truth. Augustine's astute theological orientation prevents him from making the Donatist error of making the efficacy of preaching dependent on the preacher, but when he turns to the topic of the preacher's person he is, nonetheless, uncritical in his assessment of rhetoric's power among the hearers. Augustine leaves unanswered questions, such as the relationship of efficacy to persuasion and the source for one's standards of credibility in *ēthos* portrayal — from the culture or from the gospel message itself.

Barth sought to put an end to all analysis of preaching from a rhetorical frame of reference. His exclusively theological approach to preaching as God's word spoken virtually eliminates talk about the human person in the pulpit. Ritschl offers an example of Barth's homiletic drawn to its logical conclusion; nowhere does Ritschl broach the issue of the preacher as human (other than Jesus), hence he fails to address the nature of the preacher's character.

The rebirth of the hearer-driven model for homiletics is seen perhaps most clearly in Baumann, Fant, and Meyers. These all operate explicitly from a rhetorical frame of reference, seeking to take advantage of insights from empirical fields of research. In many ways, these new homiletical approaches represent a return to Augustine and the belief that rhetoric is neutral and we must avail ourselves of its wisdom in order faithfully to bear witness to the gospel and gain as great a hearing as possi-

---

*Heart of the Yale Lectures,* and Don M. Aycock, *Preaching with Purpose and Power: Selected E. Y. Mullins Lectures on Preaching* (Macon, GA: Mercer University Press, 1982).

ble for its truth. Nevertheless, these theorists fail to see the ideologically freighted character of rhetoric, that it shapes what one sees and how one proceeds. Under its influence "efficacy" is reduced to persuasion or influence and becomes a matter of human manipulation. In addition, issues of "real" character often become obscured by the essential veil that exists between the "real" and the "perceived" in any rhetorical situation. And finally, from a rhetorical frame of reference, matters of credibility become primarily an issue of audience analysis, in the search for those standards of credibility which the audience holds.

In the Apostle Paul's correspondence with the Corinthian community of faith, we discover yet another approach to the relationship between the rhetorical and theological frames of reference, and one that holds promise for overcoming the present impasse in homiletical theory. Chapter three will be an examination of Paul's own understanding of *ēthos*, one neglected in the homiletical tradition, yet one that can reorient homiletical theory to the primacy of the gospel, without rejecting the role which rhetoric and *ēthos* always play.

# 3. *Ēthos* in Paul

Orators, we know, are naughty in their art of persuasion, but to
be no orator is to be truly naughty in mischievous subversion
of art by art itself.

*David Jasper*[1]

## Introduction

Paul shows an acute awareness of classical rhetoric in his letters. He uses
rhetoric even as he sublimates it in his theological critique of it. Unlike
Augustine, Paul did not consider rhetoric to be ideologically neutral.
Rhetoric for Paul was a powerful frame of rationality which postured
hearers, speaker, and subjects in certain ways, some of which conflicted
with the message of the gospel. Yet even though Paul is clearly message-
driven in his approach to all matters pertaining to the situation of
preaching, he does not abandon rhetoric. He continues to use it, especially rhetorical *ēthos*. He does so, however, in ways that are consistent
with, even demanded by, the gospel and the kind of community that the
gospel forms.

The Apostle Paul, in discussing the proclamation of the gospel, ex-
hibits a distinctive *ēthos* argument which provides an alternative to the
theologically problematic use of classical rhetoric's category of *ēthos*. This

---

1. David Jasper, "The Christian Art of Missing the Joke," in *Rhetoric, Power and Community* (Louisville: Westminster/John Knox Press, 1993), 136.

chapter will deal with the following: (1) Paul's understanding of the *kērygma* and *kēryx;* rather than being hostile to *ēthos* considerations they necessitate them, but in a theologically informed way. (2) Paul uses rhetoric in a highly ironic way due to the gospel's constraints on its use. (3) In 1 Cor. 1–4 Paul uses conventional forms of classical deliberative rhetoric in order to persuade the Corinthian church to unity and a rightful view of themselves and their leaders. (4) As an aspect of his deliberative argument, Paul develops an ironic or reverse-*ēthos* argument which is consistent with the cross-event-proclaimed.

Although Paul develops *ēthos* arguments elsewhere in his letters, this discussion will focus on Paul's *ēthos* defense in 1 Cor. 1–4.[2] My reasons for doing so are threefold: (1) 1 Cor. 1–4 is the most concentrated place in the Pauline literature where matters of classical rhetoric, proclamation of the gospel, and the role of the preacher as person are treated. (2) Though 1 Cor. 1–4 is a part of correspondences (the letters of Paul to Corinth) about which there is intense debate regarding matters of literary and theological integrity, there is wide scholarly agreement about the literary integrity of the section 1:10–4:21.[3] (3) Among recent scholars employing rhe-

2. For discussions of Paul's *ēthos* defense elsewhere in the Pauline literature see especially Stephen J. Kraftchick, *Ethos and Pathos Appeals in Galatians Five and Six: A Rhetorical Analysis* (Ph.D. diss., Emory University, 1985); Mario DiCicco, *Paul's Use of Ethos, Pathos, and Logos in 2 Corinthians 10–13* (Lewiston, NY: Mellen Biblical Press, 1995); and Richard Ward, *Paul and the Politics of Performance* (Ph.D. diss., Northwestern University, 1987).

3. Though, as Nils Dahl states in his seminal article on 1 Cor. 1–4, "there is no consensus with regard to the background and nature of the controversies [about which these introductory chapters in 1 Cor. consist]," there is wide consensus among both historical and literary scholars that 1 Cor. 1:10–4:21 is a coherent unit of material. See Dahl's "Paul and the Church at Corinth According to 1 Corinthians 1:10–4:21," in *Christian History and Interpretation: Studies Presented to John Knox,* ed. W. R. Farmer, C. F. D. Moule, and R. R. Niebuhr (Cambridge: Cambridge University Press, 1967), 315. For scholars who argue for the coherency of 1 Cor. 1–4, see the following commentaries on 1 Corinthians: C. K. Barrett, *The First Epistle to the Corinthians* (New York: Harper and Row, 1967); Hans Conzelmann, *1 Corinthians* (Philadelphia: Fortress Press, 1975); Gordon Fee, *The First Epistle to the Corinthians* (Grand Rapids: William B. Eerdmans Publishing Company, 1987); Margaret M. Mitchell, *Paul and the Rhetoric of Reconciliation: An Exegetical Investigation of the Language and Composition of 1 Corinthians* (Louisville: Westminster/John Knox Press, 1991); Richard E. Oster, *1 Corinthians* (Joplin, MO: College Press Publishing Company, 1995); Ben Witherington III, *Conflict and Community in Corinth: A Socio-Rhetorical Commentary on 1 and 2 Corinthians* (Grand Rapids: William B. Eerdmans Publishing Company, 1995). There are as well a number of special studies that are devoted to the thought of this unit of material: Alexandra R. Brown, *The Cross and Human Transformation: Paul's Apocalyptic Word in 1 Corinthians*

torical criticism in the study of 1 Cor. 1–4, there is a growing consensus concerning the subject matter and theological import of these chapters.[4]

## Kerygmatic Theology: Hostile to *Ēthos* Considerations?[5]

In this century, influential readings of Paul have accentuated the idea of the preacher as "herald" in such a way as to be hostile to *ēthos* considerations. Key persons in this interpretation of the preacher as "herald" were Karl Barth, Rudolf Bultmann, and Gerhard Friedrich. Most recently, Duane Litfin continues this way of interpreting Paul regarding the person of the preacher.

For Bultmann, the preaching of the gospel is not the mere recitation of past acts or of certain doctrinal content regarding God or even Jesus. Rather, the preaching of the gospel as word of God "is *kerygma,* personal address [*Anrede*], demand [*Forderung*], and promise [*Verheissung*]; it is the very act of divine grace."[6] Because of the nature of the word as *kērygma,*

(Minneapolis: Fortress Press, 1995); Martin Hengel, *Crucifixion in the Ancient World and the Folly of the Message of the Cross* (Philadelphia: Fortress Press, 1977); Duane Litfin, *St. Paul's Theology of Proclamation: 1 Corinthians 1–4 and Greco-Roman Rhetoric* (Cambridge: Cambridge University Press, 1994); Karl A. Plank, *Paul and the Irony of Affliction* (Atlanta: Scholars Press, 1987); and Stephen M. Pogoloff, *Logos and Sophia: The Rhetorical Situation of 1 Corinthians* (Atlanta: Scholars Press, 1992). Though there continues to be great debate about the literary integrity of the Corinthian correspondence as a whole, Duane Litfin has summarized recent scholarly opinion concerning the divided state of opinion about the nature of the whole of the Corinthian correspondence with regard to 1 Corinthians 1–4: "The rhetorical interpretation of 1 Cor. 1–4 does not depend on any given structural theory or particular reconstruction of Paul's contacts with the Corinthians. In the final analysis, virtually any of them will do." See Litfin, *St. Paul's Theology of Proclamation,* 148.

4. See especially Duane Litfin, *St. Paul's Theology of Proclamation;* Margaret M. Mitchell, *Paul and the Rhetoric of Reconciliation;* Stephen M. Pogoloff, *Logos and Sophia;* and Ben Witherington III, *Conflict and Community in Corinth.*

5. For important discussions of Paul's theology of preaching see especially John William Beaudean, Jr., *Paul's Theology of Preaching,* National Association of Baptist Professors of Religion Dissertation Series, No. 6 (Macon, GA: Mercer University Press, 1988); Duane Litfin, *St. Paul's Theology of Proclamation;* and Jerome Murphy-O'Connor, *Paul on Preaching* (New York: Sheed & Ward, 1963).

6. Rudolf Bultmann, *Theology of the New Testament,* 2 vols., trans. Kendrick Grobel (New York: Charles Scribner's Sons, 1954), 1:319, cited in James F. Kay, *Christus Praesens: A Reconsideration of Rudolf Bultmann's Christology* (Grand Rapids: William B. Eerdmans Publishing Company, 1994), 45-46. Kay's treatment of Bultmann and Bultmann's interpretation of Paul on *kērygma* substantially informs what follows.

God's own word personally encountering hearers, it demands bearers of that word who perform the task faithfully: the *kēryx*, or herald. As Bultmann himself explains:

> In the "word," then, the salvation-occurence is present. For the proclaimed word is neither an enlightening *Weltanschauung* flowing out in general truths, nor a merely historical account which, like a reporter's story, reminds a public of important but by-gone facts. Rather it is *kerygma* — herald's service — in the literal sense — authorized, plenipotent proclamation, edict from a sovereign. Its promulgation requires authorized messengers, "heralds," "apostles" (= sent men) (Rom. 10:13-17). So it is, by nature, personal address which accosts each individual, throwing the person himself into question by rendering his self-understanding problematic, and demanding decision of him.[7]

The single most significant study to fix the herald image on the minds of those who interpret Paul's conception of the person of the preacher is Gerhard Friedrich's essay on *"kēryx"* in the *Theological Dictionary of the New Testament* (hereafter *TDNT*). Adhering to the format of *TDNT*, Friedrich traces the background of the term and notes that as a messenger of the gods the *kēryx* delivers the word of the god who sends him. "Through him God Himself speaks. His teaching is revelation, his preaching the word of God." Yet, it is precisely at this point that Friedrich notes what he calls an important difference between the Christian preacher as herald and the Greek philosophical preacher:

> When the Stoic [preacher] calls himself *angelos kai kataskopos kai kēryx tōn theōn*, it is the word *kataskopos* which best distinguishes him from the early Christian missionary. His task is to observe men, to inspect them, and then to declare his message on the basis of these observations. The Christian missionary, however, is not a *kataskopos* of human relations. He is a preacher of the Word of God.

For Friedrich, therefore, the preacher of the gospel does not consider with great seriousness the situation of the hearers, as say a Greek rhetor would. Rather, the gospel-preacher functions largely as a mouthpiece of another, namely God, who is in fact the real preacher in preaching. This explains for Friedrich why the term *kēryx* is only used three times in the New Testament:

---

7. Bultmann, *Theology of the New Testament*, 1:307.

For the true preacher [of the gospel] is God or Christ Himself. Hence there is little place for the herald. The Bible is not telling us about human preachers; it is telling us about the preaching. . . . Hence *kērussein* is more important than the *kēryx* in the NT.

In this way Friedrich downplays the human preacher:

Sinful men are commissioned by God to declare this message to men. These men are neither miracle-workers nor philosophers. They are neither profound scholars who can convince all by their learning nor skilled orators who can bind men by their powerful speech. They are heralds — no more (1 Cor. 1:22f; 2:4). It is not their moral blamelessness nor their Christianity which decides the worth or efficacy of their preaching. Otherwise the Word of God would be dependent on men.[8]

Thomas G. Long distills into three points this understanding of the herald image: (1) With the preacher viewed as herald, the message is what is truly important. The herald is simply commissioned "to get the message straight and to speak it plainly." (2) With the emphasis on the message of preaching, the herald image "deemphasizes the personality of the preacher. . . . The task of the herald is not to *be* somebody, but to *do* something. . . . Only the message is important, and once the message is spoken, the herald is thoroughly dispensable." (3) The preacher as herald stands in a paradoxical relationship to the congregation in that God uses the person of the preacher to speak a word to the congregation, which includes the preacher. "Thus the herald metaphor underscores the conviction that the primary movement of preaching is *from* God *through* the herald *to* the hearers."[9]

Duane Litfin is the most recent example of those who read Paul as a proponent of a strictly herald concept of the person of the preacher. This fits Litfin's primary supposition that Paul did everything possible to be anti-rhetorical in his preaching. Litfin writes:

---

8. Gerhard Friedrich, "Kēryx," in *Theological Dictionary of the New Testament*, ed. G. Kittel, trans. G. W. Bromiley (Grand Rapids: William B. Eerdmans Publishing Company, 1965), 693-94, 696, 710. For important critique of the methodology of *TDNT*, as well as measured advice on how it may benefit the user, see James Barr, *The Semantics of Biblical Language* (New York: Oxford University Press), 1961.

9. Thomas G. Long, *The Witness of Preaching* (Louisville: Westminster/John Knox Press, 1989), 24-30. Emphasis is Long's.

The principles of rhetorical adaptation are irrelevant to the *kēryx*. . . .
The herald's task is not to create a persuasive message at all, but to convey effectively the already articulated message of another. . . . Paul's mission was simply to placard Christ crucified. Such an approach could not
have been in starker contrast to the principles of Greco-Roman rhetoric.

In his conclusion, Litfin attempts to explain Paul's obvious use of rhetoric
and adaptation to specific readers and hearers. Yet, having waved a hand at
such a critique of his own position, Litfin reaffirms his fundamental point
that Paul fastidiously avoided rhetoric in preaching because "it was only in
this realm [self-consciously using classical rhetoric] that one began to
tread beyond the role of the herald and impinge upon the work of the
Spirit in inducing *pistis*."[10]

One of Long's criticisms of the herald image is that, from a
phenomenological perspective, the character of the preacher is an important factor for those who hear preaching. Long echoes Aristotle's insight,
which Augustine functionally canonized for homiletical theory: "Whether
or not the congregation believes and trusts the preacher, whether or not
the preacher is perceived to have integrity, undeniably affects to some degree the receptivity of the hearers."[11] Similarly, even Friedrich concedes
that "the life of the preacher is not negligible." Commenting on Paul,
Friedrich acknowledges an insight that, if he had developed it, would have
edged him closer to Paul's reverse-*ēthos* argument. Friedrich writes:
"There should not be a discrepancy between the message and the conduct
of the preacher. . . . 'I keep under my body, and make it a slave, in order
that I should not preach to others and myself be rejected' (1 Cor. 9:27)."[12]

The strong "herald" reading of Paul, typical of theoreticians who
tend toward a kind of homiletical Docetism, is dependent on a kerygmatic
theology which is selective in its use of the Pauline material. Barth, Ritschl,
Friedrich, and Litfin — all — fail to factor into their negative homiletical
assessments of the preacher's person the fuller range of the Apostle Paul's
theological and rhetorical argument.

Bultmann, however, cannot be criticized as harshly in this regard. As
James F. Kay shows, Bultmann in his more exegetical writings goes beyond
Friedrich, Barth, and others toward a position very close to what can be
called a reverse-*ēthos* argument.

10. Litfin, *St. Paul's Theology of Proclamation*, 196, 262.
11. Long, *The Witness of Preaching*, 30.
12. Friedrich, *"Kēryx,"* 710.

In his discussion of "The Kerygma and Christ: Patterns of Predication," Kay argues that Bultmann's reading of Paul allows for a series of synonomous predications.

> With respect to their soteriological benefits, the event of Christ is synonomous with the event of Christ proclaimed. . . . By bestowing the same eschatological predicates on preaching that he gives to Christ, namely, "power" and "righteousness," Paul testifies to the soteriological synonymy of Christ and the kerygma. Hence, Paul can name either the kerygma or Christ as the object of faith.[13]

What is more, the preacher becomes synonymous both with Christ and with the event of Christ proclaimed. Bultmann claims that

> it is the apostle himself who is . . . identical with the *logos tou theou* [Word of God] which he proclaims [2 Cor. 2:17]. . . . As the Word, so the apostle himself belongs to the eschatological saving event described in verse 16. . . . Paul as it were proclaims himself.

The nature of the preaching situation binds the preacher to both the *kērygma* and the Christ in such a way that "the decision for the gospel and for Paul is one and the same (2 Cor. 5:12)." It is not, however, the moral uprightness of the preacher or any culturally prized attribute that the preacher possesses which form the basis of the hearers' decision for Paul and the gospel. For in faithfully proclaiming the gospel of Jesus Christ crucified, the preacher's goal is less to acquire for himself culturally acceptable marks of credibility and more to manifest in his own person "the pattern of Christ himself, in whom '*astheneia* [weakness] and *dunamis* [power] are joined (2 Cor. 13:4).'"[14] Bultmann argues from 2 Cor. 6:3-10 (one of the *peristasis* catalogues) that this is the way that Paul countered the charge that he was

> a pitiful, powerless apostle by arguing paradoxically, and on analogy with 4:7-12, that 'the power of the efficacious *zōē* [life] in the proclamation reveals itself exactly in the lowliness of the proclaimer.' Thus, the eschatological life of the new creation is manifested both in the 'power' of

---

13. Kay, *Christus Praesens*, 49.

14. Rudolf Bultmann, *The Second Letter to the Corinthians*, ed. Erich Dinkler and trans. Roy A. Harrisville (Minneapolis: Augsburg Press, 1985), 66-67, 107, 148, 242-43. Cited in Kay, *Christus Praesens*, 50-52.

the apostolic proclamation and in the 'weakness' of the apostolic pro-claimer.[15]

In these exegetical observations on Paul, Bultmann goes far beyond Barth, Friedrich, and others in the "herald" tradition. As Kay comments, "Thus, despite the oft-repeated accusation of Bultmann's Docetism, this label may better fit many of his opponents. Why? Because both idealism and liberalism shuck the kerygma where alone Christ is enfleshed for faith."[16] Moreover, Bultmann insists that the enfleshing of the gospel does not exclude, but requires the person of the preacher. Although he never ex-presses this view in rhetorical terms, Bultmann does recognize in Paul a role for the preacher's person in preaching. Bultmann shows that Paul's understanding of *kērygma* and *kēryx* is not in fact hostile to *ēthos* consider-ations. I shall argue in this chapter that the role of Paul's herald or preacher may be best characterized in terms of reverse-*ēthos*.

## Rhetoric and Paul

Nowhere in the canonical literature is the intersection between classical rhetoric and Christian proclamation more evident than in the letters of the Apostle Paul. Recognizing this, scholars have turned renewed attention to the Greco-Roman rhetorical tradition as an important backdrop to Paul's dealings with predominately gentile Christian communities.[17]

Paul envisioned himself as sent to be Jesus Christ's own spokesper-son of the gospel (Gal. 2:9; 1 Cor. 1:17) to a first-century gentile world which was profoundly shaped by the classical rhetorical tradition. When Paul stood up and began to proclaim "his gospel" he would have found gentile audiences composed of rhetorically astute hearers predisposed to analyzing the entire rhetorical situation in certain ways.

15. Bultmann, "Exegetische Probleme des zweiten Korintherbriefes [1947]," in *Exegetica: Aufsatze zur Erforschung des Neuen Testaments*, ed. Erich Dinkler (Tübingen: J. C. B. Mohr [Paul Siebeck], 1967), 306. Cited in Kay, *Christus Praesens*, 54. See also Bultmann, *The Second Letter to the Corinthians*, 145-46, 167.

16. Kay, *Christus Praesens*, 61.

17. For a brief summary of this history of research, with pertinent bibliographical ci-tations, see Hans Dieter Betz, "The Problem of Rhetoric and Theology according to the Apostle Paul," *L'Apôtre Paul: personnalité, style et conception du ministère*, ed. A. VanHoye (Leuven: Leuven University Press, 1986), 16-21.

Greek and Roman hearers of Paul's day would have had primary contact with Christianity via the orated word *(logos)*. Such an introduction to a "new philosophy" would not have been novel. For this was the customary means by which new ideas were promulgated. Orated philosophies competed for allegiances in the first-century marketplace.

Such a background means that Paul's hearers would have organized his address within the frame of their dominant experience of oratorical address, namely the rhetoric which was a prominent feature of their culture and life. As George A. Kennedy asserts, "When early Christians spoke, wrote, heard, or read religious discourse in Greek, even if relatively uneducated, they had expectations of the form the message would take and of what would be persuasive."[18] Professional rhetors from various philosophical schools as well as many more popular-style preachers (e.g., the Cynics)[19] "were constantly attempting to get the ear of a public who appreciated a good speech."[20] Classicist Henry Marrou comments:

> Nothing is more characteristic of Hellenistic civilization than this category [of preachers] that included wandering poets, artists, philosophers, rhetors, and specialists in hygiene, who went from city to city, from one end of the Greek world to the other, armed with fine speeches and sure of an enthusiastic reception. The lecture became the most vital form of literature. . . . Hellenistic culture was above all things a rhetorical culture, and its typical literature form was the public lecture.[21]

Duane Litfin underscores the importance of rhetoric in Paul's day:

> The practice of eloquence was not something which merely existed during Paul's day; it was pervasive in Greece and had been for centuries. It was a prime ingredient in the cultural heritage which defined Hellenism and gave the Greek mind its shape. . . . The reach of rhetoric was all but inescapable during the life of Paul, from city to town to village. The Greco-Roman people thrived on eloquence and lionized its practitioners in a way that is difficult for moderns even to conceive. . . . The truth

18. George A. Kennedy, *A New History of Classical Rhetoric* (Princeton: Princeton University Press, 1994), 258.

19. On popular preachers in Paul's day, see Abraham Malherbe, *Paul and the Popular Philosophers* (Minneapolis: Fortress Press, 1989).

20. Pogoloff, *Logos and Sophia*, 53.

21. Henry I. Marrou, *A History of Education in Antiquity,* trans. George Lamb (New York: Sheed & Ward, 1956), 187, 195. Cited in Pogoloff, *Logos and Sophia*, 53.

is that rhetoric was not merely ubiquitous in the Greco-Roman culture; more than that, it was endemic, an inherent part of life. . . .[22]

Thus, to understand even the discourse of a Tarsus-bred, Pharisee-trained man in a Jewish sect of the first century c.e., one would have to take into account the prevailing oratorical climate as shaped by the *paideia* tradition of Greco-Roman rhetoric.[23] As E. A. Judge states,

> The fact remains that it [the NT] was written in Greek if not by rhetorically literate Greeks, at least partly for them. . . . Such is the subtlety of the lost rhetorical art, that until we have it back under control we can hardly think we know how to read passages which both by style and content belong to Paul's struggle with rhetorically trained opponents for the support of his rhetorically fastidious converts.[24]

For this reason, exegetical tone-deafness to classical rhetoric distorts Pauline interpretation.

It is likely, as Stephen Pogoloff posits, that many biblical scholars of the nineteenth and early twentieth centuries failed to set Paul's arguments (especially in 1 Cor. 1–4) against the backdrop of classical rhetoric because of a misunderstanding of what rhetoric was in the ancient world. These scholars were so influenced by the way in which rhetoric had become devalued in their time, that it clouded their interpretation of the value of rhetoric in Paul's day. As Samuel Ijsseling points out,

> Towards the end of the nineteenth century, rhetoric fell into disrepute and was no longer taught in various educational institutions. The word "rhetoric" received a pejorative meaning, suggesting the use of underhanded tricks, fraud and deceit, or the stringing together of hollow words, hackneyed expressions and mere platitudes. To be rhetorical was to be bombastic.[25]

Thus, many biblical scholars of this period eschewed the value of classical rhetoric as a background to Paul.[26]

22. Litfin, *St. Paul's Theology of Proclamation*, 13-14.

23. See Henry Marrou, *A History of Education in Antiquity.*

24. E. A. Judge, "Paul's Boasting in Relation to Contemporary Professional Practice," *Australian Biblical Review* 16 (1968): 46-48. Cited in Pogoloff, *Logos and Sophia*, 221.

25. Samuel Ijsseling, *Rhetoric and Philosophy in Conflict: An Historical Survey* (The Hague, Netherlands: Martinus Nijhoff, 1976), 1.

26. Notable exceptions to this trend include Johannes Weiss and his student, Rudolf

Part of this modern devaluation of rhetoric was due to a misunderstanding of the nature of rhetoric. Pogoloff identifies influential New Testament scholars (e.g., W. Schmithals, U. Wilckens) who understood rhetoric to be little more than stylistic embellishment, a form of adornment with which any content might be fashioned. Pogoloff shows how these scholars, with their defective view of the nature of ancient rhetoric, failed to appreciate Paul's argument:

> Again and again we find scholars underestimating the importance of the meaning of *sophia logou* as rhetoric because they understand rhetoric as no more than form. But can form and content be so neatly split? If we examine the rhetoric to which Paul refers, we will find the answer to be not as straightforward as NT scholars seem to have assumed.[27]

Nevertheless, Paul has been read through classical rhetorical lenses at different junctures of the church's history (e.g., Augustine and Melanchthon). Johannes Weiss provides the last attempt to do so before the twentieth century.[28] A major figure in biblical studies at the end of the nineteenth century who turned against reading Paul in rhetorical terms is Eduard Norden. He argues that Paul's epistles lack the artifice of classical rhetoric and that Paul represents a more "Asian" form of rhetoric.[29]

Several ways of viewing the relation of Paul and classical rhetoric emerge in the history of New Testament interpretation. First are those scholars who do not acknowledge the possibility of classical rhetoric being the prime backdrop for Paul since they misunderstand rhetoric as trickery or embellishment. Second, there are those scholars who do posit such a classical rhetorical background but who argue that Paul dismisses it as a

---

Bultmann, who devoted his doctoral dissertation to a study of the Cynic-Stoic diatribe form in the Pauline literature. See his *Der Stil der paulinischen Predigt und die kynisch-stoische Diatribe* (Göttingen: Vandenhoeck & Ruprecht, 1910, reprinted 1984).

27. Pogoloff, *Logos and Sophia*, 10. Duane Litfin, *St. Paul's Theology of Proclamation*, 3-4, identifies *sophia* and its meaning as "the key issue" in understanding Paul's argument in 1 Cor. 1–4. Litfin categorizes the history of interpretation on this issue into three groups: (1) those scholars who see *sophia* referring to the rhetorical tradition, (2) those who interpret *sophia* in terms of gnostic mythology, and (3) those who understand the background to *sophia* to be "the later Hellenistic-Jewish tradition represented by Philo and 'the Wisdom of Solomon.'"

28. Johannes Weiss, *Beiträge zur paulinischen Rhetorik* (Göttingen: Vandenhoeck & Ruprecht, 1897).

29. Eduard Norden, *Die antika Kunstprosa*, 2 vols. (Stuttgart: B. G. Teubner, 1915).

potential means of expression for the gospel. Third are those scholars who take a mediating position, understanding that Paul used rhetoric, though in an inferior manner to those better trained in the art.

The scholars of whom Pogoloff speaks belong to the second category. They seem to assume that Paul entirely dismissed classical rhetoric as a vehicle for the gospel. This view is expressed well by the contemporary historian of rhetoric, George Kennedy. Commenting on 1 Cor. 2:6-13 Kennedy states: "This passage may be said to reject the whole of classical philosophy and rhetoric."[30] Here Kennedy utterly fails to take account of the rhetorically sophisticated way in which Paul is said to be rejecting "the whole of classical philosophy and rhetoric." For Paul's "rejection of rhetoric" comes in the midst of a tightly argued section of deliberative rhetoric![31] Kennedy argues that Paul replaces classical rhetoric with what he calls "radical Christian rhetoric." Radical Christian rhetoric proclaims rather than proves. It asserts without attempting to argue. Regarding *ēthos* in radical Christian rhetoric, Kennedy comments: "The orator himself is nothing; his words are not plausible; all lies with God."[32] This comment fails to recognize the irony in Paul's words. Indeed, Paul's argument travels the route of high irony in that he carries out a strident critique of rhetoric by means of rhetoric.

Duane Litfin attempts to dodge the implications of Paul's ironic rhetoric. Litfin argues that Paul's statements, especially 1 Cor. 1:17–2:5, have to do only with the Apostle's explicit rejection of classical *oral* rhetoric. Litfin fears that the inclusion of any aspect of classical rhetoric by Paul in his preaching would have made the gospel dependent on Paul's rhetorical adaptability rather than on God's working. So Litfin is forced to assume that Paul's liberal use of classical forms of epistolary rhetoric exacted no compromise for the gospel and contributed nothing essential to its proclamation. Elaborating on the practice that he believes Paul would have avoided, Litfin writes,

> Like an inventor attempting to build a machine out of makeshift parts, the orator's efforts were always bound and directed both by the nature

30. George Kennedy, *Classical Rhetoric,* 131-32.

31. See below, pp. 98-105 for a treatment of 1 Cor. 1–4 as deliberative rhetoric.

32. Kennedy, *Classical Rhetoric,* 131. In contradiction to this claim, Kennedy shows awareness elsewhere that Paul does use conventional, not just "radical Christian," rhetoric in his letters. His *New Testament Interpretation Through Rhetorical Criticism* (Chapel Hill: University of North Carolina Press, 1984) represents a fine example of the contemporary turn to classical rhetoric in New Testament interpretation.

of the available materials and the purpose of the thing. And the genius of the orator, like the genius of the inventor, lay in how well he could adapt to these constraints successfully. Given this audience, given this subject, given this occasion, in the light of this goal, what are the various rhetorical possibilities? . . . It is precisely this dynamic — the dynamic of Greco-Roman rhetoric — that Paul is here disavowing.[33]

Litfin argues for a division in Paul's use of genre. According to Litfin, in letter-writing Paul felt free to use virtually any classical categories he deemed necessary to persuade Christians of the gospel's implications. But in oral proclamation he is to be understood as taking none of these factors into account. Indeed, Litfin argues, to do so would usurp God's activity and authority, to "empty the cross of its power," to exalt the preacher over the preached. "Paul seemed to conceive of these two persuasive dynamics — that of the rhetor and the cross — as mutually exclusive. To utilize the one was to abandon the other." Litfin argues that Paul's preaching "was not the manipulated variable by which the equation was made to work; it was instead a sturdy, unchanging constant — Christ crucified, simply proclaimed."[34]

What Litfin means by "a sturdy, unchanging constant — Christ crucified, simply proclaimed" is not altogether clear. He appears to mean that in his preaching Paul simply spoke about Christ as crucified, literally and woodenly. Since Litfin never explicitly describes what such proclamation actually looked like, one is left to assume that Paul simply repeated the assertion — "Christ crucified" — again and again. Using the "herald" image in an extreme manner, Litfin says that

the *modus operandi* Paul adopted to avoid usurping the power of the cross is summed up in the term proclamation — the simple, straightforward "placarding" of the cross. The essential difference between proclamation and the approach of the rhetor focuses upon the process of adaptation. Whereas the genius of the rhetorical dynamic was its emphasis upon adaptation with a view to engineering *pistis,* the emphasis of proclamation was precisely the opposite. The herald was one who carried the message of another. It was not the herald's task to persuade, but to announce. In contrast to the shrewd and ingenious modulations of the rhetor, each calculated for its effect, the proclaimer took essentially the

33. Litfin, *St. Paul's Theology of Proclamation,* 191-92.
34. Litfin, *St. Paul's Theology of Proclamation,* 192, 208.

same message with him from audience to audience. If he fulfilled his role faithfully, this message remained fixed and unchanged, not a variable at all but a *Constant*. . . . The matter of the listener's *pistis* must be left to the Spirit alone. As for Paul, straightforward proclamation would constitute the essence of his *modus operandi* as a preacher.[35]

Litfin sketches here a dramatic caricature of the classical rhetor in contrast to the Christian preacher in order to make his point. Unfortunately, such overstatement weakens the very point he attempts to strengthen, since his distinction between Paul's oral and written discourse is not an adequate representation of either the rhetorical situation that Paul faced or the extant evidence of Paul's response.

In the first place, Litfin fails to take into account the various ways that Paul adapted his gospel and message throughout his letters. This is the kind of question which remains central for Pauline scholars. J. Christiaan Beker's work in Pauline studies focuses the discussion of Pauline theology in helpful ways on the manner of Paul's adaptation of his understanding of the core of the Christian gospel with the contingent situations which constantly needed specific application and adaptation of that core gospel.[36] The new series on Pauline theology edited by David M. Hay and Jouette M. Bassler continues to ask these same questions, questions which are at the center of understanding the nature of Pauline theology.[37] To posit as Litfin does that Paul's preaching would not have carried on this same kind of hermeneutical interaction with gospel and situation is ludicrous, especially in view of the fact that his letters are our only evidence of his hermeneutical practice. It is to dismiss the conviction of Pauline scholars that Paul's gospel is truly a word on target, not oblivious to context, but very much context-sensitive.

Second, if Paul's letters do not provide a written remnant of his oral gospel, then we have no access to the gospel he preached. Thus, Litfin bases his argument on evidence — Paul's oral discourse — to which there is no access, if he is correct in his genre-split. If, however, Paul's written discourses provide at least a shadow of his oral proclamation then it is certain

---

35. Litfin, *St. Paul's Theology of Proclamation*, 247-48. Emphasis is Litfin's.

36. See Beker's *Paul the Apostle* (Philadelphia: Fortress Press, 1980); and "Recasting Pauline Theology: The Coherence-Contingency Scheme as Interpretive Model," in Jouette M. Bassler, ed., *Pauline Theology I: Thessalonians, Philippians, Galatians, and Philemon* (Minneapolis: Fortress Press, 1991).

37. See Jouette M. Bassler, ed., *Pauline Theology, Volume I*, and David M. Hay, ed., *Pauline Theology, Volume II: 1 & 2 Corinthians* (Minneapolis: Fortress Press, 1993).

that he was neither ignorant nor exclusionary of rhetorical conventions. Indeed, in spite of Litfin's suggested split of Paul's oral and written discourses, many posit a close relationship between Paul's letters and his oral preaching. Raymond Bailey comments:

> Epistles, of all written materials, may come closest to oral communication. . . . We can see that Paul dictated, so close is the written to the spoken word. . . . There may be another reason for the distinctively oral character of Paul's epistles. Richard Ward has argued convincingly that they were written as performance literature; that is, Paul intended them to be read publicly in the churches and dictated them in a fashion conducive to that purpose.[38]

Bo Reicke, too, argues for a close relationship between Paul's oral and written discourse:

> Great parts of [Paul's letters] were obviously influenced by oral discourses, such as were commonly delivered by the Apostles, and they may often be regarded as literary substitutes for personal addresses (cf. 2 Cor. 10:10). Phrases such as 'brethren,' 'I say,' 'you know yourselves,' are numerous in the Pauline epistles, and together with the general stylistic character of the epistles and many other facts they prove that the Apostle, when he wrote, imagined himself to be speaking to the collective audience, and not writing to individual readers. The dialogue character of his writing was probably influenced by the Greek diatribe (cf. Bultmann, *Stil*). It is also an established fact that the epistles were meant to be read in the churches (Col. 4:16).[39]

In spite of Litfin's claims, the issue is not simply handled by positing an impossible-to-substantiate split between Paul's use of genre in oral and written discourse. The question is no longer a matter of "if" Paul used rhetoric in both his written and oral discourses, but "how" in fact he did use it, and with what sort of theological discretion.

The solution to understanding Paul's discourse in 1 Corinthians is not to assume with Kennedy that Paul rejects the whole of the classical rhetorical tradition; nor is it to argue with Litfin that in oral discourse Paul

---

38. Raymond Bailey, *Paul the Preacher* (Nashville: Broadman Publishing Company, 1991), 17-18. See also Ward, *Paul and the Politics of Performance*.

39. Bo Reicke, "A Synopsis of Early Christian Preaching," in *The Fruit of the Vine*, ed. A. Friedrichsen (Westminster: Dacre Press, 1953), 145.

eschewed rhetoric in favor of a simple placarding of a message heedless of the classical communication context; nor is it to posit with Schmithals and Wilckens that rhetoric simply had to do with flowery embellishment, and thus had to be rejected, leaving the gospel as content; nor is it to devalue Paul's rhetoric, à la Norden, via a comparison test as inferior to others. Rather the solution lies in seeing *how Paul uses rhetoric* in expressing the gospel — both in epistle and in proclamation — *even as he critiques rhetoric.* As Karl Plank comments: Paul's "every protest of ineloquence bows to the force of his masterful irony and paradox."[40] Further discussion of this point will be taken up when we come to the treatment of 1 Cor. 1–4 later in this chapter. What we shall observe there is that a prime example of Paul's inverted and ironical use of rhetoric occurs as he employs the rhetorical category of *ēthos* to substantiate his cruciform apostleship.

## Paul's Use of Deliberative Rhetoric in 1 Corinthians

Before we observe the way in which Paul develops his *ēthos* defense, we must understand the rhetorical situation of 1 Corinthians. The problems that Paul addresses in that letter include matters pertaining to sex (ch. 5), lawsuits (ch. 6), marriage (ch. 7), food (ch. 8), ministerial patronage (ch. 9), worship (chs. 10-11), spiritual gifts (chs. 12-14), the resurrection (ch. 15), and the Jerusalem collection (ch. 16).

Though this array of problems existed, and Paul's correspondence is largely an attempt to deal with these problems, there is an even deeper problem that interpenetrates all of them, especially regarding the Corinthians' receptivity to Paul's advice. This is because Paul himself is ultimately the problem at Corinth. Underlying all the problems in Corinth, Paul is a problem himself because of a fundamental disagreement between Paul and some in Corinth over the kind of person that God's messenger of the gospel ought to be. These differing points of view as to the nature of the preacher are due to differing criteria that are being exerted for evaluating the preacher. Some at Corinth are attempting to erode Paul's apostolic authority by applying criteria for his credibility derived from the sociocultural expectations for orators as described in the classical rhetorical tradition.

Thus, from a social standpoint, the most likely accounting for the di-

---

40. Plank, *Paul and the Irony of Affliction*, 1.

vision of groups around community orators (1 Cor. 1:10) is due to the social conventions of urban Corinth. Richard Oster comments:

> Three realities of city life that could well have contributed [to the attack on Paul's person] are: (1) personal patronage — house churches, (2) philosopher-student loyalty, and (3) urban party loyalties. . . . The human soil from which the church of God at Corinth grew had been watered and cultivated for generations with party strife and loyalties.[41]

Paul counters this in 1 Cor. 1–4 by arguing that the criteria for the Christian orator ought to derive, not from the culturally cultivated soil of classical rhetoric, but from the nature of the message with which the preacher is entrusted, from the God who gives and empowers the message, and from the community which is formed by the message. Paul's strategy, then, in reestablishing his own authority as a preacher to whom the Corinthians should listen, is to reframe their categories of orator evaluation by way of a new framework for discernment which has been revealed in the cross.

Paul's Corinthian letters are, thus, largely an apologetic for the legitimacy of his apostleship.[42] Karl Plank describes the nature of apologetic discourse:

> In terms of argumentation, apologetic discourse presupposes two basic elements: first, to engage in apologetic, speakers must perceive or anticipate a challenge against themselves or their actions; and second, that challenge, if unmet, must be sufficient to obstruct the performance of a chosen or required task. Apology is not idle discourse. It responds to a perceived criticism which the speaker cannot ignore without consequence.[43]

The immediate context of 1 Cor. 1–4 reveals several aspects of the criticism levied against Paul and Paul's response. Paul does not deny the

---

41. Oster, *1 Corinthians*, 50.

42. Research on Pauline opposition has been thorough. See Dieter Georgi, *The Opponents of Paul in 2 Corinthians* (Philadelphia: Fortress Press, 1986); John J. Gunther, *St. Paul's Opponents and Their Background* (Leiden: Brill, 1973); John H. Schütz, *Paul and the Anatomy of Apostolic Authority* (Cambridge: Cambridge University Press, 1975); E. Earle Ellis, "Paul and His Opponents: Trends in Research," in *Christianity, Judaism, and Other Greco-Roman Cults: Studies for Morton Smith at Sixty* (Leiden: Brill, 1975).

43. Plank, *Paul and the Irony of Affliction*, 13.

fact that the evaluation of community orators is legitimate. In 4:2 he uses the term "steward" to refer to one of the essential requirements of community orators: trustworthiness. Even so, with this concession he rejects their standards for judging trustworthiness. In a classical rhetorical situation one could say that the audience is "lord" insofar as it is the final judge. For it is the hearer who decides on the persuasiveness of the orator and his speech. In view of this sociocultural reality, the speaker must orient his person, his speech, and his appeals to the nature of the hearer in such a way that they will be convinced of his argument and decide favorably on his behalf. As we noted in chapter one, the astute orator in antiquity would "base his persuasive arguments on notions possessed by most people. . . . He will adapt his methods to his audience."[44] Paul seeks to sober their judgment of him by reminding them that his Lord of judgment is Jesus Christ (the divine-human sender and hearer) not them (the human receivers and hearers):

> But with me it is a very small thing that I should be judged by you or by any human court. I do not even judge myself. I am not aware of anything against myself, but I am not thereby acquitted. It is the Lord who judges me. Therefore do not pronounce judgment before the time, before the Lord comes, who will bring to light the things now hidden in darkness and will disclose the purposes of the heart. Then each one will receive commendation from God. (1 Cor. 4:3-5)

Both Paul and the Corinthian congregation stand under the watchful eye of God who knows what cannot be known to the mere human observer. Therefore, Paul is willing to withstand the charges that his critics have brought against him because he knows they cannot ultimately stand up in the eschatological and divine court. His goal in the meantime is to convince them of the authenticity of his own *ēthos* (which God knows) within the temporal frame of their judgment. To do so he must readjust the man-

---

44. Donald Lemen Clark, *Rhetoric in Greco-Roman Education* (New York: Columbia University Press, 1957), 49. As was noted in chapter one, rhetoricians of antiquity delineated the specific traits of various types of audiences to help rhetors tailor their discourses most appropriately to the group they would address. According to Aristotle, invention, arrangement, style, and delivery all are formatted with the hearer foremost in mind. John Jesse Rudin II argues that this is especially true for invention, the category in which the speaker develops his or her appeals to *ēthos, pathos,* and *logos.* See Rudin, *The Concept of Ethos in Late American Preaching* (Ph.D. diss., Northwestern University, 1950), 364-68.

ner of their judgment, bringing it into line with the same manner of judgment that God will use in the *eschaton.*

Specifically, Paul's Corinthian opponents are questioning Paul's reliability because several matters within their field of vision appear to discredit him. Criticism of Paul first shows itself in the factions that Paul describes in 1 Cor. 1:10-16. Though we cannot ultimately know what is meant by these factions or their slogans ("I belong to Paul," "I belong to Apollos," etc.), as C. K. Barrett observes,

> The existence of a 'Paul' group itself implies opposition to Paul in Corinth. That some made a point of standing by the founder of the church shows that there were others who if they did not assail his position at least regarded him as *demode,* and preferred new missionaries.[45]

Another criticism which lurks behind 1 Cor. 1–4 is that his preaching lacked the numerical success (1 Cor. 1:14-17) and rhetorical polish of others (1:17; 2:1-4). It could have been Apollos with whom some in Corinth were comparing Paul, since Paul brings Apollos up several times in this section (1:12; 3:4; 3:22), and Apollos had a reputation as a man of eloquence (Acts 18:24). Paul's fight does not, however, appear to be with Apollos, but with some in Corinth who were using Apollos as an example of a good preacher, especially vis-à-vis Paul.[46]

Criticisms which come to the surface in 2 Corinthians are tempting to consider, for they fill out the need for Paul to defend himself to the Corinthians. Moreover, it is likely that criticisms which surface in 2 Corinthians existed at the time 1 Corinthians was written. Without claiming that

---

45. C. K. Barrett, *The First Epistle to the Corinthians,* 43. Scholars using social science criteria have suggested that, given the paucity of information about the hypothetical doctrinal nature of these groups, our best alternative in understanding the factions in Corinth is to see them as ethical in nature, not doctrinal. The history of interpretation on the factions in Corinth is extensive. See Pogoloff, *Logos and Sophia,* 99-104, for a lucid and concise summary. Pogoloff and Peter Marshall, *Enmity at Corinth: Social Conventions in Paul's Relations with the Corinthians* (Tübingen: J. C. B. Mohr, 1987), reject the older view associated with an influential article by Nils Dahl (a view that Dahl has himself since retracted) that the factions were divided over doctrinal matters. See Dahl's "Paul and the Church at Corinth According to 1 Cor. 1:10–4:21," 313-35. See also Dahl's retraction in "Paul and the Church at Corinth According to 1 Cor. 1:10–4:21," in *Studies in Paul* (Minneapolis: Augsburg/Fortress Press, 1977), 61, n. 50.

46. Paul states in 1 Cor. 16:12 that he had asked Apollos to return to Corinth. Despite the scanty evidence, some have developed quite elaborate theories about Apollos's role at Corinth. See J. H. A. Hart, "Apollos," *Journal of Theological Studies* 7 (1906), 16-28.

these later attacks on Paul's person actually existed prior to his writing 1 Cor. 1–4, I believe their consideration here suggests the fuller picture of all with which Paul had to contend in his relationship with Corinth.

In 2 Corinthians we see a lack of trust on the part of some of the Corinthians due to a belief that his failure to visit them as he said he would showed "a lack of affection on his part or perhaps [indicated] that Paul was a flatterer who promised one thing and did another."[47] Moreover, he was to some an incompetent and insincere orator (2 Cor. 1:12; 2:17, 3:5, 5:11; 6:3). His personal demeanor was socially problematic (2 Cor. 4:7-15; 6:4-10). Moreover, he showed an insufficient demonstration of charismatic gifts thought by his opponents as indicative of apostolic office (2 Cor. 5:12-13a). Surely, other teachers were better representatives of the gospel than Paul. Kraftchick notes that because of these things, "The Corinthians failed to see in Paul enough evidence of the power of God."[48] In sum, the primary problem in Corinth is Paul's own person, a matter to which he must respond if he is to have any authority to speak to the other serious problems there.

In order to substantiate his authority for advising them on these matters in chapters 5–16, Paul prefaces his argument in chapters 1–4 with an *ethos* defense. Kennedy notes this move by Paul in 1 Cor. 1–4,

> where Paul develops his authoritative ethos and lays a theological basis for his subsequent admonitions to the Corinthians by working out and reiterating a small number of concepts which are the 'topics' of his invention.[49]

47. Kraftchick, "Death in Us, Life in You," in *Pauline Theology I*, Jouette M. Bassler, ed., 165; Some felt that Paul had lied to them, or at least had proven to be unreliable, in his travel plans. He promised to visit them, but subsequently did not show up (1 Cor. 4:14-21; 2 Cor. 1:15–2:4). Peter Marshall describes Paul as the "flatterer" to the Corinthians: "His enemies ridiculed him as a servile, fickle and insincere person who consciously adapted to his circumstances and associates for his own ends." See Marshall, *Enmity in Corinth*, 398.

Citing 2 Cor. 1:17-20, Plank argues that Paul saw much at stake in this indictment regarding his personal character (*ethos*) and influence among the Corinthians. "Paul links his apparent failure to fulfill his travel plans with the issue of his integrity, the trustworthiness of his speech, and ultimately the reliability of his proclamation." See Plank, *Paul and the Irony of Affliction*, 14.

48. Kraftchick, "Death in Us, Life in You," 165.

49. George Kennedy, *New Testament Interpretation Through Rhetorical Criticism*, 22. Kennedy fails, however, to explain the relationship of Paul's "radical Christian rhetoric" and his use of conventional rhetoric. Nor does he discuss how Paul's *ethos* argument in 1 Cor. 1–4 is both like and unlike classical rhetoric's use of the category.

Before turning specifically to the details of Paul's *ēthos* argument —
an argument in response to the criticisms of his personal integrity and apostolic authority which we have summarized here — it is important to
note how such defenses typically functioned within classical deliberative
discourse. First Corinthians provides an example of just such a discourse.

Margaret M. Mitchell persuasively argues that 1 Corinthians is a letter which functions as deliberative rhetoric. Having exhaustively combed
through the ancient sources, including both manuals of rhetoric and actual discourses, Mitchell establishes the genre of deliberative rhetoric as
consisting of the following features:

> 1) a focus on future time as the subject of deliberation; 2) employment
> of a determined set of appeals or ends, the most distinctive of which is
> the advantageous *(to sumpheron)*; 3) proof by example *(paradeigma)*;
> and 4) appropriate subjects for deliberation, of which factionalism and
> concord are especially common.[50]

Paul's first epistle to the Corinthians reflects each of these generic
characteristics. In the first instance, Paul is using the letter to urge the Corinthian community to decisions about their community life that they
must make in the near future.[51] Matters concerning ethics in sexual relationships (ch. 5), marriage (ch. 7), food (ch. 8), ministerial patronage (ch.
9), worship (chs. 10–11), and the impending Jerusalem collection (ch. 16)
all demanded their deliberation for future action. Paul's letter is intended
to be an authoritative guide as the Corinthians deliberate toward making
appropriate decisions on these imminent matters.

Second, Paul uses words from the stem *sumpher-* ("what is advantageous") five times in the letter.[52] Even though commentators on Paul have
often commented that appealing to self-interest was an ignoble practice
for an apostle, Mitchell shows that this way of arguing "lies at the heart of

---

50. Mitchell, *Paul and the Rhetoric of Reconciliation,* 23. The following section is dependent upon Mitchell.

51. As Mitchell observes, "In contrast [to deliberative rhetoric], forensic rhetoric
deals with the past, and epideictic with the present." See Mitchell, *Paul and the Rhetoric of
Reconciliation,* 24.

52. Mitchell notes that in addition to the *sumpher-*root "other terms describing 'advantage' or 'gain' are also found throughout 1 Corinthians: *misthos* in 9:18; *kerdainein* in
9:20; *ōphelein* in 13:3; *ōphelos* in 15:32; and, *ouk estin kenos* in 15:58. These are all ways of expressing the deliberative appeal to advantage." See Mitchell, *Paul and the Rhetoric of Reconciliation,* 33, n. 57.

deliberative rhetoric, and it is what Paul uses to persuade the Corinthians to work for a new standard of 'common advantage,' and dissuade them from selfish behavior." This reorientation of the Corinthians regarding their considerations of personal advantage reaches a high point in 10:23–11:1 where Paul leads them "to deduce that the advantageous act is that which builds up the community."[53]

Third, "of the three rhetorical species [forensic, deliberative, epideictic], the deliberative most appropriately employs proof by example. Even more telling than the mere presence of examples, however, for determining the rhetorical species, is the *function* which those examples play in the argument." Speakers and writers would often introduce examples for their hearers and readers to follow. These examples would function paradigmatically for the audience's future behavior. "An orator can even present himself as the *paradeigma* which his audience should imitate." Indeed, if this was done well it could be the most influential move the rhetor could make. Mitchell quotes Aristotle's by now familiar words: "'Now the proofs furnished by the speech are of three kinds. The first depends upon the moral character *(ēthos)* of the speaker'. . . . The speaker's personal qualities are essential to the success of any speech, for 'moral character, so to say, constitutes the most effective means of proof.'" Even when the speaker is not explicit in his *ēthos* appeals, the important role that his perceived character plays in argumentation, especially deliberative argumentation, is implicit and ever-present.

Lastly, Mitchell argues that matters of factionalism and concord were typical issues in deliberative rhetoric. "Deliberative rhetoric, the rhetoric of the assembly, is often primarily concerned with such matters as political stability and unity."[54] Since the presenting problem from Paul's informants ("Chloe's people" in 1:10) is factionalism, Paul's use of deliberative discourse is entirely appropriate.

Following Mitchell, I take 1 Corinthians as a discourse of deliberative

---

53. Mitchell, *Paul and the Rhetoric of Reconciliation*, 35, 37. Mitchell cites Epictetus, *Diss.* 2.22.15: "It is a general rule — be not deceived — that every living thing is to nothing so devoted as to its own interest [*tō idiō sumpheronti*]." In modern times, this principle has been called "Social Action Theory." Rather than abandoning this insight, Paul throughout Corinthians attempts to "baptize it into Christ" by, as Mitchell puts it, "defining the basic sphere of advantage for the Christian not as the individual, but as the entire *ekklēsia*." See Mitchell, ibid., 36.

54. Mitchell, *Paul and the Rhetoric of Reconciliation*, 37, 42, 45, 61. See Mitchell in this context for the wealth of ancient texts which bear out this point.

rhetoric which aims to persuade the Corinthian Christian community to unity and to a proper view of themselves and their leaders. The primary point of division in Corinth centers around the church modeling its attitudes and behaviors after the social and cultural standards of the outside world, actions which Paul believes betray the heart of the gospel.[55] This larger problem is the source of the Corinthians' misunderstanding of communal Christian identity and the role of church leaders (orators), especially with regard to social and rhetorical standards of credibility (*ēthos*). Paul addresses these problems by means of deliberative rhetoric. Paul's *ēthos* argument is an aspect of his proof (*pistis*) by example. As we saw in the rhetorical handbooks in chapter one, the first proof depended on "the moral character (*ēthos*) of the speaker."[56] Quintilian drove home the importance of *ēthos* arguments in deliberative rhetoric:

> What really carries greatest weight in deliberative speeches is the authority of the speaker. For he, who would have all men trust his judgement as to what is expedient and honorable, should both possess and be regarded as possessing genuine wisdom and exellence of character.[57]

This is precisely why Paul's opponents in Corinth were succeeding in defaming Paul before the Corinthian Christians. From the cultural credibility standards current in Corinth he could not be considered as honorable, nor as possessing genuine wisdom and excellence of character. Yet, rather than giving up on *ēthos* as a viable means of winning back the confidence of the Corinthians because his own *ēthos* might offend the Corinthians' social sensitivities, Paul shows them how the gospel of Jesus Christ crucified inverts all credibility standards, thus ironically validating his unusual *logos* and *ēthos* appeals.

## Paul's Proof by Example: Reverse-*Ēthos*

As an aspect of his deliberative discourse in 1 Corinthians, Paul argues for his legitimacy and authority by means of an unusual *ēthos* argument. Normally rhetors construct an honorable picture of their own person based upon the properties of character that the target audience deems

---

55. Pogoloff, *Logos and Sophia*, 275.
56. Aristotle, *On Rhetoric*, 1.2.4.
57. Quintilian, *Institutes of Oratory* (London: Bell, 1875-76), 3.8.13.

credible and honorable. Playing to an audience's own standards of credibility, and accentuating how the speaker fits its picture of what is credible, the rhetor could then use that as a basis on which to argue other matters.[58]

Paul's *ēthos* argument is unusual in that he attempts to reframe his readers' expectations for what makes any orator/leader credible within the Christian community. Rather than implicitly approving of their own *ēthos* standards, which were conditioned by their classical rhetorical heritage, Paul questions them from the standpoint of a countervailing Christian perspective. For Paul, the only context within which to know what to expect of a community orator is that entailed by the message of the gospel — the cross-event-proclaimed.

## Christological Orientation: The Christian Community's New Framework for Discernment

Paul grounds his *ēthos* appeal to the Corinthians in his christology. This is epitomized by the opening ten verses of 1 Corinthians. Scholars often note that Paul sets up the arguments of his letters in the salutation and thanksgiving.[59] This is no less true of 1 Corinthians, where Paul introduces several key themes (e.g., gifts, call, gnosis, speech) that he takes up more pointedly later in the letter. Scholars fail to note, however, that Paul sets up his christological argument as well by referring to Jesus Christ ten times in the first ten verses.[60] This emphasis on Christ Jesus as Lord gives Paul a common touchpoint with the Corinthians which he will very quickly reinterpret to fit their situation, just as he does on the other matters raised in the introduction. Gaining their nod regarding their God-given spiritual giftedness, their gifts of speech, and their knowledge, Paul then proceeds to explain to them the theological and ethical import of those gifts. Similarly, gaining their nod about Jesus the Messiah who is their Lord, he then proceeds to explain that this Messiah is the crucified Messiah whose lordship consists of suffering ignominy. The implication of this christological ori-

---

58. For numerous examples of this, see DiCicco, *Paul's Use of Ethos, Pathos, and Logos in 2 Corinthians 10–13*, ch. 2.

59. See P. Schubert, *Form and Function of the Pauline Thanksgivings* (Berlin: Töpelmann, 1939); and P. T. O'Brien, *Introductory Thanksgivings in the Letters of Paul*, Supplements to Novum Testamentum no. 49 (Leiden: Brill, 1977), 107-37.

60. In all ten verses Paul uses *Christos;* in nine, *Iēsous;* in six, *kurios,* all of which refer to Jesus as Lord.

entation is profound for the estimation of those who are called to preach this message in this community.

Before Paul moves on to his first appeal (*parakaleō* in the *propositio* of 1:10), he prefaces his personal *ēthos* argument with a divine *ēthos* assertion: "God is faithful; by him you were called into the fellowship of his Son, Jesus Christ our Lord" (1:9). It is not the human preacher's *ēthos* which makes efficacious the gospel. Rather, it is God's trustworthiness. A better question than the one which was common in classical rhetorical situations ("Can this human orator be trusted?") is the question which the cross-event-proclaimed necessitates: "Can this God be trusted?" Thus, preacher *ēthos* ironically consists in the preacher not being morally pure or credible by means of his or her own accomplishments, since this is in fact in conflict with the message of Jesus Christ crucified. The preacher must be sinner in need, not "saint," if by this is meant living above the mire of the human predicament. This means that far from being morally pure ("good"), or culturally credible in such a way as to predispose the hearer to accepting the message (antecedent *ēthos*), part of the preacher's role includes having an ongoing cognizance and humility to acknowledge his or her own complicity in sin — sin for which Christ's sacrifice was alone efficacious ("he was crucified for you" [1:13]). Refocusing his audience from himself as preacher to God as guarantor allows the theology of the cross (1:18–2:5) to inform the way in which the *ēthos* of the preacher in the Christian rhetorical situation is to be differentiated from the classical rhetorical perspective. For "the cross brings home the full seriousness of sin, declares the powerlessness of fallen humanity to achieve salvation and exposes human delusions of self-righteousness."[61] This indictment includes the human preacher.

Compounding the irony, this refocusing and shifting of emphasis away from self as preacher and to God as source of preaching's power acts to build and project the kind of preacher-*ēthos* which does attribute credibility to the preacher of the gospel. But such credibility takes the form of self-effacement, i.e., the pointing away from oneself and toward God who calls, commissions, and empowers God's own message. Paul points the community to God who alone is faithful in making this message efficacious for salvation.

In deflecting attention from himself to God, Paul asserts the ultimate

---

61. Alister McGrath, "Cross, Theology of the," in *Dictionary of Paul and His Letters*, ed. Gerald F. Hawthorne and Ralph P. Martin (Downers Grove, IL: InterVarsity Press, 1993), 193.

trustworthiness of God's character *(ēthos):* "God is faithful *(pistos);* by him you were called into the fellowship of his Son, Jesus Christ our Lord" (1 Cor. 1:9). The Greek backdrop to *pistos* connects it to meanings that have to do with "trusting," "trustworthy," "faithful," "reliable," and even a "means of proof" in the classical rhetorical sense of a proof in argumentation. The Old Testament backdrop pictures a God who is faithful in keeping covenant and showing steadfast love (Deut. 7:9; 1 Kings 8:23; Neh. 1:3; 9:32; Dan. 9:4).[62] When God calls humans into covenant with himself he is faithful to keep covenant even when they break it.[63] For Paul, God's steadfast faithfulness is nowhere more clearly seen than in the call to fellowship that God makes in Christ Jesus. Moreover, it is the faithfulness of God which guarantees Paul's own word (2 Cor. 1:18).[64] Paul is convinced that, in the relationship that God has created with humankind, God's faithfulness extends even to the point of God preventing unbearable situations of temptation (1 Cor. 10:13; 2 Thess. 3:3) while it works an ongoing sanctification of the believers within the faith community (1 Thess. 5:23-24).

It is God's faithfulness, then, which guarantees the efficacy of the proclaimed word's saving power and not any human being's personal attributes. The orated phenomenon we call preaching the gospel is not just another rhetorical event. It may have the appearance of such from the perspective of one who sees it as just another rhetorical situation. But from the vantage point of one who is "in Christ," there is more than meets the eye. This is because Paul perceives a fundamental difference between those who are in Christ and those who are outside of Christ regarding their orientation for discerning reality.

For Paul, the basic orientation for discernment that one has outside of Christ is *kata sarka* ("according to the flesh"). In 1 Cor. 2:6–3:4 Paul uses *psychikos* ("the natural person") as an equivalent to *kata sarka.* In the new

62. *Theological Dictionary of the New Testament,* s.v. *"pistis,"* by Rudolf Bultmann and s.v. *"hsd,"* by H.-J. Zobel.

63. This is a prominent theme throughout the Old Testament. God consistently calls humans into fellowship with himself and remains faithful to the relationship. The greatest fissure in Israel's understanding of God's faithfulness came in 587 B.C.E. with the destruction of Jerusalem, the Temple, and the subsequent exile to Babylon. It appeared that God had abandoned his promise to be faithful. Numerous voices dot the Old Testament landscape in an attempt to understand this most fundamental theological problem. See Ralph W. Klein, *Israel in Exile* (Philadelphia: Fortress Press, 1979).

64. On the theme of God's faithfulness see s.v. "God," by Donald Guthrie and Ralph P. Martin, and "Faith," by Leon Morris, in *Dictionary of Paul and His Letters,* ed. Gerald F. Hawthorne and Ralph P. Martin.

community created by God through the gospel, Christians are not "to be-have as ordinary men" (1 Cor. 3:3), *kata sarka* (1 Cor. 1:26; 2 Cor. 1:17; 5:16; 10:2-3; 11:18). By necessity, *kata sarka* judgments place a premium on externals, since that is what they can observe and test. As Rudolf Bultmann comments: *sarx* refers to "the whole sphere of that which is earthy or 'natural.'"[65] The "sphere of the *sarx*" is that "of the visible and demonstrable (Rom. 2:28-29; 2 Cor. 4:18), whether in the form of natural phenomena, of historical circumstances or of palpable achievements."[66] Paul asserts that this manner of perception is ultimately deceptive since it cannot be trusted in matters which are unseen (matters pertaining to faith) and eternal. For one may have all the outward marks of credibility (cf. Paul's own list in Phil. 3:2ff.), yet remain in a state of estrangement be-fore God. It is likely that Paul would charge any hyper-hearer-driven homiletic that uncritically appropriates classical rhetorical categories (i.e., *ēthos*) with operating *kata sarka*, outside of Jesus Christ. Paul's alternative is a way of knowing that is shaped by the new framework for discernment grounded in, and proceeding from, the cross-event-proclaimed.[67]

Faith in the God who gives and empowers the gospel of salvation constrains one to ascribe to this word of the cross, which proves itself so-cially stigmatic, foolish, weak, and even theologically objectionable (cf. Deut. 21:23, "anyone who is hung on a tree is under God's curse"), the power of God. Paul remains self-effacing in his ministry of the gospel — pointing away from himself and to the work which God does in Jesus Christ which alone is capable of saving him and his hearers — knowing that a cruciform orientation is not achievable by means of *kata sarka* ave-nues (1 Cor. 1:17; 2:1ff.). This is so "your faith might rest not on human wisdom, but on the power of God" (1 Cor. 2:5).[68]

Paul's position on the all-sufficiency of God in the proclamation of the gospel keeps him from the error of "homiletical Donatism." In his let-ter to the Philippian church (1:15-18) we catch sight of Paul addressing the problem of immoral preachers. Apparently there were some who preached Christ in order to try to worsen Paul's treatment while he was in prison.

---

65. Bultmann, *Theology of the New Testament,* 1:233-35.

66. *Theological Dictionary of the New Testament,* s.v. "*thanatos,*" by Rudolf Bultmann.

67. See pp. 110-18 below for an extended discussion of the new "epistemology" granted by the cross.

68. A central Pauline irony consists in Paul's self-effacing character to point to God who is alone faithful and capable while at the same time pointing to himself as one for oth-ers to imitate. We will treat this irony in the final section of this chapter.

Rather than defame their message, Paul rejoices in the fact that Christ is preached. The extent to which God will use proclamation which springs from impure motives does not hinge on the preachers' morals or motives. God remains free to work his word through whatever vessels he chooses. For ultimately it is the treasure which God chooses to put within the vessel which exerts the power: "So that it may be clear that this extraordinary power belongs to God and does not come from us" (cf. 2 Cor. 4:7; Rom. 3:3-4).

## The *Logos* of the Cross

Paul's primary task in correcting the Corinthians' problems consists in orienting the community to a new "epistemology" grounded in the cross-event-proclaimed.[69] Alister McGrath comments on the epistemological character of this message:

> The cross — more accurately, the crucified Christ — thus acts as both the foundation of authentically Christian ways of thinking about God and as a judge of those ways of thinking about God which humans absorb uncritically from the world around them and unconsciously incorporate into theological thinking.[70]

Paul expects the cross-event-proclaimed to "deform" and "remint" the Corinthians' linguistic and ideological worlds.[71] The nature of the *kērygma* necessitates an ongoing test of all that the Christian community does and thinks.

---

69. I use the term "epistemology" guardedly recognizing that it does conjure up for many ideas of systematic, scientific inquiry *(Wissenschaft)*. I choose to use it, however, because it does express something important with respect to the new orientation that persons are given in Christ. From the cross-event-proclaimed comes a new framework for understanding and discernment in community and world. This new framework for discernment "in Christ" is what I mean by "epistemology." See the similar approach taken by J. Louis Martyn, "Epistemology at the Turn of the Ages: 2 Corinthians 5:16," in W. R. Farmer, C. F. D. Moule, and R. R. Niebuhr, eds., *Christian History and Interpretation,* 269-87. Martyn's classic essay has been republished in his *Theological Issues in the Letters of Paul* (Nashville: Abingdon Press, 1997).

70. Alister McGrath, "Cross, Theology of the," in *Dictionary of Paul and His Letters,* 194.

71. Robert W. Funk, "Word and World in 1 Corinthians 2:6-16," in his *Language, Hermeneutic, and Word of God* (New York: Harper and Row, 1966), 275.

Paul's message is Jesus the Messiah crucified. There is a power inherent to this message, but it is a power only evident to those "being saved" (1 Cor. 1:18). To others, "those who are perishing," this same message is not the antithesis of power, i.e., "weakness," but foolishness *(mōria)* (1 Cor. 1:18). It is this message of foolishness that Paul was called to proclaim.

Moreover, it is a message that conflicts with the structures of logic and decency in both Jewish and Greek frameworks of rationality and morality. Martin Hengel comments on this:

> To believe that the one pre-existent Son of the one true God, the mediator at the creation and the redeemer of the world, had appeared in very recent times in out-of-the-way Galilee as a member of the obscure people of the Jews, and even worse, had died the death of a common criminal on the cross, could only be regarded as a sign of madness. The real gods of Greece and Rome could be distinguished from mortal men by the very fact that they were *immortal* — they had absolutely nothing in common with the cross as a sign of shame *(aischunē)* (Hebrews 12:2), the infamous stake *(infamis stipes)*, the 'barren' *(infelix lignum)* or 'criminal wood' *(panourgikon Xulon)*, the 'terrible cross' *(maxuma mala crux)* of the slaves of Plautus, and thus of the one who, in the words of Celsus, was 'bound in the most ignominious fashion' and 'executed in a shameful way.'[72]

This was a message which caused the Jews to stumble *(skandalon)* and Greeks to scoff in derision *(mōria)* (1 Cor. 1:23). This message is a constant challenge to all *kata sarka* approaches to life in Christian community. But in the new community formed by the cross-event-proclaimed, *kata sarka* judgments have been dethroned. For in this new community, Christ — the crucified — is Lord. Therefore, in view of the cross-event-proclaimed, *kata sarka* judgments and conclusions no longer accord with "reality" as seen through the cruciform lens of Christian existence.

"What saves is the 'power of the cross,' a formulation that is nonsensical in the perspective of worldly wisdom. . . . The cross continues to break powerfully into the old world's 'dominant system of convictions' wherever it is proclaimed."[73] As such, this message is indeed a mystery of

---

72. Martin Hengel, *Crucifixion in the Ancient World and the Folly of the Message of the Cross*, 6-7.

73. Brown, *The Cross and Human Transformation*, 75.

God (1 Cor. 2:1; 4:1) that has been put in the trust of some, like Paul, to deliver in a trustworthy manner.

As I noted earlier, the cross-event-proclaimed is more than the mere recitation of past, countercultural events, as Hengel describes them. Rather, as Bultmann describes it, Paul's *kērygma* announces "Jesus Christ the Crucified and Risen One — to be God's eschatological act of salvation."[74] This eschatological event that broke into history, even more importantly, continues to happen in our history whenever it is proclaimed anew.

As we have observed in his use of deliberative rhetoric with its *ēthos* appeals, Paul appropriates classical rhetoric for his use in preaching and writing. But he always puts such means through the epistemological test of the crucifixion, thus employing means of expression which are consistent with the word of the cross. Perhaps better, he does so in ways that this message itself shapes.

The clearest example of this is to be seen in Paul's use of *logos* and *ēthos*. Paul's central *logos* is the message of "Christ crucified," virtually an expletive, as Hengel shows. But Paul insists it is the only thing he decided to know in his ministry with the Corinthians (1 Cor. 2:2). Morever, this disdainful *logos* functioned even in his personal presence, and perhaps also in his style of proclaimed delivery (1 Cor. 2:3-4). Paul's *logos* is indeed a kind of "logic," but one that makes "sense" and is persuasive only for those who are willing to see from the perspective that the cross itself provides. In extending the implications of this unusual *logos* to his own person *(ēthos)*, Paul will show how this particular message even validates his hardships — sufferings which had apparently shamed the Corinthians socially and that were being used by Paul's opponents to prove that he was a fraud.

Thus, we can now see Paul's hermeneutical strategy in using rhetorical categories. A countercultural event for both Jewish and gentile audiences — the crucifixion of Jesus the Messiah — becomes the organizing principle and center for all the factors in the rhetorical situation of Christian proclamation. All aspects of the rhetorical situation of the proclamation of the gospel are seen through the cruciform lens of the gospel message. This is one way in which Paul's fundamental *modus operandi* differed from those of classical rhetoric, which operate in a typical hearer-driven manner.

There is, therefore, the decisive aspect of the crucified Christ, the

---

74. Bultmann, *Theology of the New Testament*, 1:3.

cruciform community, and the cruciform preacher in the Christian rhetorical situation. No doubt, this will be perpetually repugnant to the outsider. Indeed, to outsiders this *logos* will reek of death (2 Cor. 2:14-17). Even so, Paul refuses to "clean it up" so that it (or he!) might sell better. "For we are not peddlers of God's word like so many; but in Christ we speak as persons of sincerity, as persons sent from God and standing in his presence" (2 Cor. 2:17). Regardless of this inherent revulsion, which would necessarily jeopardize its acceptance in the world of his time (or any time, if the heinous nature of the crucifixion message is grasped), Paul persists in allowing this center to determine the peripheries. For to change the center of the gospel message — Christ crucified — would be to allow the cultural exigencies to eclipse the gospel's exigencies. The culture must be accommodated in certain ways because of the constraints of historical situatedness,[75] but ultimately it is the culturally enmeshed people who hear the gospel who must accommodate themselves to the gospel's claims, if they are to receive the salvation and subsequent community life of the saved that the gospel offers. This is why the typical human response demanded by the gospel is radical change of heart — repentance, confession, surrender, and praise of the all-sufficiency of God.

This demand on hearers to shift their perception of reality is undoubtedly one of the things that makes Paul's gospel such a stumbling block *(skandalon)*.[76] For those outside the Christian community would have to suspend their cultural and social standards of credibility and credulity to entertain the possibility of this word *(logos)* being true and this preacher *(ēthos)* being believable. As Brown suggests, "The world created by the cross is characterized by strange reversals; it is a world in which wis-

---

75. On the nature of historical situatedness see Hans-Georg Gadamer, *Truth and Method*, ed. Garrett Barden and John Cummings (New York: Seabury Press, 1975), passim, but esp. 341-80.

76. This is a way of describing what Brown argues that Paul is doing in his letter of 1 Corinthians. She writes: "In 1 Corinthians 1–2, Paul strikes at the heart of schism in the church. His principal weapon is the Word of the Cross (1:18); with it he breaches the barriers of ego and ideology — even Christian ideology — that divide believers at Corinth. His battleground is the realm of human perception; wielding the Word of the Cross, he invades the perceptual landscape of his hearers, cutting across their accustomed (and, he believes, false) ways of knowing with the sharp expression of a new reality. The effectiveness of this strike, Paul's letter suggests, rests in the power of the Word he preaches to liberate both minds and bodies from the grasp of the false world to which he elsewhere refers as 'the present evil age' (Gal 1:4)." See Brown, *The Cross and Human Transformation: Paul's Apocalyptic Word in 1 Corinthians*, xvii.

dom is characterized as folly, the least become the greatest, strength resides in weakness, and fullness of being arises from emptiness."[77]

It is not too much to say that there is an entirely new epistemology at work for those in Christ. Working from 2 Cor. 2:14–6:10, J. Louis Martyn maintains that Paul's defense of himself hinges on "the turn of the ages" which occurs at the cross. This turn of the ages is a juncture at which one is granted a "new means of perception which enables him to distinguish true from false apostles." Thus, "Paul's statements establish an inextricable connexion between eschatology and epistemology." The turn of the ages in the event of Christ's cross means that life is now manifested in death. "Therefore we are each day given up to death for Jesus' sake, so that the life of Jesus may be shown in our dying." The true apostle's "daily death is his daily renewal, and it points to his ultimate life." Living life at the juncture means having a way of perceiving reality that comes from the end of the ages even while one lives under the shadow of the old age. Such a situation is bound to cause confusion and misunderstanding, especially by those who use old-age criteria to judge end-of-the-age apostles: "Since the old-age ways of knowing are past, the old standards for identifying an apostle are shown to be invalid."[78]

There are, therefore, two ways of knowing according to Paul. These distinct ways of knowing are separated from one another by the death and resurrection of Christ. The way of knowing associated with the old age is, as we have already noted, that which Paul calls *kata sarka* ("according to the flesh"). It operates primarily on the basis of sensory perception. Martyn musters numerous ancient authorities on the concept to demonstrate that Paul's original readers would have understood quite well what he meant by the phrase *kata sarka*.

In contrast, the way of knowing associated with the new age is that which many commentators on Paul have called *kata pneuma* ("according to the spirit"). But Martyn is careful to point out that Paul refrained from neatly juxtaposing the orientations of *kata sarka* and *kata pneuma*, since this was more likely a way that "Gnostics" in Corinth would frame the issue. In so doing, these "Gnostics" boast in their *kata pneuma* orientation in a quite *kata sarka* manner. Paul cannot argue for a pure *kata pneuma* epistemological orientation since "he does not live entirely in the new age, but rather at the painful juncture where some are being saved and some

---

77. Brown, *The Cross and Human Transformation*, 93.
78. Martyn, "Epistemology at the Turn of the Ages," 271-73, citing 2 Cor. 4:11.

are perishing (2 Cor. 2:15)." Therefore Paul's way of knowing is not to be characterized as *kata pneuma,* but as *kata stauron* ("according to the cross"). Until one is completely in the new age, one's "knowing *kata pneuma* can occur only in the form of knowing *kata stauron.*"

The new way of knowing afforded by the cross necessitates a new way of being in the world which is destined to conflict with old-age ways of knowing, such as the ways that people adjudicate authenticity and credibility. Thus, paradoxically, those who seek to know in a *kata sarka* or in a *kata pneuma* manner both prove deceived in discerning truly in the present. This is because the present is a violent and often muddled mixture of two fundamentally different ages. "For now we see in a mirror, dimly" (1 Cor. 13:12). Martyn summarizes:

> The new way of knowing is not in some ethereal sense a spiritual way of knowing. It is not effected in a mystic trance, as the superapostles claimed, but rather right in the midst of rough-and-tumble life. To be sure, the veil is taken away, the creation is new, the old has passed away, look!, the new has come. Yet all of this can be seen only by the new eyes granted at the *juncture* of the ages. Thus, the man who knows *kata pneuma* cannot show that he knows *kata pneuma* by performing mighty works. Seeing in a partial way has not yet been replaced by seeing face to face. On the contrary it has been replaced by faith (2 Cor. 5:17). The marks of the new age are at present hidden *in* the old age. At the juncture of the ages the marks of the resurrection are hidden and revealed in the cross of the disciple's daily death, and *only* there.

The epistemological positioning of the disciple of Jesus — at the turn of the ages — provides the mandate for the kind of life that he or she lives in witness to the gospel. In this way epistemology is bound up with ontology. The event of Christ's death and resurrection "involves far more than the granting of a new way of knowing." It involves a new way of being in the world. Martyn expresses the interconnectedness of epistemology and ontology in this way: "Until we all stand before the *bēma tou Christou* ('the judgment seat of Christ'), there is only one point at which the epistemological question can be legitimately posed: the death/resurrection of Christ and the daily death/life of the disciple."[79] The message of the cross puts to death *kata sarka* standards of what makes preaching preaching, and what makes preachers preachers. The cross is thus the

79. Martyn, "Epistemology at the Turn of the Ages," 285-87, 287, n. 2.

epistemological key for Paul, for in the cross the church has a new way of knowing in the time frame in which it currently exists, the painful and often perplexing juncture between the ages. The church thus operates *kata stauron* in its manner of judgment in that it sees that God has put to death, and continues to put to death, the instantiations of death which come from *kata sarka* judgments.

Kennedy attempts to describe Paul's gospel and his manner of presentation of that gospel as "radical Christian rhetoric." But is the term "radical" extreme enough to describe it as we have seen that gospel unfold from Paul's writings? For Paul goes so far as to "reverse" rhetoric in his gospel communication, and in his description of preaching, thus using rhetoric for the purpose of rhetoric's own humiliation. In like manner, God uses preachers in an event which, culturally defined, functions to elevate orators competitively, thereby creating rivalry among them and their adherents. But because of what the gospel accomplishes, the cross-event-proclaimed actually humiliates preachers and hearers alike by demolishing the arena and occasion of competition and the resultant party rivalry. God uses preachers to humble preachers. As Bultmann stresses, what is true of the cross is true of the word of the cross. Moreover, what is true of the word of the cross is true of the proclaimer of the cross.[80] After all these proclaimers have done, they are still mere servants and stewards (1 Cor. 4:1ff.). Brown summarizes Paul's argument in 1 Cor. 1:

> Thus far in Paul's discourse the cross has functioned in three central ways. First, it has dislocated its hearers by calling into question their ways of knowing (1:18). Second, it has revealed God's purpose to save, not through wisdom, but through the "folly of the cross itself" (1:21-25); and third, it has demonstrated God's destruction of the old world (with its valued human assets of strength, wisdom, nobility) and creation of the new world (into which he calls the weak, the ignoble, the nonexistent; 1:26-31).[81]

Perhaps this explains why such a message appealed to those whose experience of the dominant culture was not the best (1 Cor. 1:26-31). Since the dominant cultural and social world tends to harm those who are not in power, those on the margins ("the weak, the ignoble, the nonexistent" [1 Cor. 2:26]), a word *(logos)* that stood outside of that dominant and op-

---

80. See Kay, *Christus Praesens,* 49-53.
81. Brown, *The Cross and Human Transformation,* 96.

pressive realm could be entertained as freeing. The apocalyptic or eschatological reality of the cross constitutes in this world the new world of the eschatological *ekklēsia*, thus forming newly remade persons into an
alternative community, a subculture, if you will, wherein forms of oppression found in the wider culture are no longer operative. Such a community subverts the dominant, and domineering patterns of culture. Formerly
societally controlled people, such as slaves, women, and gentiles, were now
set free to be full citizens of God's kingdom.

The paradox which attends the message (1 Cor. 1:18-25) is thus evident in the makeup of the church (1 Cor. 1:26-31), as it is in the way that
Paul proclaimed that message (1 Cor. 2:1-5). Paul's "demonstration"
*(apodeixis)* of its truth was not carried out *kata sarka*, nor in a way that the
*pyschikos* (1 Cor. 2:14), "the natural person," would comprehend. Rather it
was something that the Spirit of God undertook "so that your faith might
not rest on human wisdom but on the power of God" (1 Cor. 2:5).

An *apodeixis* is a technical rhetorical proof which Quintilian called
"a clear proof," or "a means of proving what is not certain by means of
what is certain."[82] Paul's proof is based on what happened to the Corinthians themselves in their hearing of the gospel, i.e., their salvation and initia-
tion into the "being saved" community (1 Cor. 1:24). When the Corinthian
Christians divided themselves up as they apparently did, they showed that
they were "immature," that they were following a "wisdom of this age,"
that they were acting "naturally" and not as spiritually discerning Christians. Over against a mindset of division based in preacher and party rivalry, Paul asserts that they have the mind of Christ by virtue of the grace
of God given them in their salvation. As Witherington comments,

> Though all the Corinthian Christians have the Spirit they are not living
> as spiritual persons ought to live. They are acting like non-Christians,
> and Paul's basic response is "Stop!" Their practice has not caught up
> with what they have accepted in principle. Their cultural assumptions
> have not been critically evaluated in light of their Christian faith and of
> the presence of God in their lives.[83]

Paul reminds them: "But we have the mind of Christ" (1 Cor. 2:16).
This assertion caps the discussion begun in 1:10 where he urges the Corin-

---

82. Quintilian, *Institutes,* 5.10.7. Cited in Witherington, *Conflict and Community in
Corinth,* 125.

83. Witherington, *Conflict and Community in Corinth,* 129.

thian Christians to "be united in the same mind." That "mind" of unity is the mind of the crucified Christ. It is a community mindset that is shaped christologically. "What was begun in the dismantling of intellectual and social structures by the rhetoric of the cross now reaches its completion in the consciously cruciform mind."[84] This "consciously cruciform mind" will result in a cruciform community of faith that lives out the gospel, that communicates the gospel, and that understands its community orators in ways that are consistent with the cruciform mindset.[85]

## The Role of Community Orators in Christian Community

One of Paul's tasks in 1 Cor. 1–4 is the condemnation of hero worship. The classical rhetorical world in which the Corinthians lived was one which involved the comparison of orators. The issue of Paul's *ēthos* and the basis for the evaluation of community orators is tied integrally to this cultural phenomenon.

The entire context of 1:10–4:21 deals with the problem of party strife, which proved to be disruptive to community unity as well as disloyal to Paul as their founding apostle. Paul's use of the *parakaleō* formula of appeal in 1:10 and 4:16 confronts both of these issues and stylistically frames the section by his appeal to unity in the community and to a right view of himself as community leader.[86] Though this kind of orator-loyalty might be expected in any other community in the world, for Paul this was a serious breach of the nature of Christian community. L. L. Wellborn states it succinctly: "What threatened the survival of the community of chosen people was not seductive gnostic theology or infectious Judaistic propaganda, but the possibility that its adherents

84. Brown, *The Cross and Human Transformation*, 139.

85. Wendell Willis comments similarly: "Based upon both other Pauline usage and the immediate context, then, the appeal to 'have the mind of Christ' does not mean to think Christ's thoughts after him, nor to have ecstatic experiences, nor to know proper dogma. The 'mind of Christ' is not focussed upon special wisdom or experiences, but on community life." See Willis, "The Mind of Christ in 1 Corinthians 2,16," *Biblica* 70 (1989): 119.

86. On the *parakaleō* formula in ancient letter writing see Peter T. O'Brien, "Letters, Letter Form," in *Dictionary of Paul and His Letters*, 552. See also C. J. Bjerkelund, *Parakaleō: Form, Funktion, und Sinn der parakalō Sätze in den paulinischen Briefen*, Bibliotheca theologica Norvegica 1 (Oslo: Universitetsforlaget, 1967); and K. Grayston, "A Problem of Translation: The Meaning of *parakaleō, paraclēsis* in the New Testament," *Scripture Bulletin* 11 (1980): 27-31.

might 'behave like ordinary men' (3:3)."[87] Marshall arrives at a very similar conclusion,

> that the judgement against him was a social one according to conventional values and that the conflict over apostleship was primarily sociocultural in character. . . . The rival apostles were Hellenistic Jews who had been educated in rhetoric and belonged to the mainstream of Graeco-Roman cultural tradition.[88]

Socially, the Corinthian Christians are following the cultural practice of competing for social status by dividing up over who has the wiser teacher, "i.e., one whose cultured eloquence indicates and confers status."[89] This perfectly normal social and cultural activity creates an enormous ethical problem in the context of Christian community.

The ethical problem is centered in party strife and division. Such divisions were "culturally acceptable consequences of patronage and personal loyalties, [but] they were unacceptable to Paul and his theology of the corporate fellowship which they had in the Lord Jesus Christ." Consequently, Paul diverts the Corinthians' attention away from himself, Cephas, and Apollos by means of three rhetorical questions in 1:13, each of which expects a negative answer: "Has Christ been divided? Was Paul crucified for you? Or were you baptized in the name of Paul?" Paul's strategy in asking these rhetorical questions

> consists of destroying party loyalty by undermining the inflated significance attributed to the three personalities of Paul, Cephas, and Apollos. . . . What better way for one of the principals in this issue to defuse the strife than by acknowledging his own insignificance and his personal ineptitude.[90]

The import of Paul's argument is a refocusing on Christ, for the questions rephrased into assertions would read: (1) Christ is not divided,

---

87. L. L. Wellborn, "On the Discord in Corinth: 1 Corinthians 1–4 and Ancient Politics," *Journal of Biblical Literature* 106 (1987): 88.

88. Marshall, *Enmity at Corinth,* 398-99.

89. Pogoloff, *Logos and Sophia,* 197.

90. Oster, *1 Corinthians,* 52, 55. Though Paul asserts the right to ministerial patronage (1 Cor. 9), he avoids it himself knowing that the sociocultural assumptions attendant to the patronage of itinerant philosophers carried baggage which could cause some to misinterpret the nature of Christian preachers, the Christian gospel, and Christian community.

neither should we be as his body, the church. (2) Christ was crucified for us, therefore he ought to be our ultimate source of allegiance, not any factional leader. (3) We were baptized into the name of Christ, therefore his name alone ought to be our defining identity as well as that of the whole church, not any other "big name" leader. Moreover, this christological reorientation forces his readers to remember that the efficacy of their salvation is not tied to any orator but to Christ alone.

Paul fears, however, that the use of *sophia logou* ("eloquent wisdom") will empty the gospel message of its power. At this point of his argument Paul appears to cross the line into "homiletical Donatism" by suggesting that preachers have the power to hollow out the gospel's potency. Lurking behind Paul's seeming theological lapse is what Alexandra Brown calls "a central Pauline irony":

> On the one hand, the power of the crucifixion lies in the self-emptying action of Christ, just as in Phil 2:5-11 "emptiness" is understood as a power-rendering condition. Only those who boast of *this* emptiness boast legitimately. At the same time, those who boast in the Christ-event from other than the experience of emptiness (i.e., the Corinthians) are in effect *emptying* the cross. In this second sense, the "emptiness of the cross" is the nullification of its meaning and power. At Corinth, "wise talk," party strife, and exalted ego (1:12-13) empty the cross precisely because people have not experienced the paradigmatic emptiness that the cross, properly perceived, produces.[91]

Paul's goal, partly, in this context is to reorient the Corinthians to a right estimation of community orators. In view of that, his point here is that those who make much (i.e., "boast") of a particular community orator who proclaims, instead of making much of the Christ who is proclaimed, create a situation wherein the message is compromised. Paul's goal in what he says, as well as in how he says it, is to lift up the cross of Christ — in word and deed — so that his hearers' experience of that witness depends upon God, points to God's all-sufficiency to save, and leads to the praise of God's glory, not any human's oratorical ability. As Brown points out, conventional social forms from the culture were being allowed to dominate the Corinthians' experience of hearing the gospel, resulting in party-strife over various human orators rather than community concord based in the unity of the one God. As

91. Brown, *The Cross and Human Transformation*, 74. Emphasis is Brown's.

the ultimate resolution of their problem, Paul points them to the *logos* of the cross.

The new framework for discernment which was given to the Corinthian Christians in the cross-event-proclaimed lays the basis for a new approach to evaluating community orators. Unfortunately, they were not making use of these new epistemological resources and were thus acting like *sarkinoi* ("fleshly people" = *kata sarka* = *psychikoi*) (1 Cor. 3:1). As such, they show that even though they have received a new birth into a new community that they are still *nēpioi* ("babies") in terms of spiritual maturity (1 Cor. 3:1).[92] The proof of this is to be found in his fundamental charge against them that he sounded in 1:12 and now repeats in 3:2b-4:

> Even now you are still not ready, for you are still of the flesh *(sarkikoi)*. For as long as there is jealousy and quarreling among you, are you not of the flesh, and behaving according to human inclinations *(kata anthropon)?* For when one says, "I belong to Paul," and another, "I belong to Apollos," are you not merely human?

Paul, however, with the cross-event-proclaimed functioning as the Corinthian church's new framework for discernment, begins to explain more precisely the role of orators in the cruciform community.

In 3:5-17 Paul insists that the proper way to view their community orators is in relationship to God's designs for them in the community. They are fundamentally "*diakonoi* ('servants') through whom you believed" (1 Cor. 3:5; cf. 4:1 and 2 Cor. 4:7). Preachers are servants fulfilling tasks assigned to them by the Lord (1 Cor. 3:5). God and only God gives the growth that comes of ministerial labor. When ministers take credit for growth, they are trying to make something of themselves when they are actually nothing (1 Cor. 3:6-7). Those who are served, i.e., the Corinthian church, are not to equate the success of any servant's work to the power of that individual, for servants only plant seed that has been given them. They water with water given them. Any growth is due entirely to God. Neither are the servants to be seen as in competition with one another. They are co-laborers in territory that does not even belong to them. They receive

---

92. Fee comments on Paul's use of *nēpios.* "Paul regularly uses the imagery of 'children' in a positive sense to reflect his own apostolic relationship with his converts. In such cases the word is always *teknon* ('child'); the word used here (*nēpios,* 'baby' or 'mere infant') almost always has a pejorative sense, in contrast to being adult, and refers to thinking or behavior that is not fitting." See Fee, *1 Corinthians,* 124-25.

common wages and work together, not against each other. Neither gains on another, even as they build on the other's work. "For we are God's servants, working together; you are God's field, God's building" (1 Cor. 3:9). The judge of all the servants' work is God and the time of judgment is eschatologically imminent. Nevertheless, premature judgment of one another must be avoided, especially the kind which exalts one servant over another in a way that implies a competitive environment, thus creating factions.

It is only by God's grace given to Paul that any skillful construction on "God's building" is able to be done (1 Cor. 3:10). Moreover, Jesus Christ is the foundation (1 Cor. 3:11) upon which all subsequent building is erected. And every worker who adds to the building is held accountable to God, who alone is the final judge (1 Cor. 3:12-15). To divide the community in *kata sarka* ways destroys God's very Temple, and God will destroy those who do so (1 Cor. 3:16-17).

Paul, therefore, calls upon the Corinthian Christians to give up their humanly derived ways of discerning since, in the cruciform community in Christ, they are dependent upon God. For Paul, God's wisdom and value system has inverted the world's (1 Cor. 3:18-20). Therefore, Christian community orators are not to be evaluated in the same way that orators in conventional rhetorical situations are (3:21-23). Rather, in this new community they are to be thought of as "servants of Christ and stewards of God's mysteries" and, thus, wholly accountable to God (4:1-5).

Far from individual church members gaining status from huddling under the greater preacher,[93] Paul asserts that all community orators belong to the Corinthian church, not as status figures, but as slaves for Christ's sake. What does Paul mean by these preacher images, "servant of Christ" and a "steward of God's mysteries"?

"Servant" is arguably Paul's favorite term of self-designation.[94] The rhetorical impact of Paul's questions to them about their orators in 3:5 ("What then is Apollos? What is Paul?") is, as Fee suggests, to express disdain. "You are of Paul, or Apollos? Are they lords of some kind to whom you may attach yourselves, to whom you may belong? Do you not know,

---

93. See Pogoloff, *Logos and Sophia*, 129.

94. Paul used various terms for "servant" *(doulos, diakonos, hypēretas)* throughout his letters in reference to his identity and role as given by God. The word in 3:5 is *diakonos* and in 4:1 *hypēretas*. On *diakonos* see E. Earle Ellis, *Prophecy and Hermeneutic in Early Christianity: New Testament Essays* (Grand Rapids: Eerdmans Publishing Company, 1978), 6-15; and H. W. Beyer, *Theological Dictionary of the New Testament*, II, 81-93.

after all, what Apollos and Paul really are?"[95] They are, Paul insists, "servants."

The servant imagery *(diakonoi)* of 3:5-15 in reference to God's field and building shifts in 4:1-5 to a servant imagery that has to do with God's household goods. In both instances the idea of a steward in trust of another's belongings is present, but this stewardship concept is explicit in 4:1. "Think of us in this way, as servants of Christ and stewards of God's mysteries." The word for servant here *(hypēretas)* is the only occurrence in Paul. It originally was used in reference to slaves who rowed in the lower tier of a trireme.[96] Paul employs it in 1 Cor. 4 as a functional synonym to *diakonos* and as a parallel term to *oikonomos*. The "steward" was often a slave who had primary management responsibilities of the owner's household. The term implies the kind of delegated authority that Paul has been arguing for throughout this context. As God's stewards they are accountable to God, who is the owner.[97]

Paul caps his thoughts in 4:6-7 before moving to the *peristasis* catalogue of 4:8-13 with two key summary points: (1) "I have applied *(metaschēmatizo)* all this to Apollos and myself for your benefit" (4:6). Stephen Pogoloff comments: "Paul describes his own rhetoric: he has 'transferred as in a figure of speech *(metaschēmatizo)* the rhetoric of status to himself and Apollos. But the rhetoric is reversed: he and Apollos are not to be spoken of as sources of status enhancing wisdom, but as mere servants."[98] In the same vein Benjamin Fiore writes:

> Paul is intent on awakening his audience's attention to the fact that things are not what they seem to be. In fact, in using the term *metaschematizein* ("to transfer in a figure") . . . Paul expressly states the parenetic purpose behind his remarks. . . . At least the Christian patrons [wish] to resemble those of other groups around sophists and professional rhetoricians. If, then, it was these same highly placed Christians who were guilty of lionizing one teacher over another (1:10; 3:4), of vaunting their own knowledge (3:1; 6:12; 8:13), of making distinctions

95. Fee, *1 Corinthians*, 130.

96. Fee, *1 Corinthians*, 159.

97. On *oikonomos* see John Reumann, "'Servants of God' — Pre-Christian Religious Application of the *oikonomos* in Greek," *Journal of Biblical Literature* 77 (1958): 339-49; and idem, "*Oikonomia*-Terms in Paul in Comparison with Lucan *Heilsgeschichte*," *New Testament Studies* 13 (1966/67): 147-67.

98. Pogoloff, *Logos and Sophia*, 214.

in the community rooted in pride (4:7; 5:2), or of slighting the poor at the assemblies (11:17-34), then Paul would have to proceed with caution. . . . Paul offers his own example . . . as a help for the community to see things for what they are and not take them as they seem to the world.[99]

Paul drives home his second point by three rhetorical questions in 4:7: "Who makes you different? What do you have that you did not receive? And if you received it, why do you boast as if it were not a gift?" Paul wants them to apply this principle to themselves in the same way that he has applied it to Apollos and himself, for they are no different, all being in the same cruciform community. Moreover, he wants them to be grateful rather than boastful. That one difference — gratefulness vs. boastfulness — marks the difference between the person who understands himself to be a "steward" and an "owner." In taking on the mindset of grateful recipient of God's blessings, the Corinthians will take on Paul's own God-given mindset ("the mind of Christ," 2:16) and thus prove themselves to be imitators of Paul (4:16).[100]

Dale Martin notes Paul's inversion of status as he reveals what it means to be "Christ's slave *oikonomos*":

> Paul's choice of imagery emphasized that he, their first leader, is a high-status person who has taken on low status. He challenges the other leading Christians to do the same. . . . His rhetoric overturns the clear categories of his contemporary readers, who assume that leaders are free, exercise authority, and do not work, whereas lower-status persons do work. Paul's language forces his readers who share upper-class views to think of leadership in confusing ways that stress the ambiguity — not the "givenness" — of normal status indicators.[101]

All of this sets up Paul's *peristasis* argument which climaxes Paul's *ēthos* argument and creates a new vision for the person of the preacher. Paul's *peristasis* argument is the climax to his presentation in 1 Cor. 1–4.

---

99. Benjamin Fiore, "'Covert Allusion' in 1 Corinthians 1–4," *Catholic Biblical Quarterly* 47 (1985): 89-101. Cited in Pogoloff, *Logos and Sophia*, 214.

100. Imitation of Paul is thus to be construed as imitation of Christ. Insofar as Paul embodies the nature of the crucified Christ he shows himself to have the mind of Christ and thus provides a present, incarnate version of the gospel. Cf. Kay, *Christus Praesens*, 52.

101. Dale Martin, *Slavery as Salvation: The Metaphor of Slavery in Pauline Christianity* (New Haven: Yale University Press, 1990), 79-80, 82. Cited in Pogoloff, *Logos and Sophia*, 215.

These hardship catalogues are at the heart of his reverse-rhetoric argument. They represent the implications of the *logos* of the cross for the *ēthos* of the one who would orate that *logos,* i.e., the preacher. For Paul the *ēthos* of the preacher is derivative of and organically related to the nature of the *logos* of the cross.

Paul employs several hardship catalogues in the Corinthian correspondence to authenticate his ministry (1 Cor. 4:9-13; 2 Cor. 4:7-12; 6:4-10; 11:23-29). Günther Bornkamm notes that in 1 and 2 Cor. Paul has "several lists of the vicissitudes and acts which in Paul's view legitimate the true apostle."[102] To deploy hardship catalogues within one's argument of self-justification was not without precedent in Paul's world. In fact it was one way that a wise, but suffering, sage would orient his audience to the true (usually divinely appointed) reasons for his hardships. John T. Fitzgerald describes the way a sage of Paul's day would use the hardship list:

> *Peristasis* [hardship] catalogues frequently serve as rhetorical and literary foils for the depiction of the wise man's existence and character. . . . They serve to depict such characteristics as 1) the sage's serenity despite the direst calamities of life, 2) his virtue, especially his courage, 3) his endurance of the greatest and most demanding hardships, 4) his perseverance in doing noble deeds despite the dangers involved and his refusal, at any cost, to depart from what justice dictates, 5) his contempt for Fortune, 6) his victory over adversity, 7) his *askēsis* [weakness] and the role it plays in his victory, 8) his invincibility and invulnerability as a person, 9) his perfect rationality, 10) his demeanor and his response to his adversaries, 11) his consent to the conformity to the will of God and the place of his suffering within the divine plan. In short, the catalogues depict and celebrate the greatness of his invincible virtue, the power and tranquility of his philosophically informed mind.

Though Paul's hardships embarrassed the Corinthians, and in their thinking shame him, Paul wants to show them that "the [hardship] catalogue presents the suffering apostolic existence as the praiseworthy paradigm for Christian existence." Observe Paul's *peristasis* catalogue of 1 Cor. 4:9-13:

> For I think that God has exhibited us apostles as last of all, as though sentenced to death, because we have become a spectacle to the world, to

---

102. Günther Bornkamm, *Paul* (New York: Harper and Row, 1969), 169.

angels and to mortals. We are fools for the sake of Christ, but you are
wise in Christ. We are weak, but you are strong. You are held in honor,
but we in disrepute. To the present hour we are hungry and thirsty, we
are poorly clothed and beaten and homeless, and we grow weary from
the work of our own hands. When reviled, we bless; when persecuted,
we endure; when slandered, we speak kindly. We have become like the
rubbish of the world, the dregs of all things, to this very day.

As servants of God's servant who suffered, Jesus Christ, "the divine is
said to exhibit [the apostles] as a model." The suffering of those who minister
the gospel becomes a part of their witness to the gospel. It is not that the gospel
depends upon the commensurate suffering of its messengers to be efficacious
for salvation, but rather that such a linking of ministerial life with the God-
empowered message functions to point to Christ's suffering death which alone
is sufficient, and which alone gives meaning and hope to their suffering.
Paul's use of the ironic *peristasis* catalogues

> is informed by OT traditions about the afflicted righteous man and suf-
> fering prophet, and it is transformed by his fixation on the cross of
> Christ. His *peristasis* catalogues thus represent the convergence of sev-
> eral traditions and reflect his own personal experiences of suffering and
> divine power. They take us to the center of Paul's understanding of God
> and his own self-understanding, yet anchor him in the culture and con-
> ventions of his time.[103]

One aspect of preacher *ēthos* consists in the preacher entering
into, with his whole self, the ministry of Christ Jesus, a ministry which
Paul describes in terms of agency (2 Cor. 2:14-17; 4:5-12).[104] This is a
ministry of suffering as Christ suffered.[105] The message of the gospel

---

103. John T. Fitzgerald, *Cracks in an Earthen Vessel: An Examination of the Catalogues
of Hardships in the Corinthian Correspondence*, SBL Dissertation Series, #99 (Atlanta:
Scholars Press, 1988), 115, 122, 204, 207.

104. Jeffrey A. Crafton, *The Agency of the Apostle: A Dramatist Analysis of Paul's Responses to Conflict in 2 Corinthians*, Journal for the Study of the New Testament, Supplement
Series 51 (Sheffield, England: Sheffield Academic Press, 1991), 62, uses Kenneth Burke's rhetorical categories of Agent/Agency to explain Paul's conception of the ministry in 2 Corinthians. Crafton writes: "In Paul's agency orientation God is the agent; all matters of authority, sufficiency, purpose or goal, therefore, are deferred to the divine actor. Adequacy belongs
to God and can only be attributed to the apostle by association (2 Cor. 2.16b-17; 3.5-6)."

105. Alister McGrath, "Cross, Theology of the," in *Dictionary of Paul and His Letters*,
196, notes three key texts in Paul (2 Cor. 4:7-15; Gal. 6:14; Phil. 3:8-12) where "Christ and

does not gain validation, or even any help in achieving its God-directed goals, from the preacher patterning his person, his dress, his hair, his morality or any aspect of his character according to the sociocultural standards of his hearers. Rather, just as the gospel is at its heart a countercultural *logos* which establishes and funds a countercultural community, this word and community, at least implicitly, exist partly as a prophetic and eschatological challenge to the exclusive and hierarchical, the social and economic structures that have been constructed in the world *kata sarka*, which work against God's purposes as revealed in the gospel. The preacher's person participates in that same challenge as an embodied witness to God's gospel. Thus, the weakness and power of the preacher mirror that of Jesus Christ himself. Karl Plank comments on Paul's use of ironic language to tie his *ēthos* to the *logos* of the cross:

> Paul parades apostolic weakness before the eyes of his audience. Forsaking second-order description, he forces his readers to witness specific manifestations of weakness: hunger, thirst, exposure, beatings. He etches weakness upon their imaginations and gives it an immediate presence through his forceful and imaginative style. In doing so he brings weakness into the readers' world — not just any world, but that near world they call to mind in their reading — and makes its claim unavoidable. Moreover, he brings not just any weakness for, through their reading, they themselves come to know the reality of apostolic weakness. At least in that real world of their imagination, the weakness Paul brings is their own, the weakness which binds both apostle and community to the realities of the cross and the divine call to salvation. Struck by the presence of weakness, Paul's readers stand vulnerable to the force of his irony and the power of his paradoxical gospel.[106]

Paul forces all who would seek the power that oratory confers, and all who attempt to tuck themselves under the cloak of the power that supposedly exists within an orator, to reconsider the nature of power in the oratory of the gospel. "Essentially Paul sees no reason why there should be a power struggle focussing on one or another leader since the divine power

---

his cross are the cause and the paradigm of the suffering of the believer. There is a strong sense of the believer sharing in the life — and hence in the sufferings — of Christ, an idea perhaps expressed most fully at Romans 8:17 (cf. Col. 1:24)."

106. Plank, *The Irony of Affliction*, 89-90.

that authenticates all ministries is available to the whole church in the word of the cross."[107]

Paul's call to his churches to imitate himself and others (e.g., Timothy, Titus, Philemon, Stephanus, Fortunatus, Achaicus, Phoebe, Epaphroditus) does not negate the point being made here nor insinuate that Paul is actually donatistic. Paul Sampley comments: "Paul is a valid model because he patterns himself after Christ, because he understands the gospel and the life appropriate to it, and because his actions and comportment openly reflect God's grace."[108] In pointing to himself and others as worthy models to imitate, Paul is attempting to show what Christ looks like "in the flesh" even as Christ indwells those who are "in him." Seen in the context of Paul's Agent/Agency model of 2 Cor. 4:7ff., where the earthen vessel is the chosen means by which God allows his own treasure to be seen, Paul's argument does not fall prey to donatistic tendencies.

As I have pointed out, Paul does not dismiss rhetoric or refrain from using rhetorical categories in his preaching or teaching. Rather, he "baptizes them into Christ." He uses them, especially *logos* and *ēthos* appeals, but under the criticizing gaze of the gospel itself. In other words, with regard to *ēthos*, the standards for perceived credibility shift from the sociocultural to the theological as shaped by the cross-event-proclaimed. Paul would even agree with the classical rhetorical dictum that his credibility hinges on the perception of those who were to judge him in the rhetorical situation of Christian proclamation. Paul, however, perceived his judge to be God and not any human court (1 Cor. 4:1-6) which would stand outside of him and judge him before the appropriate time and with inappropriate criteria.

Paul, therefore, wants his hearers to perceive God to be his judge, not them. He also wants to shift their expectations for *ēthos* in two specific ways. First, he wants them to consider God as the one whose credibility ultimately is at stake in the preaching of the gospel. Second, he wants his own preacher *ēthos* to be judged in terms of the criteria that the gospel message — the cross-event-proclaimed — demands.

---

107. Charles Cousar, *A Theology of the Cross: The Death of Jesus in the Pauline Letters* (Minneapolis: Fortress Press, 1990), 34.

108. Paul Sampley, *Walking Between the Times: Paul's Moral Reasoning* (Minneapolis: Fortress Press, 1991), 88.

## Conclusion

Though the "herald" image has been the dominant manner of characterizing Paul's view of the preacher, this is a reading of Paul which is selective and reductive in its use of the Pauline materials. Nevertheless, Rudolf Bultmann's more textured reading of Paul points to the inextricably intertwined relationship between the heralding messenger and the heralded message. Bultmann raises the possibility that Paul's understanding of the *kērygma* and *kēryx* are not hostile to *ēthos* considerations.

Indeed, as I have shown, the categories of classical rhetoric were pervasive in Paul's day. Modern exegetical tone-deafness to classical categories misses a vital note for Pauline interpretation. Instead of resorting to a reductive account of the nature of classical rhetoric (Schmithals and Wilckens), or positing a split between Paul's use of genre in oral and written communication (Litfin), the better question to ask of Paul's writings is how in fact he did use rhetoric, and with what sort of theological discretion. As I have shown, Paul employs a classical *ēthos* defense of his ministry within the deliberative discourse of 1 Corinthians.

Paul's chief problem in Corinth regarding his own person had to do with the differing standards which he and the Corinthians used for determining speaker credibility. Paul does not measure up to the Corinthians' credibility standards, standards which they had borrowed unreflectively from their rhetorically-enmeshed environment. Paul's task in face of this was to reorient the Corinthian Christians to a different expectation for and perception of preacher-*ēthos*. He does this by linking ministerial *ēthos* to the exigencies of the gospel message of Jesus Christ crucified rather than to the exigencies of the sociocultural situation of first-century Corinth. In this we see that Paul's homiletic is message-driven. The cross-event-proclaimed becomes dominant to the point of functioning as a new epistemological lens for the preacher and the church. Moreover, the message of the cross puts to death *kata sarka* standards of what makes preaching preaching, and what makes preachers preachers. The cross is the epistemological key for Paul, for in the cross the church has a new way of knowing in the time frame in which it currently exists, the painful and often perplexing juncture between the ages. The church thus operates *kata stauron* in its manner of judgment in that it sees that God has put to death, and continues to put to death, the instantiations of death which come from *kata sarka* judgments. In the delivery of the word of the cross, God creates and sustains a new community — the cruciform community.

Within this new and alternative community, the preacher, by God's design, is a servant of Christ and a steward of God's mysteries — primarily that mystery which is the *logos* of Christ crucified.

For Paul, true *ēthos* is derivative not of a social and cultural expectation but of an expectation (a divine call, commission, and empowerment) that arises from the nature of the gospel and the community of faith that is formed and sustained by the God-given and empowered *logos* (the cross-event-proclaimed). Any talk, therefore, of Paul's conception of *ēthos* must be couched in a discussion of his reverse-*logos* (the gospel message) and the alternative community that this strange *logos* of the cross forms and funds. One could argue that for Paul, then, it still is the expectation of the social and cultural group that sets one's *ēthos* construction and projection. But it is the radically reconceived social constraints of the faith community that sets the expectation.

Paul's reverse-*ēthos* argument is a defense of his own person and ministry. It takes the form of both direct and indirect responses to critics who were attempting to erode his credibility as a community leader. The direct response against his critics consists of Paul's ironic use of his sufferings (*peristasis* catalogues) and his supposed deficiencies. Paul takes up the very charges that have been levied against him and, rather than denying them, acknowledges them, claiming that these deficiencies actually authenticate his ministry when viewed from a christologically corrected faith perspective.

These direct, while ironic, arguments about Paul's person are set against the backdrop of his indirect defense: the theology of the cross. It is, in fact, the theology of the cross which makes possible and persuasive Paul's reverse-*ēthos* argument. For the cross is the reverse, or ironic, *logos*. This reverse-*logos* not only legitimizes, but even necessitates a reverse-*ēthos*. Even though Paul claims that in preaching all is dependent on God, he does not negate the category of *ēthos* as unimportant or inconsequential. Rather he reframes it given the new epistemology of the cross. The preacher's life is to be a cruciform life, consonant with the message of the cross. The preacher's own sufferings do not, however, prove efficacious for salvation. The preacher's sufferings function as witness to Christ's own salvific sufferings.

In sum, Paul's deliberative argument was designed to convince the Corinthian church of his own authority and of their need to end party strife and reunify as one body. Paul wants the Corinthian Christians to decide for him as a true apostle of Jesus Christ based upon a reverse-*ēthos* appeal. To accomplish this he must reverse their criteria of orator evaluation. He does this by grounding them in the new way of knowing (epistemological reframing) that the cross-event-proclaimed provides them. The cruciform *logos* calls for a cruciform *ēthos,* just as it forms a cruciform *ekklēsia* which now reasons with a cruciform consciousness ("the mind of Christ," 1 Cor. 2:16). Such a reframed view of *ēthos* ironically turns sociological criticisms against Paul into theological arguments for his legitimacy. It is, thus, a reverse-*ēthos* appeal which proves both adequate and appropriate given the nature of the Christian rhetorical situation.

With this reorientation, we can now turn to contemporary homiletics. In light of Paul's theology of the cross, ministerial *ēthos* can legitimately become an essential component of homiletical theory. To show how this can take place in the context of practical theology is the task of chapter four.

# 4. *Ēthos* for Contemporary Homiletical Theory

Being disciplined by the Word entails allowing our lives to be patterned in Christ. As such, we are to have a character that reflects neither that egocentric reading and witness in which God gets (at best) second-billing, nor that faceless reading and witness in which it is presumed that the messenger is irrelevant to the message. Rather, it involves a willingness to have our lives formed and transformed in and through particular Christian communities so that the words we use become means of pointing to the Word we follow.

*Stephen E. Fowl and L. Gregory Jones*[1]

If it were only texts or men we had to handle! But we have to handle the gospel.

*P. T. Forsyth*

---

1. Stephen E. Fowl and L. Gregory Jones, *Reading in Communion: Scripture and Ethics in Christian Life* (Grand Rapids: William B. Eerdmans Publishing Company, 1991), 34.

## Summary and Review

This study has traced the origin of the homiletic discussion regarding the preacher's person back through Augustine to the key theorists in the Greek and Roman classical rhetorical heritage. I have noted a persistent tension that exists between the logically diverse frameworks of rationality that have been used to describe "what is really going on" in the preaching situation, namely rhetoric and theology. I have traced the history of homiletical theory on this topic as essentially a tug-of-war between two frames of reference over which is the legitimate standard to judge the nature and function of the preacher's person in preaching. Some, operating with rhetorical principles as primary, have followed Aristotle to draw the conclusion that the person of the preacher, as with any orator, is perhaps the most important factor in the persuasion of the hearers. Others, operating with theological assumptions as primary, have argued that since preaching is nothing less than God's word for which God alone is responsible and which God alone makes efficacious, then any talk of the human person making the word "more efficacious" is idolatrous.

Amid this conflict between rival interpretations, I reexamined the apostle Paul's *ēthos* defense in his Corinthian correspondence. Though influential readings of Paul have tried to reduce Paul's conception of preaching to an exclusively herald model, I noted that Paul did not play the "either-or" game of choosing only one frame of reference, i.e., the theological, to the denial of the other, i.e., the rhetorical. Rather, Paul makes extensive use of classical rhetoric in defending the theological understanding of his own person. His *ēthos* defense — a thoroughly rhetorical phenomenon — is shaped, however, in ways that overturn a fundamental stance of Aristotelian-style rhetoric by his turn for guidance first to the *logos* of the cross, not to the prejudices and expectations of his hearers. Paul is thus message-driven, but not to the exclusion or dismissal of rhetoric. Rather, since he recognizes that there is no non-rhetorical way of communicating, he puts the rhetoric he uses through rigorous testing by the message of Jesus Christ crucified. In addition, he attempts to reframe the position of his hearers/readers, i.e., those who are "in Christ," in light of the "turning of the ages" wrought in the cross of Christ. To be more precise, in relation to Paul's apocalyptic understanding of the cross, a reframed understanding of rhetorical *ēthos* — "reverse-*ēthos*" — mediates between rhetorical and theological homiletic theories. Designating the nature of preacher *ēthos* as "reverse-*ēthos*" indicates the theological discrimination that is necessary in the appropriation of the rhetorical category of *ēthos* for preaching. Such a designation differentiates it from Aristotelian *ēthos* in that the criteria for assessing a speaker's *ēthos* is shifted from hearer to message.

In view of these findings, chapter four will develop the theoretical and practical implications of Paul's reverse-*ēthos* for contemporary homiletics. These implications can be conveniently grouped into three categories: (1) the relationship between theology and rhetoric in homiletics; (2) preaching's message and "real" *ēthos;* and (3) preaching's message and "perceived" *ēthos.*

## The Relationship between Theology and Rhetoric in Homiletics

One implication of this study has to do with the way in which one conceives the relationship between rhetoric and theology in describing preaching. Though preaching the gospel is a unified whole in the actual event of preaching itself (in the primary discourse of proclamation), in the secondary discourse of reflective analysis on the church's proclamation two intrinsically diverse ways of describing the event persistently emerge. The singular road of proclamation's primary discourse reaches a fork in the analysis of secondary discourse: one branches to rhetorically oriented analyses, the other to theologically oriented analyses.

The brief history of homiletical history on the person of the preacher in chapter two revealed significant conflict over the way the rhetorical frame of reference should relate to the theological. I noted the scorn of the early Latin fathers and twentieth-century Barthians for any means of analysis deemed extra-theological. And yet, other homiletical theorists, such as Augustine in the early church and Daniel Baumann, Clyde Fant, and Robin Meyers in this century, endorsed thorough engagement with what can be learned from rhetoric based upon the assumption that such phenomenologically assembled knowledge is essentially neutral with respect to theological claims.

In the critical analysis of preaching, then, an impasse is reached, an impasse that has its corollary in the other subdisciplines of practical theology. Philosopher of Christian education James E. Loder has called this fundamental impasse practical theology's "generative problematic." The generative problematic at the heart of the study of the preacher's person has to do with the logically diverse means of discourse which can be, even must be, brought to bear on this topic's analysis.

Perhaps the fundamental way in which the theological and rhetorical frames of reference are logically diverse is in the way that each deals with the role of God. For though the theological frame of reference itself comes "from below" as an enterprise of utterly human reflection, it nevertheless, and in contradistinction from other scientific modes of discourse, factors into its analysis confessional convictions about the reality of God — God's true involvement — in the matters under contemplation. Analyses from rhetoric and communication theory, on the other hand, bracket God out of their investigation. "God," as such, is not a legitimate field of inquiry for the sciences, insofar as these treat what can be empirically tested. In this sense, the human sciences are phenomenological, relying on data derived from human experience obtained through the senses. This mode of inquiry is thus largely descriptive. It attempts to define what is "really going on" in a particular situation under observation from an empirical perspective. Only after such empirical observation does it sometimes move to prescription — guiding what "ought to be." It thus moves to prescription by way of description. As a means of prescription based in description, rhetoric is fundamentally hearer-driven and tends to look upon theologically oriented prescriptions as quaint, if not downright ignorant, ostrich-with-head-in-sand approaches to preaching. Fred Craddock, for example, bewails the hearers of the Barthian preacher as javelin catchers, thus highlighting the violence he saw the purely theological mode of preaching inflicting on the "real" situation of preaching.

Homiletical theorists who operate primarily from the theological frame of reference recoil at what they perceive to be the idolatrous anthropocentric perspective of the rhetorical frame of reference. The theologically framed analyst starts with preaching's claim to be the word of God spoken. It is a revelatory word in which God promises to be active even unto salvation. To bracket out the work of God in preaching as beyond the pale of analysis is to be ultimately reductionistic — even idolatrous — in that preaching is turned from an act of God into a set of communicative processes which can be manipulated on the human plane to effect results which are both measurable and predictable. From a theological vantage point, what is "really going on" in the preaching situation is accessible only to faith, since it is an apocalyptic occurrence of God's action in the present word of the cross.

These are, perhaps, overdrawn pictures in order to illustrate the divide between frames of reference. But we did see some respective examples (e.g., Ritschl and Meyers) for whom this way of characterizing the situation is not a caricature. Reconceiving homiletics as I am suggesting is a call for one to become more self-conscious in one's analysis of preaching from the logically diverse conversation partners which are brought to bear on preaching's analysis. It means that one resists a kind of reductionism which occurs when one discipline pejoratively declares of its cognate counterpart, whether theology or one of the human sciences, that it is in effect "'nothing but' a subcategory of its own structure, and, consequently, the fundamental claims of the other discipline are explained away."[2] This kind of reductionism is seen in discussions of the person of the preacher especially with respect to the issue of efficacy and persuasion.

From the perspective of Aristotelian-style rhetoric, one is most interested in matters pertaining to persuasion, meaning, the convincing or winning over of one's hearers to one's position. This is, in large part, the goal of preaching from a rhetorical perspective. Moreover, following Aristotelian-style rhetoric, if persuasion is deemed to be the goal of preaching, then the *ēthos* of the preacher often becomes the chief matter of concern. By contrast, from a theological frame of reference, preaching is confessed to be the power of God for salvation. As such, preaching — by God's free grace, power, and providence — proves efficacious for the hearer's salvation. From this vantage point, God is the chief matter of concern, and any talk of the human preacher affecting or effecting the situation of God's activity borders on idolatry. Rhetorically framed homileticians have concluded that theological talk of efficacy is really "nothing but" persuasion. Some, for example, Baumann, Fant, and Meyers, seem to think that persuasion is actually "nothing but" efficacy. The terms "persuasion" and "efficacy" are thus used as functional synonyms in approaches that fail to differentiate between the paradigmatic frames of reference to which each term belongs.

These two important, ideologically freighted concepts — persuasion and efficacy — make sense within their given frames of reference. When, however, they are imported to another ideologically framed paradigm they become problematic in meaning and function. For efficacy issues, which have ultimately to do with confessional faith convictions about God and God's working, cannot legitimately or meaningfully function within a

---

2. James E. Loder, "Theology and Psychology," in *Dictionary of Pastoral Care and Counseling,* ed. Rodney J. Hunter (Nashville: Abingdon, 1990), 1267.

frame of reference which deliberately brackets out any notion of divine activity. And persuasion issues, which ultimately have to do with matters like human invention and image projection, conflict in significant ways within a frame of reference which brackets out humanity's role in the efficacy of preaching. What we see in the efficacy/persuasion problem is that each frame of reference has eclipsed the logically diverse aspects of the other frame's key concept. Each concept has its meaning and validity within its own frame of reference. However, the concepts are not simply interchangeable between frames. I contend that the efficacy/persuasion problem has been at the heart of the problem of describing and understanding the nature of the preacher's person throughout the history of homiletical theory and continues to be at the heart of the problem in contemporary homiletical theory.

The way that Paul dealt with criticisms of his own person as minister of the gospel, and the way he reframed the issues rhetorically and theologically, in 1 Cor. helps us out of our dilemma. Chapter three demonstrated the intimate connection that Paul insisted exists between preacher and message. This predominately theological way of construing the preaching situation differs from a classical rhetorical interpretation of the situation.

From an Aristotelian perspective, the speaker ought to consider the relationship between *pathos* (audience reaction/emotion) and *ēthos* (speaker character) to be more important than the relationship that exists between *logos* (message) and *ēthos*. *Ēthos* is an audience construct according to rhetoric's frame of reference. It is a construct based upon information that the hearers have about the speaker primarily in the rhetorical situation of the speech itself (though we have expanded Aristotle's conception to include the reality of antecedent *ēthos*, what is known of the speaker by reputation or through relationship prior to the speaking event). The astute speaker must recognize this audience expectation in some way if he or she is to be successful in persuasion. Thus aware of, and using, audience predispositions, the speaker is perceived to be credible to the hearers and has a greater chance for being heard and believed. If the speaker's projected *ēthos* deliberately conflicts with audience prejudice, then the possibility for persuasion is lessened. One could argue that speakers who deliberately project an *ēthos* that conflicts with their hearers' predispositions regarding credibility commit nothing less than rhetorical suicide.

Paul shows deliberate disregard for his readers' negative assessment of his problematic personhood in that he does not try to change his own projected person in order to be perceived better in view of the Corinthians' criteria for assessment. This is because in Paul's way of thinking the message of preaching, the word of the cross, has paradigmatic influence on the preacher's person — as it does over every matter in the rhetorical situation of Christian proclamation. Thus, for Paul, *logos* concerns take priority over *pathos* concerns in determining and assessing his projected *ēthos*. Paul, in contradistinction from Aristotle, considers the relationship between *logos* and *ēthos* to hold a priority over all other matters in the rhetorical situation of Christian proclamation. What is at stake for Paul is faithfulness in his person to the message entrusted to him. An *ēthos* which was "out of character" with the message would be a poor witness and thus a breach of service to Christ and a compromising of his stewardship of God's mysteries.[3]

Therefore, Paul urges the Corinthian Christians to alter their expectations of what ought to make the Christian preacher credible. Paul wants the Corinthian Christians to assess their own corporate character as the church of Jesus Christ in view of the message of the gospel before they assess his own character and credibility. With this reframed view of reality provided by the *logos* of the cross-event-proclaimed, they will be able to see that Paul's person does not in fact invalidate his credibility and thus cast a shadow of doubt concerning his message. Rather, his person embodies the cross he proclaims. Yet, Paul refrains from tying the efficacy of the preached word to the person of the preacher and his or her ability to live blamelessly according to the paradigm of the cross. Rather, the efficacy of the word preached is due to the power of God in the ever-efficacious crucifixion and resurrection of Jesus Christ. The preacher's life is implicated in the proclamation, however, since this message is about life. It makes claims on life and demands a decision from its hearers about their lives as brought before the cross of Christ. Preachers are not exempt from the word of the cross. They, too, stand under its death and life, at the juncture of its judgment of the old age and dawn of the new.

This brings us back again to the vexing problem of efficacy and persuasion. In analyzing the nature of the preacher's person, it is persistently difficult to unhinge *ēthos* from efficacy. This is because homileticians who analyze the person of the preacher typically fail to differentiate between

---

3. There is a similarity to Plato's rhetoric here in that Plato believed that the rhetor's task was faithful witness to the Truth even at the cost of martyrdom. A primary difference between Paul and Plato on *ēthos*, however, is in their radically different understandings of what the Truth is, and what, therefore, would be worth dying for.

the rhetorical and theological frames of reference when describing the person of the preacher. Efficacy and persuasion ought to be differentiated from one another in terms of the paradigmatic frame of which each is an organic part. When each concept is treated within its own frame of reference, each has something to offer the homiletician as he or she attempts to understand preaching's situation.

Persuasion, from a rhetorical standpoint, reminds the preacher that the situation of Christian proclamation is "one which could be otherwise" — decisions for or against faith are being made every time the gospel is proclaimed — and that the preacher's perceived person is intimately bound up in the hearers' decisions about the message. This forces the preacher constantly to reevaluate the nature of his or her implied *ēthos*. What do the people see and perceive me to be? How does this relate to who we are to be together as God's people? Such questions become important in the preacher's overall call to witness to the gospel as a servant and steward.

Efficacy, from a theological standpoint, reminds the preacher that the situation of Christian proclamation is one that is ultimately in God's control. The preacher, like a good gardener, simply plants and waters seeds. Faithful constancy to these tasks of service and stewardship are ministry's call, but do not necessarily constrain the word to "work" or fail. For salvation is something only God can effect. "God gives the growth" is the continual confession of the preacher who knows that true hearing unto salvation is a mysterious activity of which only God truly knows the whence and whither.

Paul's approach to the person of the preacher gives clear priority to the message. He is message-driven in his understanding of preaching because he believes that the ultimate issue in preaching has to do with God and the claims for God's promises and actions in the proclaimed word. This does not cause Paul to eliminate all concern for rhetoric or for what the rhetorical frame of reference allows one to see. Rather, Paul engages rhetorical concerns but subordinates such concerns in view of the claims of the cross-event-proclaimed. What is annulled at the cross, then, is not rhetoric as such but its *kata sarka* ("according to the flesh") enslavement. Without the theological insight that comes *kata stauron* ("according to the cross"), rhetoric cannot be used faithfully, i.e., in a way that accords with the nature of the message of preaching.

Reverse-*ēthos*, then, is a theologically informed rhetorical category which describes the nature and function of the preacher's person in the rhetorical situation of Christian proclamation. It is designated "reverse" or "ironic" *ēthos* to differentiate it from an Aristotelian notion of *ēthos* which derives its meaning and function primarily from paying attention to audience expectation for how a speaker is to be deemed credible. Reverse or ironic *ēthos* highlights the turn first to the message of Christian proclamation and considers the demands that it exacts on the rhetorical situation.

It is clear from a study of the homiletical literature, however, that just what preaching's message is cannot be assumed. Lack of clarity over preaching's message is behind much of the confusion over how to describe and assess *ēthos* for preaching. In view of this, it is not redundant to inquire more specifically as to preaching's contemporary message.

## Preaching's Message and "Real" *Ēthos*

Just what preaching's message consists of is an arguable point in the homiletical tradition. Yet, much depends for *ēthos* construals on what one conceives the message to be and on how one conceives the message to function in the appropriation of rhetorical guidelines in the preaching situation.[4]

One of the most fascinating areas of study in homiletical history is that of searching out just what homiletical theorists have named preaching's message to be. In the literature by homileticians (such as Clyde Fant, Daniel Baumann, and Robin Meyers), one finds more often than not that the message of preaching is assumed, or vaguely described as "preaching the Bible."[5] The greater weight in these approaches is given to the nature of preaching, the person of the preacher, the putting together of the communicational en-

---

4. Even if one regarded the message of preaching to be the guiding hand in understanding the nature of the preacher's person, this does not mean that reverse-*ēthos* is a natural consequence. For one may construe the message to be about "health and wealth." If so, then one's preacher-*ēthos* would likely exude health and wealth in order to be persuasive.

5. It is striking that there is no specific category on preaching's message in Richard Lischer's fine anthology, *Theories of Preaching: Selected Readings in the Homiletical Tradition* (Durham, NC: The Labyrinth Press, 1987), or in Batsell Barrett Baxter's *Heart of the Yale Lectures* (New York: Macmillan Publishers, 1947). Recent work by Thomas G. Long and Edward Farley on the relationship of preaching the gospel to preaching the Bible holds great promise for this once assumed, but now debated, aspect of preaching. See Long, "The Use of Scripture in Contemporary Preaching," *Interpretation* 44 (1990): 341-52; Farley, "Preaching the Bible and Preaching the Gospel," *Theology Today* 51 (1994): 90-103; and idem, "Toward a New Paradigm for Preaching," in *Preaching as a Theological Task*, ed. Thomas G. Long and Edward Farley (Louisville: Westminster/John Knox Press, 1996), 165-75.

tity of the sermon, and the articulation of the sermon. No clear and organic connection is indicated in these works about how the message itself serves as both resource and critique of every aspect of the preaching situation.[6]

Theologians who write about preaching, on the other hand, deal quite substantively with the nature of preaching's message. I noted this in regard to Karl Barth and Dietrich Ritschl. But rather than seeing that rhetoric is reversed in view of preaching's message (as Paul did), Barth concludes that the *logos* of the cross effectively annuls any concerns for rhetorical advice. His theological convictions concerning preaching's message cause him generally to forswear rhetorical counsel, and with it *ēthos* concerns.[7]

Therefore, to assert that preacher-*ēthos* ought to be conceived as an aspect of preaching's *logos* may reveal why the person of the preacher has been largely a neglected category (in Barthian homiletics) or one that has been usually formatted according to classical rhetorical standards. Lack of clarity over what preaching's message is (for rhetorically shaped homiletics), or how preaching's message guides one in the use of rhetorical categories (as in Barthian homiletics), leads to a lack of clarity over how *ēthos* is to be construed for preaching. As we saw in Paul, clarity about the gospel led to clarity about ecclesiology and about the nature and role of community orators in Christian community. That is why it is of first importance to establish just what preaching's message is and how it relates to the use of rhetoric. Without a clear understanding of preaching's message, we are without clear guidelines for how we ought to conceive the preacher's person. Or, perhaps better, without a clear idea of just what the message of preaching is and how it has priority in the situation of Christian proclamation, the guidelines for conceiving the nature of preacher-*ēthos* naturally slip to those which are either rhetorically shaped, i.e., hearer-driven, or are abandoned altogether in the name of theological purity.

My argument for a reconceived *ēthos* for preachers hinges on the assumption that preaching's message continues in our time, as it was for Paul's, to be the gospel of Jesus Christ crucified and risen — on the condition that the crucifixion places the faith community's life at the juncture of

---

6. Clyde Fant, in *Preaching for Today* (New York: Harper and Row, 1975), attempted to do this by using the doctrine of the Incarnation as a guiding theological concept in defining especially the person of the preacher. As I noted in chapter two, however, his theological insights fail to critique his appropriation of rhetorical guidelines for the preacher's person.

7. See in this regard the more detailed analysis of Barth's *Homiletics*, trans. Geoffrey W. Bromiley and Donald E. Daniels (Louisville: Westminster/John Knox Press, 1991), chapter two.

the ages. Before proceeding with a restatement of the word of the cross and its implications for preacher-*ēthos,* it is important, however, to respond to a significant voice of protest against the contemporary viability of a theology of the cross.

Does the word of the cross compound the damage done to people who are already suffering under an imposed load of servitude? Based upon some feminist and liberation presuppositions, it most definitely does. John Cobb, in a sermon on the Markan call to take up one's cross, names the dilemma well:

> What really happens . . . when the church calls for people to "take up their crosses"? Perhaps for the men who hear the call it is a healthy check to their ambition and self-assertion. . . . But what happens to the majority of the audience — the women? From infancy, they have been brought up to understand that the woman's role is to serve her menfolk — her husband and her children. She brings with her to church both this socialization and her conscious or unconscious desire to discover her own capacities and to express them, to function in the family and in society in a role equal to that of men, to find her own identity in distinction from her service role. Then in church she hears that she should "deny herself and take up her cross." Whereas for the man these words may have only the vaguest relation to the immediate decisions of life, the woman knows very well what they mean. They call her to give up her hopes for her own life and to subordinate herself to the welfare of the other members of her family.

Cobb notes that for a variety of reasons — God is masculine; Christianity points to a male savior; Christianity is part of a patriarchal culture, and sanctions that culture; Christianity resists giving full equality to women — women are leaving the church or only remaining by radically reconceiving it. Yet these reasons are not foremost:

> But for some women who have understood themselves as Christians, the deepest problem with continuing [their] identification [with Christianity] is their correct understanding that the Christian message calls for self-sacrificial love. Their need, they are convinced, is for self-love and for nurturing in one another the willingness to take the risk of asserting the self and its needs. The call to "take up the cross" works directly against their liberation.[8]

8. William A. Beardslee, John B. Cobb, Jr., David J. Lull, Russell Pregeant, Theodore J. Weeden, Jr., and Barry A. Woodbridge, *Biblical Preaching on the Death of Jesus* (Nashville: Abingdon Press, 1989), 133-34.

Delores S. Williams, in the construction of a womanist, black-liberation theology, sharpens the edge of this voice of protest. She argues that the history of classical Christian doctrine is the story of attempts to interpret Jesus' death on the cross as an atonement of various kinds — ransom, satisfaction, substitution, or moral. Williams understands these theories in terms of their use of "the language and sociopolitical thought of [their] time to render Christian ideas and principles understandable." Given the oppression, especially of black women in our time, such atonement theories concerning Jesus' death on the cross are not only inappropriate but heighten their oppression. Jesus' salvific value for black women today consists not in his yielding (or being forced) to death,

> rather their salvation is assured by Jesus' life of resistance and by the survival strategies he used to help people survive the death of identity caused by their exchange of inherited cultural meanings for a new identity shaped by the gospel ethics and world view. . . . This kind of account of Jesus' salvific value — made compatible and understandable by use of African-American women's sociopolitical patterns — frees redemption from the cross and frees the cross from the 'sacred aura' put around it by existing patriarchal responses to the question of what Jesus' death represents.

Williams' reinterpretation of Jesus' salvific significance for black women entails a rejection of Paul's reflections on Jesus' death. Instead, she mines the Synoptic Gospels for Jesus' *ministerial* vision, one which was intended to show humans life, not death. Jesus' resurrection was the righting of the horrible wrong of the cross:

> [The cross was] the evil of humankind trying to kill the *ministerial* vision of life in relation that Jesus brought to humanity. The resurrection does not depend upon the cross for life, for the cross only represents historical evil trying to defeat good.

Because so much evil and sin blatantly exists in the world today, Williams believes it is problematic to believe in an interpretation of Jesus' death that holds that he defeated such atrocities on the cross once and for all:

> Rather, it seems more intelligent and more scriptural to understand that redemption had to do with God, through Jesus, giving humankind new

144

vision to see the resources for positive, abundant relational life. Redemption had to do with God, through the *ministerial* vision, giving humankind the ethical thought and practice upon which to build positive, productive quality of life.[9]

Jesus' purpose, then, was to set forth a vision of healthy community life in order to show what was possible for human beings to become in their relations with one another. His work of redemption must be redefined as a visionary activity which promotes a greater quality of life rather than an atoning activity. The death of Jesus is thus reinterpreted as a demonic interruption to Jesus' vision-casting and is virtually dispensable for Williams's version of womanist theology:

> Humankind is, then, redeemed through Jesus' *ministerial* vision of life and not through his death. There is nothing divine in the blood of the cross. . . . Jesus came for life, to show humans a perfect vision of ministerial relation that humans had very little knowledge of. As Christians, black women cannot forget the cross, but neither can they glorify it. To do so is to glorify suffering and to render their exploitation sacred. To do so is to glorify the sin of defilement.[10]

Williams' project is reminiscent of the older liberal project which reduced the significance of Jesus to that of a great teacher of new ethical vision. Indeed, to make her case she must cash in not only the atonement theories of more traditional theologians, but those of Paul and Hebrews as well. She must also dismiss clear overtones throughout the gospel accounts concerning the salvific necessity of Jesus' death on the cross.[11] Thus, one wonders how Williams' suggested new interpretation of Jesus' role in redemption is "more scriptural," as she claims, when it entails the spurning of most of scripture's own testimony on the relation of redemption to Jesus' cross. Moreover, it is ironic that Williams seeks to ground her reconception of how Jesus redeems in the Synoptic Gospels, for a theology of the cross undergirds them (especially Mark). Indeed, most of the New Testament can be seen as the attempt to prepare early Christians to withstand, partly by means of a

9. Delores S. Williams, *Sisters in the Wilderness: The Challenge of Womanist God-Talk* (Maryknoll, NY: Orbis Books, 1993), 164-65.

10. Williams, *Sisters in the Wilderness,* 167.

11. Cf. Mark 10:45; 14:24; Matt. 20:28; 26:28.

theology of the cross, the persecution that they are currently facing or are about to encounter.[12]

Do Cobb's and Williams' objections render the cross unusable theologically in our time? Does the cross's (mis)use empty it of its redemptive power? Or, is our constant call within theology to reclaim the misused, not allowing the abuser to extend his or her abuse by causing us to abandon crucial and paradigmatic Christian concepts? When we abandon the cross of Christ as God's apocalyptic act of atonement and reorientation of value, are we in fact exchanging the gospel for something much less, namely a better "quality of life"?

This is not to dismiss the very real misuse of the cross by people in power which has intensified the suffering especially of women and non-whites. I would argue, though, that misuse of the cross by ignorant or unscrupulous people does not invalidate the true cross of Christ through which God reveals God's own salvific ends for humanity. Indeed, when the cross is used in a profane manner to crucify the life out of people, Paul would want such misuse itself to be crucified. What needs to die in Christendom, then, is not the theology of the cross, but masochistic manifestations of a misinterpreted and mishandled cross.

Sally Purvis goes beyond the harmful abuses of the cross in her apocalyptic reading of the cross's meaning. She claims that the cross "can only be used to harm and suppress within certain shared assumptions about power. . . . Properly understood, the 'power of the cross' subverts its own nature as harmful and oppressive."[13] Even though in our time the message of the cross may be more than foolishness to some, and a seemingly insurmountable stumbling stone to others, with Paul we still assert that the cross-event-proclaimed is paradoxically the power of God for salvation. And this is not a power that can be simply replaced with any ethical vision. Indeed, as in Paul's thought, the cross is the power for any Christian vision which can be called ethical. Williams rightly notes that true salvation consists in being saved from "the death of identity caused by the exchange of inherited cultural meanings for a new identity shaped by the gospel ethics and world view."[14] The theology

---

12. Cf. Charles Cousar's discussion of "The Suffering of the Church" in *A Theology of the Cross: The Death of Jesus in the Pauline Letters* (Minneapolis: Fortress Press, 1990), 170-75.

13. Sally Purvis, *The Power of the Cross: Foundations for a Christian Feminist Ethic of Community* (Nashville: Abingdon, 1993), 14. Cf. Roberta Bondi's powerful personal journey toward reframing the meaning of the crucifixion of Jesus in her *Memories of God: Theological Reflections on a Life* (Nashville: Abingdon, 1995), 111-44.

14. Williams, *Sisters in the Wilderness*, 164.

of the cross which undergirds Paul claims the same thing. In the cross of Christ the categories that demean human beings and force humans into abasing subjection simply because of their color or gender, categories that have been assigned by the power structure, are identified as not ultimately definitive. They are named as evil and are judged in view of the cross. The new worldview of which Williams speaks is more appropriately understood as that new epistemological orientation at the juncture of the ages which the cross reveals. Moreover, the cross reveals an apocalyptic righting of culturally inherited wrongs (cf. Gal. 3:27-29) which are perpetuated in our contemporary American context against minorities. Thus, the cross, rather than compounding one's suffering, is that power of God which renders evil as evil and which orients one to survive as an agent of redemption in a world "not yet" fully inhabited by God's shalom, yet one in which it is promised and guaranteed in Jesus' death and resurrection.

The cross-event-proclaimed is not only indispensable for Christian theology, it is the fundamental means by which the "epistemic values" of the faith community — including personal identity — are oriented and re-oriented.[15] The cross-event-proclaimed functions, therefore, as a "meta-lens" for the church's discernment. It serves a watchdog function since "the 'theology of the cross' loses its original meaning if it is used non-polemically. It was always a critical attack on the dominating traditional interpretation of the Christian message, and it was not by chance that it characterized Protestant beginnings."[16] That is how we saw it function in Paul's reverse-*ēthos* argument against the Corinthians. The theology of the cross was a polemic against preacher-*ēthos* standards and identities that were derived apart from the gospel of Christ crucified and apart from the cruciform community to which it gives rise.

Reverse-*ēthos* continues to be a theology-of-the-cross-informed critical attack on countervailing construals of preacher-*ēthos* in homiletical theory when such construals derive their credibility standards from social and cultural standards rather than from the gospel's core cri-

---

15. "Epistemic values" is Richard Osmer's helpful phrase, which I borrow here to show how the epistemology of the cross-event-proclaimed takes hold of the community's vision of "reality." Osmer explains how these function: "Epistemic values are those values that influence the way knowledge is constructed and evaluated in the rational communications of a particular discourse community." See Osmer, "Practical Theology as Argument, Rhetoric, and Conversation," *The Princeton Seminary Bulletin* 18 (1997): 51.

16. Ernst Käsemann, "The Saving Significance of Jesus' Death in the Letters of Paul," in *Perspectives on Paul* (Philadelphia: Fortress Press, 1971), 34.

teria, criteria which radiate from the cross-event-proclaimed. "Once more Paul proves to be of lasting value and fateful significance."[17] This core orients the faith community's choices for action and its development as a people of character who conform to this peculiar vision of the good news.

Ernst Käsemann points out that Paul underscores his hard polemical edge by his preferred manner of expressing the gospel center as "the cross," and referring to Jesus as "the crucified." By expressing the matter in terms of the cross, Paul intentionally scandalizes his message and his hearers both socially and religiously. Religiously, the cross stamped Jesus' death as a curse from the deity (Deut. 21:23; Gal. 2:19, 21; 3:13). Even gentiles would have recognized the death on the cross outside "the limits of consecrated ground" as a sign of rejection by the gods. Paul's verbally-expressed cruciform message was functionally an expletive in his social and religious context.

Herein lies part of our problem today. For though the cross began as a statement of bald-faced scandal, it became in time an icon of Christian piety, religious jewelry, and recently even a faddish pop-culture bauble for rock stars, rappers, and athletes with no organic connection to Christian community or message. The cross thus functions today for many as a pious icon or a fashion accessory,

> but [in Paul's day], if it was set up in territory outside divine influence, the honoring of anyone who hung on that cross was from the outset a scandal of the most profound kind. This is what 1 Cor. 1:23 means by 'a stumbling block' to the Jews and folly to the Gentiles.' These words have come to be embedded in so much pious cotton-wool that we are no longer conscious of their aggressiveness. In fact, elevating tendencies of this kind do more to hinder the gospel than the most radical demythologizing. For they free us from the brutal clutches of Christ's message and turn us into observers of a religious pageant.

This is the crucial point of contact between the cross of Jesus and the contemporary disciple of Jesus. For the same hostility and revulsion which Jesus' cross evokes, often becomes reduplicated in the lives of those who align themselves with the crucified one. The very character of the person who associates with Jesus in his contemporaneous gospel ministry becomes altered because of the association. As Käsemann states, "The Chris-

---

17. Käsemann, "The Saving Significance," 34.

tian's existence is most deeply stamped by the fact that through Jesus' cross the world is crucified to him and he is crucified to the world."[18]

A basic definition of "character" is "stamp" or "imprint." This way of understanding character emphasizes the indelible impression that is made by that outside pressure which has had the greatest influence on one's identity. Jesus' cross-event, and its contemporaneous expression in the world of the disciple, becomes that ever present outside influence on the Christian's life which shapes the Christian's character with an indelible imprint:

> Christ is our life and according to II Cor 4:10 we only manifest Jesus' life if we carry his death about with us. For what the apostle says about himself here, applies to every messenger of the gospel; that is to say, it is true of every Christian. He is only a disciple as long as he stands in the shadow of the cross.

When one stands in the cross's shadow, the same stigmata attend to the follower as they did to the master. In fact, the attending stigmata are the disciple's marks of genuineness or credibility:

> It is not only according to Gal 6:17 that Paul views the stigmata of the one who was crucified (stigmata which assumed physical form) as the sign of his belonging to Christ and as the mark of a true apostle and follower of Jesus. He was unable to separate faith from these stigmata.[19]

To preach the cross of Christ and not to live out the cross for others effects a separation of witness: one's lived witness is separated from one's verbal witness. Søren Kierkegaard was critical of theologians, professors, and preachers who might think profoundly about central Christian matters and articulate eloquently the true matters of the cross of Christ but who in their actual existences remained far from the cross's contemporaneous embodiment of that witness:

> What nonsense it is therefore that instead of following Christ or the Apostles and suffering as they suffered, one should become professor — of what? Why, of the fact that Christ was crucified and the Apostles scourged . . . one would be tempted to laugh involuntarily if in that passage where it is said that God appointed some to be prophets, others to

---

18. Käsemann, "The Saving Significance," 37.
19. Käsemann, "The Saving Significance," 37-38.

be apostles, others to be pastors — one would be prompted to laugh involuntarily if it were added, some to be professors of theology.[20]

Similarly, Käsemann chastises a "separated theology," one which admiringly views the character-imprint of the cross from afar yet remains existentially untouched:

Faith which is lived and suffered is obscured in our theological thinking by what have become bloodless convictions, either vague or material. Dogmatic beliefs which do not realize themselves in suffering discipleship are turning the church's piety today into an illusion; and the world is not interested in a Christianity which has become an abstraction. . . . What the world inevitably clashes with is whatever reflects the true image of Jesus in his cross. Here unrest and passionate disputes arise, even among Christians.[21]

One might say that this kind of dispute happens "especially among Christians." For the most violent disputes about the faithful embodiment of the gospel are always intramural.

The recoil from ēthos as a viable category theologically is due precisely to an aversion to the idea that human manipulation of the situation (by means of a credible or attractive ēthos) can definitively constrain God either one way or the other. If, however, we recognize the presuppositions and limits of the rhetorical frame of reference, then those observations and recommendations can benefit the homiletician.

For example, with regard to ēthos, we learn from rhetoric that people do judge a speaker's words in view of their perception of that speaker's lived witness. This reminds us that because people are reading and interpreting our life in view of our words that our life has the possibility to extend our call to witness to the gospel beyond our mere words. This creates a new arena — the embodied word — in which to proclaim the gospel as Christ's servants and God's stewards. Knowing, however, that neither our lives nor our words effect salvation for those who view, hear, and interpret what they see in us, our task is not just to leave our hearers and viewers with their way of judging us. Rather, part of our stewardship consists in

20. Walter Lowrie, *A Short Life of Kierkegaard* (Princeton: Princeton University Press, 1942, 1970), 228, 230. His attack on the minister who is likewise separated from the gospel message is also well documented. See especially his *Attack Upon "Christendom": 1854-1855* (Boston: Beacon Press, 1944, 1956).

21. Käsemann, "The Saving Significance," 38.

reframing the way they are to judge us, namely from the frame of reference that the cross itself provides. In doing this for our hearers we remind them that what they see and hear in us may be deceptive and even concealing of God's revelation.

On the other hand, those who operate from a theological frame of reference must not be reactionary in thinking that everything described and prescribed by the phenomenological frame of rhetoric is necessarily a mandate for formatting the way the church does its thinking and working. The descriptions offered by rhetoric conceivably can help clarify aspects of the Christian community's convictions about self-identity, expression, and action, even when such marks of self-identity and action run counter to the "rhetorically advisable" self-descriptions and actions.

Preachers, though, often feel pressured to bow to sociocultural credibility standards for various reasons, the best of which is usually phrased, "in order to get a greater hearing for the word." Indeed, the "reward system" in North American churches is clear about who "will move up." But preachers who remember the core message entrusted to their stewardship, who are in a faith community which holds its members accountable to the epistemic values of the cross-event-proclaimed, and whose lives are stamped with the character of this message are equipped to resist temptations to use culturally-prized standards of credibility: "the cross leads us back from illusory heroism to the humanity of creatureliness."[22] The submission to the cross as our fundamental epistemic value and norm simultaneously exalts God as Creator and Redeemer and puts the dynamics of the proclamation moment in the proper perspective. What is excluded is any sense that God is dependent upon, or aided by, human "endorsements" which "market" the gospel.

One might say that the cross is crucial for preaching and, in the mystery of God's working, preaching is crucial to the cross. "The cross helps no one who does not hear the word of the cross and ground his faith on that. . . . The theology of the cross and the theology of the Word belong together and are won or thrown away together." What it means to hear, believe, and ground our faith on the cross is the point of claim and demand on the disciple. This is the point at which lives and message can converge and become harmonious witnesses together of the gospel or become estranged from one another, creating a dissonance of sorts to the attentive listener and watcher:

22. Käsemann, "The Saving Significance," 41.

Christianity carries the victory of Jesus into the world, but can only do so if and in so far as it takes up Jesus' cross after him. Its glory is hidden in being crucified with Jesus. Paul never tires of showing the same things in his own case, as the catalogue of his sufferings and his general exposition in II Cor. 10–13 show. At a time when the subject of the apostolic succession plays the greatest part in ecumenical discussions and in questions of church union, Paul's self-characterization is, however, passed over with staggering facility. . . . The only infallible token [Paul] offers the enthusiasts and his rebellious congregations [of the sign of his genuine apostleship] is being crucified with Jesus and the service which is realized in this way.[23]

Paul's call to "imitate me" is not a plea for a pragmatics of persuasion. Nor does it suggest that either Paul's right living or his readers' right imitation of Paul makes efficacious the gospel message. Rather, his imitation call is ethical in the Pauline sense of the call to the cruciform life (1 Thess. 1–2). The life so lived becomes a lived parable of the gospel message, an existential witness of the death and resurrection of Christ continuing to work its judging and redeeming power in the world.

That Paul's self-identity is that he has "no boast" and is "the least of the apostles" and yet is an agent of God's "treasure," is an aspect of what Alan Lewis has called the "ecclesiological conundrum." This pregnant phrase highlights God's paradoxical and ironic choice of embodiments for his grace and message, "God's reliance on his resisters and destroyers":

The outpouring of his Spirit . . . falls upon the city that has been rejected. God's own Son (Acts 2:22f.), and the missionary call goes precisely to the crucifiers: the Gospel for the circumcised deputed to the Galilean denier of Christ, that for the uncircumcision [to] his persecutor from Tarsus (Gal. 2:7). Our cherished cachet 'apostolicity' signifies, therefore, not sanctity and soundness, but incorporation, across the generations, into the calling and commissioning of traitors and enemies. God's own reconciling cause is surrendered to hands that have proved hostile and unstable, his *euangelion* placed on lips fearful to acknowledge truth, or once sworn to destroy it.[24]

23. Käsemann, "The Saving Significance," 50, 58.
24. Alan E. Lewis, "Kenosis and Kerygma: The Realism and the Risk of Preaching," in *Christ in Our Place*, ed. Trevor A. Hart and Daniel P. Thimell (Exeter: The Paternoster Press, 1989), 71-72.

This view of preaching asserts the theological view of *ēthos* as that of a witness of concealment. Trevor Hart, commenting on Karl Barth's theology of the word, maintains that the human components do not reveal God, but conceal him. Thus, speaking with theological precision,

> There is nothing about his human being as such, nothing about these words as such, nothing about this preaching as such, which compels faith or reveals God in any straightforward or obvious manner. It is entirely possible for intelligent humans to see and hear these human realities and not find themselves in the grip of a revelatory encounter.[25]

God remains free from captivity to any link in the chain of embodied witness to him, yet, in God's mercy, he chooses to use the chain of witness as a true avenue of his grace and salvation. In this sense, then, even the cruciform life of the preacher and faith community become concealed signs utilized for revelation by the grace of God, as God alone renders the cross efficacious through proclaimed word and deed.

Rebecca Chopp has urged: "For theology to have authority, in the present situation, it must, rhetorically and pragmatically speaking, not merely talk about suffering, but have the authority of suffering."[26] David Cunningham concurs: "To bear witness to the Gospel at the risk of death is to endow one's arguments with an ultimate appeal to *ēthos:* in this sense, one's whole life becomes an argument for a particular theological position."[27] But this is a different kind of rhetoric, for it takes the *logos* of the cross as the epistemic guide for all matters in the rhetorical situation of Christian proclamation. An *ēthos* which is characterized by this kind of witnessed martyrdom (cf. *martyr,* the original word for "witness" in the New Testament) shows that it refuses the credibility standards which society idolizes in order to shape its witness in ways commensurate with the message.

Lewis uses Arthur McGill's phrase "bronze people" to describe contemporary North American culture's materialistic ethos, one which is per-

---

25. Trevor A. Hart, "The Word, the Words, and the Witness: Proclamation as Divine and Human Reality in the Theology of Karl Barth," *Tyndale Bulletin* 46 (1995): 87.

26. Rebecca Chopp, "Theological Persuasion: Rhetoric, Warrants, and Suffering," in *Worldviews and Warrants: Plurality and Authority in Theology,* ed. William Schweiker (Lanham, MD: University Press of America, 1987), 29.

27. David S. Cunningham, *Faithful Persuasion: In Aid of a Rhetoric of Christian Theology* (Notre Dame: University of Notre Dame Press, 1990), 143.

haps the chief threat to a cruciform *ēthos*. The "bronze people" of American idealism and wishful aspiration ("if I could only hit the lotto or have Ed McMahon visit me after the Super Bowl on behalf of Publishers Clearinghouse") are those

> who cherish illusory dreams of immortality and physical perfection in cowardly evasion of death's reality and the depredations of decay and age. Collectively, yet so individualistically, we worship idols of beauty, health, and property, sanctified by a culture of having and accumulating. Forlornly optimistic, society expects the direct or vicarious experience of fullness and success to anesthetize the gnawing pain of emptiness and need, to keep at a distance the menacing monsters of sickness and dependence, and every hint of negativity.

This cultural context of aspiration and expectation is a powerfully deceptive new wilderness sphere of temptation for the church, seducing it to relinquish its call to "carry the cross" in "cruciform oneness with the least and broken of the world." The church, in an attempt to be persuasive or relevant, often conforms to the world (Rom. 12:2),

> blessing and mirroring its mighty and triumphal. Thus has kenotic ministry been pathologically inverted; for the church has not emptied herself of self-promoting pride, to find herself in lowly fellowship with those beyond her boundaries. Rather, she has emptied herself of that very servitude that makes her different through self-destroying imitation of the world's success and plentitude.[28]

Lewis paints a picture of a contemporary covenant people in pursuit of en vogue false gods of fertility. Such exchange is idolatry and is in fact a contemporary exchange of gospels (Gal. 1:6-10), since the gospel of Christ crucified does not champion bronze triumphalism in any age, even if it is buttressed by a prooftexting appeal to Paul's statement, "I have become all things to all people, that I might by all means save some" (1 Cor. 9:22). Paul continues that statement by stating, "I do it all for the sake of the gospel, so that I may share in its blessings" (1 Cor. 9:23). That gospel in the Corinthian correspondence is decidedly the gospel of Jesus Christ crucified. And the blessings in which Paul hopes to share are

---

28. Alan E. Lewis, "Unmasking Idolatries: Vocation in the *Ecclesia Crucis*," in *Incarnational Ministries: The Presence of Christ in Church, Society, and Family*, ed. Christian D. Kettler and Todd H. Speidell (Colorado Springs: Helmers and Howard, 1990), 112.

surely the community life of those who obey the gospel, both now and eschatologically.[29]

The form of ministry and the kind of ministers that we are and are becoming show whether or not it is the theology of the cross which informs and forms us. "Ministry is theology's polygraph, its infallible lie-detecting test, revealing the truth of what the church believes and the identity of whom she worships — the God of the cross or the false gods of her cultural ideology."

Over against the rhetorical theorist's advice that the preacher project an *ēthos* which would be deemed credible by his or her audience, the preacher of the cross-event-proclaimed must prophetically name the "bronze ideals" of the "bronze people" as idolatrous denials of the gospel. "Society idolizes, [and] often chooses and elects to honor, privilege and power, those whose flawless public image — cosmetic, athletic, moral, or financial — is an earnest of the well-being that awaits us all."[30] Recall Cicero's statement to the same effect:

> Virtue is above all things desirable, since honest, just, and conscientious industry is ennobled with honors, rewards, and distinctions; but the vices and frauds of mankind are punished by fines, ignominy, imprisonment, stripes, banishment, and death.[31]

Paul's reverse-*ēthos* argument was forged from a theology of the cross over against a triumphalistic theology of glory that is analogous to the present-day, culturally deceived churches with numbers-driven, success-enamored criteria for judging the church's presence, and thus the preacher's person, in the world:

> The God of the cross . . . is revealed as yielding to negativity and triumphing through failure, not its avoidance, and as inaugurating a tearless, painless, deathless future only through sacrifice, suffering, and stigmatization. Therefore vocation in the *ecclesia crucis* must be practiced by means that do not sanctify but abrogate the perfectionist cult. These means, surely, must include criteria for recognizing those called to public ministry who reflect God's strange choice, not of the "best and the

---

29. Cf. Phillips Brooks's statement: "There are some things which St. Paul will not become to any man." *Lectures on Preaching. 1877.* (New York: E. P. Dutton & Company, 1898), 30.

30. Lewis, "Unmasking Idolatries," 113, 118.

31. Cicero, *De Oratore*, trans. H. Rackham and E. W. Sutton (Cambridge, MA: Harvard University Press, 1992), 1.43.

brightest" or the fullest, but — in the *locus classicus* of the relation of vocation to the cross — "not many wise . . . powerful . . . of noble birth" (1 Cor. 1:26ff.).[32]

What kind of person is it that is called by God to a ministry of the cross-event-proclaimed? It is one whom God chooses and entrusts with God's own mysteries. It is one who serves Christ and bears witness to Christ's efficacious death and resurrection. It is one who stakes his or her identity in serving Christ through proclaiming the cross and who, in so doing, seeks to be a faithful steward to God's mysteries, primarily the mystery revealed in the gospel.

This does not mean that intellectual, physical, or spiritual gifts become unimportant. It does mean, though, that these personal characteristics are neither the reason for ministry nor the source of the preacher's identity and character. Neither does it mean that the person ought to strip these personal characteristics away. Rather they are to be viewed within the proper context — the cross-event-proclaimed — to know their meaning and significance:

> Paul, that Pharisee non pareil, makes no apology for his knowledge and his skills (2 Cor. 11:6; Phil. 3:4ff.). It is precisely not their absence that makes him a fool in and for the crucified Christ. Pedigree, training, status, even moral blamelessness and spiritual gifts — all these Paul has, and they have utility and value, not to be despised. He himself is not what he *has,* but what he *hears;* and his true identity heard and received in faith, is strictly that of Christ (Gal. 2:20). . . . [He] lives as if he has nothing, having lost it all for Christ (Phil. 3:7f.). And finding his new real self in Christ he must live as if he were indeed Christ: that is, share Christ's sufferings, bear Christ's stigmata, imitate Christ's death — and only thus be united with Christ's triumph (Phil. 3:10f., Gal. 6:17, Rom. 8:17).[33]

Lewis here brings home the implications of the gospel message for the person who is called to bear that message in both word and deed. In so doing he has highlighted the importance of "real" *ēthos.* Indeed, a primary implication of orienting oneself first to the message of the cross is in the understanding of the "real" preacher before God, in community, and as a witness. By God's grace and mercy, the gospel really does affect those persons who hear it, including the preacher.

32. Lewis, "Unmasking Idolatries," 118.
33. Lewis, "Unmasking Idolatries," 123.

In this regard, the preacher's "real" *ēthos* could be seen as an *ēthos* "given by God in Christ in the preaching and hearing (which of course also means obedience) of the Word of the cross."[34] This *ēthos* given by God as a witness to God's gospel is, thus, itself a gift and something that God effects. This is to speak with theological precision, of course, and does not preclude the fact that there is still the reality of "perceived" *ēthos* which the rhetorical frame of reference reminds us cannot be piously dismissed. The discussion of the "perceived" *ēthos* of the preacher moves us to the practical implications of this study.

## Preaching's Message and "Perceived" *Ēthos*

As we have seen, there is more than one way to look at the situation of Christian proclamation and at the preacher's person in this situation. Different frames of rationality, namely, the theological and the rhetorical, can be used, each providing quite different assessments of the exigencies of preaching.

The survey of the classical rhetorical tradition in chapter one concluded with an adaptation of Wayne Booth and Wolfgang Iser's Reader-Response model to the situation of the speech event:

| Real | Prcvd | Antcdnt | *Ēthos* | Antcdnt | Prcvd | Real |
|------|-------|---------|---------|---------|-------|------|
| Spkr | Spkr | *Ēthos* | of the | *Ēthos* | Hearer | Hearer |
| | | of the | Speech | of the | | |
| | | Spkr | | Hearers | | |
| → | → | → | X | ← | ← | ← |

**Fig. 4. Nuanced Reader-Response Chart
Applied to Speech Situation**

This chart reminds us that the "real speaker," like the "real author" of a text, is never truly accessible to the hearers in a rhetorical situation. What hearers know of the "real speaker" is an interpretive amalgam of information mediated verbally and nonverbally by the speaker in combination with the expectations and prejudices of the hearers. The speaker's person is

34. Charles L. Bartow, private correspondence with author, 23 September 1997.

157

a construct of bits and pieces of information hearers receive about the speaker both in the speech itself and in antecedent ways, such as reputation or other such means of prior relations. Thus, hearers really know only a constructed speaker, one that is a perception based upon the array of information listeners receive about the speaker, put together within the interpretative framework that hearers use to assess such information.

As a social construction, then, the person of the preacher is open to a wide variety of interpretations:

> The evaluation of character is a highly perspectival notion. The character of the speaker or writer will be evaluated differently by different audiences, and these evaluations will be influenced by a wide range of factors. Character, then, is always character as perceived by someone. The rhetor's character is not in itself persuasive. . . .[35]

Rather, the rhetor's character proves itself persuasive when it lines up with the listening community's own standards for credibility. In view of this, the preacher has a constant battle to fight both within the preacher's own self and with the hearers. The battle is the age-old one of which social construction has the final say in adjudicating character. In view of this, a large part of the preacher's ongoing task is the orientation and reorientation of him- or herself and hearers to the fundamental epistemic values they share together as shaped by the message of the cross. This ongoing orientation and reorientation process of self and congregation manifests itself most concretely in the ways in which the preacher manifests *ēthos* in actual sermons.

Though the use of the preacher's own self in preaching is rarely referred to in the homiletical literature under *ēthos* appeals, rhetorically speaking that is precisely what they are. Contemporary homileticians are mixed in their sentiments about how one should use personal information in sermons, or whether one ought to do so at all.

David Buttrick has argued forcefully against the use of "personal illustrations" in preaching. He contends that the preacher's mention of self in the sermon "will always split consciousness," by which he means that the focus of the hearers will be divided between what the preacher is trying to say and the preacher's own person. Buttrick backs up his position by unsubstantiated "research" and overstatement:

---

35. Cunningham, *Faithful Persuasion*, 112.

Research indicates that (1) congregations — even when prompted by "Has something like this happened to you?" — will *never* bring to mind similar experiences from their own recall, and (2) congregations will *always* remember the illustration as a disclosure of the *preacher's* character. The illustrations will fix like glue on the minister who is speaking. Thus, a congregation will hear the illustration and think "Our minister is sensitive," "Our minister is a voyeur of children," or something of the sort. The illustration will not illumine the idea intended.[36]

Though claiming the backing of "research" (as he does throughout his book), Buttrick cites none. Moreover, such overstatements as "never" and "always" weaken the points he tries to make. Buttrick's massive tome concludes with "a further caveat":

> We must not dally with a notion that the preacher's character is the "Word of God." Popular conviction seems to suggest that the minister's Christian personality somehow speaks through sermons so that, no matter how inept the sermon, people are drawn to God. All things considered, we should endorse loving, pious, generous ministers, but we should *not* argue that character speaks louder than words. Even when the notion is buttressed by an Aristotelian appeal to "ethos," it is theologically impossible. . . . Our character does not preach. What is more, our character does not determine the gospel or the efficacy of the gospel.

Buttrick is a good example of yet another homiletician who fails to differentiate between the rhetorical and theological frames of reference. Impaled on the horns of the homiletical dilemma, Buttrick here rejects the rhetorical frame of reference out of hand and argues for the theological. By so doing, he has no grounds for proving why we should say, "All things considered, we should endorse loving, pious, generous ministers." Moreover, he fails to see that his own denouncements of the personal character of the preacher, his standing with the Second Helvetic Confession about hearing the Word of God through the lips of sinful preachers, and his assertion that "preachers serve Christ in brokenness, trusting in grace alone," are all powerful *ēthos* appeals in their own right.[37] Just as Jerome related his renouncement of rhetoric in a rhetorically powerful dream-vision which established his own *ēthos*, so Buttrick unwittingly

36. David Buttrick, *Homiletic: Moves and Structures* (Philadelphia: Fortress Press, 1987), 142. Emphasis is Buttrick's.

37. Buttrick, *Homiletic*, 458-59.

gives his own grounds and criteria for preacher-*ēthos*, even as he attacks the very notion.

Moreover, Buttrick fails to recognize that preachers can never really avoid notice in the pulpit, even if they refrain from any and all references to self. For preachers are making unceasing statements about themselves by their choice of scripture texts, their choice of stories and characters as illustrative materials in their sermons, and even by their fastidious avoidance of any reference to self, as well as by their personal appearance and demeanor in preaching. All of these project *ēthos*, and by these the hearers most certainly construct *ēthos* portrayals. It may be that some will conclude by preachers' avoidance of personal stories that they have not themselves experienced much of the gospel. Conversely, it could be concluded by some that those preachers who refrain from telling personal experiences in sermons are quite humble people whose rich personal experience of the gospel is actually revealed covertly in the stories they tell about other people. Buttrick seems unaware, too, of the powerful act of consciousness that takes place when something is not mentioned in straightforward fashion but only indirectly or even surreptitiously. Documented research shows that real, though unnamed, information becomes more conspicuous, and perhaps even more powerful, in its influence when those involved attempt to cover it up rather than naming it overtly.[38]

Other homiletical theorists have argued for the judicious use of personal illustrations in sermons. Richard Thulin is a good example. Thulin's scope is all types of "pulpit autobiography."

Though in our time the use of personal story is gaining in frequency and force, as both Buttrick and Thulin note, Thulin recognizes that "unfortunately, little systematic inquiry has been carried out by either side [of the debate]. Assumptions have gone unquestioned. Claims and counterclaims have gone unchallenged." Thulin attempts to fill this lacuna in

---

38. Buttrick's overstatements ("never," "always") belie the nuanced nature of identity disclosure between human beings. An extensive literature exists in the psychotherapeutic realm concerning the revelation of the self in relationships. Buttrick's call for no revelation of self also opens him up to the problems associated with denial. See N. Ladany, C. E. Hill, M. M. Corbett, and E. A. Nutt, "Nature, Extent, and Importance of What Psychotherapy Trainees Do Not Disclose to Their Supervisors," *Journal of Counseling Psychology* 43: 10-24; Peter Titelman, ed., *The Therapist's Own Family: Toward the Differentiation of the Self* (Northvale, NJ: Jason Aronson, Inc., 1992, 1987), chs. 1-2; and Gerard Egan, *The Skilled Helper*, 6th ed. (Pacific Grove, CA: Brooks/Cole Publishing Company, 1998), 178-80.

homiletical theory while asserting "a clear affirmation of personal story as a vehicle for Christian proclamation."[39]

One must use caution, however, since not just any use of the first person singular in preaching is "effective," according to Thulin. There is always the possibility of inappropriate use of personal story, a use which "obstructs Christian proclamation." Three abuses stand out to Thulin: narcissism (a proclamation of self rather than Christ), privatism (an idiosyncratic use of self with which no identification is made for the hearer), and isolationism (a disconnection between the sermon and the personal story). In spite of these potential problems, Thulin believes that pulpit autobiography can be used well. When it is, it "can bolster the sagging authority of the pulpit." It does this by placing the preacher in relation to the church's past traditions and present life, thus linking the two not abstractly but concretely and existentially.

This link of past and present through the person of the preacher creates an authority for the preacher, a true authority which is not theoretically or institutionally imposed, but one forged personally and relationally:

> People will not listen seriously to what a minister says simply because he or she is ordained and speaks with the authority of the church. Nor will people be receptive to what a minister says simply because she or he quotes from the Bible or from the writings of some significant theologian. What catches the ear and urges response is the voice of a living witness . . . [a voice] that speaks the truth about one's life . . . a voice of conviction supported by a life story.

Hearers are willing to grant such authority to preachers that they hear "talk from their own lives in terms of the presence and activity of God attested to by Scripture and theology alike." Personal story is a unique vehicle in the sermon for "showing what is believed." Thus, "personal story can constitute an authoritative word and thus assist pulpit proclamation."[40]

Thulin identifies four types of personal story in preaching: illustration, reminiscence, confession, and self-portrayal. After brief descriptions of the first three, Thulin concentrates on self-portrayal. This is because, according to Thulin, "the narrative of self-portrayal can best demonstrate

39. Richard L. Thulin, *The "I" of the Sermon: Autobiography in the Sermon* (Minneapolis: Fortress Press, 1989), 9.
40. Thulin, *The "I" of the Sermon*, 12-15.

that the preacher knows what he or she is talking about." Indeed, Thulin claims that preachers themselves cannot even know what they are talking about in their sermons unless that talk "is consciously anchored in their own stories."[41]

Thulin is not an advocate for personal disclosure per se, as much as for the personal disclosure of how the preacher has experienced the gospel. His burden is not so much autobiography for aesthetic ends as it is gospel-shaped autobiography as a means of bearing witness to God's activity in the preacher's life:

> The story of the preacher must always be attached to the good news, the transmitted tradition, the Word. Only in this way can the preacher's story become a vehicle for the Word of God. Only in this way can the events of the preacher's life serve "the prismatic function of catching the gospel's rays."

Reflecting Gustaf Wingren, Thulin asserts two safeguards or checks in using self-portrayal in preaching: *scopus* (the primary aim, "that Christ may come through the word") and *simplicitas* ("that the actual text of the passage must determine what is said" and left unsaid). It is, thus, the biblical text which governs the preacher's use of self. But the text, the *simplicitas,* does not do this alone. For the *scopus* is to be understood as the aim of all preaching. The *scopus* is a hermeneutical and heuristic guide in the use of texts for preaching:

> There is a stream, Wingren insists, that flows deep down in every individual passage. It is the stream of Christ's death and resurrection. This is the center of the news about Christ. This news about Christ is the center of the New Testament, and it is toward this news that all in the Bible tends.

Ultimately, Thulin insists, the bringing together of the inherited Christian tradition and personal story can help lead God's people to a "faith-appropriation of their experiences."[42]

Thulin names three specific occasions for self-portrayal: (1) the need to state credentials; (2) the need to witness; and (3) the need to be prophetic.

---

41. Thulin, *The "I" of the Sermon,* 24-25.
42. Thulin, *The "I" of the Sermon,* 41-42, 50.

Occasions when preachers need to state their credentials are largely those where the preacher is not well-known to the hearers. In so doing the preacher shows his or her credibility, or even his or her lack of credentials for the event at hand. Primarily, Thulin believes that the speaker's most important credential to be shared is that the speaker shares a common life with the hearers. "A preacher's personal story must describe fundamental (primordial) experience if it is to demonstrate that a common life is shared by preacher and congregation."

"The need to witness" is the use of self-portrayal which "declares that what is confessed is personally owned by the preacher." Though Thulin claims that this type of personal story "invites the listener to identify rather than argue," it might be more accurate to say that it uses identification as a means of argument.[43]

"The need to be prophetic" is the use of autobiography when dealing with highly charged social, political, and ethical issues. The personal story in service of the prophetic word clarifies for the hearers the process by which the speaker arrived at his or her conclusions. It does not force a decision on their behalf, but allows them to make up their minds for themselves. Yet it points in a definite direction, since Thulin argues that the prophetic use of personal story reveals the darkness in the preacher's own life regarding the issue in question.

Thulin's work is the most helpful treatment of preacher self-disclosure in contemporary homiletical literature. His naming of narcissism as one of the deadly sins of pulpit autobiography shows how the preacher can choose to serve self rather than Christ in the pulpit. His description of self-portrayal as a concrete link of witness between the church's past traditions and its present life is what I will develop below under the rubric of "temporal instantiation." His call for the gospel to shape and temper the use of self in sermons indicates a hermeneutical discretion akin to reverse-*ēthos*. And, his description of "the need to state credentials" as an appropriate time for self-portrayal mirrors my category of polemical *ēthos* appeals, though his description of credential stating appears to be *kata sarka*.

Thulin's treatment could be strengthened by attention to several matters:

(1) The lack of differentiation between the theological and rhetorical frames of reference that I noted in homiletics also plagues Thulin. This

---

43. Thulin, *The "I" of the Sermon*, 66-69.

causes him to use a term like "effective" in confusing ways throughout the book. Speaking theologically, preaching made more "effective" by the use of personal story seems to imply "persuasion," but it does so by using a word within the semantic range of "efficacy." This creates the same kind of dissonance between paradigms that I noted in section one of this chapter.

(2) Similarly, Thulin fails to differentiate between "perceived" *ēthos* and "real" *ēthos*. Though his book is largely about "perceived" *ēthos,* since he is dealing with the effects of pulpit autobiography on hearers, to name that task appropriately would help clarify what he is and is not claiming.

(3) Another significant problem with Thulin's work is that he never clearly identifies what the message of preaching is, and thus does not clearly develop the implications of preaching's message for the use of self-portrayal in preaching. Throughout the book preaching's message is identified in various ways, all of which I assume are to be taken as synonymous with one another. Thus, the message is "Jesus," "news about Christ," "Bible," "the good news," "the transmitted tradition," "*scopus,*" "the Word," or "Christ." These terms are not unpacked, however, with the result being that it is unclear how they can function as criteria in assessing the use of pulpit autobiography since we are left to our own imaginations as to what they might mean. Moreover, these terms, which for Thulin are functionally equivalent, are not normally regarded as such in church theology or practice.

(4) Thulin's appropriation of Wingren's *scopus/simplicitas* model is his attempt to let the message act as heuristic and critical guide in use of self-portrayal. Unfortunately, Thulin simply asserts these as guides without showing how they function as such. They are suggestive, yet one is left ultimately confused by the relationship of the texts of scripture to the gospel. Thulin seems to assume that these are different, with the gospel guiding our understanding of texts, but then he claims that the preacher's use of self is to be held in subjection to biblical texts. Does he mean the gospel as it reveals itself through discrete texts of scripture, or does he mean that the texts themselves are the gospel?

(5) Thulin's description of the "need to state credentials" as an appropriate time for self-portrayal is developed in a decidedly *kata sarka* fashion, without a cross-informed orientation. "Credentials" here seems to refer to whatever might buttress one's authority with regard to one's target audience, without substantive regard for how this might function with regard to witnessing to the gospel.

(6) Finally, the primary credential Thulin believes preachers need to

establish with their hearers is that they share a "common human life" together. This notion smacks of David Tracy's notion of "common human experience," a notion that has been heavily criticized recently by scholars who emphasize that good theological connection with one's target audience is hindered more than helped when one tries to smooth over the very real differences that exist between people.[44]

In spite of these problems, Thulin points us in some helpful directions. In what follows I will build off his strengths while filling them out with what we are taught by Paul.

As I stated earlier, reverse-*ēthos* is a theologically-informed rhetorical category which describes the nature and function of the preacher's person in the rhetorical situation of Christian proclamation. The many different uses of preacher-*ēthos* in sermons can conveniently be grouped under two principal headings: (1) polemical *ēthos* and (2) apologetic *ēthos*. Both polemical and apologetic *ēthos* appeals are to be understood within the purview of the gospel itself. In this sense, the criteria judging the use of *ēthos* appeals in preaching are no different than they are for any other pragmatic aspect of ministry. Alan E. Lewis, commenting on Ray Anderson's approach to discerning how to think about the implementation of practices within the institutional church, is instructive:

> Anderson prophetically insists, "every pragmatic principle of ministry must be subjected to the critical dogmatic test: Has it gone through the death and resurrection process?" Self-subvertingly, the theology of ministry must yield to judgment and demise, to the discipline of "unteaching," so that it might prove teachable against by God's iconoclastic, renovating Word of revelation. Only as the church acknowledges the impossibility of her own life, theology, and ministry, can she recover the actuality, and so understand the possibility, of being the church of Jesus Christ. Such is the evangelically compelling, if humanly and professionally repellent, imperative that Ray Anderson has issued: the *death* — and only on the precondition of that death — and the resurrection of the theology of ministry.[45]

---

44. Cf. David Tracy, *Blessed Rage for Order* (San Francisco: Harper and Row, Publishers, 1988), and Rebecca Chopp, "Practical Theology and Liberation," in *Formation and Reflection: The Promise of Practical Theology*, ed. Louis S. Mudge and James N. Poling (Philadelphia: Fortress Press, 1987), 120-38.

45. Lewis, "Unmasking Idolatries," 110-11. Emphasis is Lewis'.

With the critical dogmatic test of the gospel message adjudicating the use of *ēthos* appeals, let us examine more closely each type.

## Polemical *Ēthos*

A polemic is a rebuttal. The polemical use of *ēthos* appeals occurs when preachers need to respond to attack or criticism. It is a self-defense against antagonists. Viewed theologically, in light of the cross-event-proclaimed, this is a defensive use of *ēthos* for the purpose of removing the wrong stumbling block for hearers of the gospel. If the hearers are scandalized in some way by the preacher, then an appropriate defense can reposition the hearers so that they can hear again the true scandal with the superimposed scandal of the preacher removed altogether, or at least put aside for the moment. Such a move need not be lengthy. It may, in fact, be quite simple, with the purpose of deflecting the attention that the criticism has caused away from oneself and back to the message.

In a sermon entitled, "Talk Is Not Always Cheap," Edmund Steimle relates a time when he was interrupted while preaching in a university chapel. He was in the first half of his sermon describing the experience of the absence of God. He was showing how God's absence is witnessed to in both the Bible and in our own experience, when a student stood up in the middle of the congregation and with a loud and clear voice declared, "This is a lot of atheistic nonsense. God is very much alive and present. This man is a false prophet." Steimle looked out at the man and said in his steady, firm voice, "That very well may be. But hear me out first and we'll see."[46] Steimle comments in the new sermon that he never had such an attentive audience from there to the end of the sermon. That itself shows how situations of attack and polemic always raise the stakes for all involved. People sit on the edge of their seats to see the outcome. In this case, Steimle adeptly refrained from overreacting to the attack on himself and redirected the hearers to the message for the day. In so doing he carried out a covert polemical *ēthos* appeal. Of interest, too, is his use of that earlier incident in the university chapel in a later sermon in order to carry out an apologetic *ēthos* appeal. I will treat that aspect of Steimle's use of this story in the next section.

---

46. Edmund Steimle, *Talk Is Not Always Cheap*, Princeton Theological Seminary, Reigner Recording Library, cassette recording, June 24, 1973.

Without the theological discretion that the cross-event-proclaimed both affords and demands, polemical *ēthos* can be carried out in *kata sarka* ways. These would be narcissistic, self-serving stories for the preacher's sake, rather than for Christ's.[47] Carried out *kata stauron,* polemical *ēthos* appeals are self-subverting in pointing people ultimately to Christ and God's work in the gospel.

Paul's *ēthos* defense in 1 Cor. 1–4 is a good example of the polemical use of *ēthos* for the purpose of repositioning the church for a consideration of the gospel itself. But Paul elsewhere in his letters shows awareness of the *kata sarka* manner of polemical *ēthos* appeals. In his defense against the "super-apostles" at Corinth he challenges them to a boasting contest. Though Paul knows that he should only boast "in the Lord," his critics have forced him to what he calls "a little foolishness." His "little foolishness" is polemical *ēthos* carried out *kata sarka.* His goal is to shame his opponents by "one-upping" them at their own game, then returning to his reverse-*ēthos* defense. In so doing he shows how such games are ultimately demeaning in the light of the gospel:

> But whatever anyone dares to boast of — I am speaking as a fool — I also dare to boast of that. Are they Hebrews? So am I. Are they Israelites? So am I. Are they descendants of Abraham? So am I. Are they ministers of Christ? I am talking like a madman — I am a better one: with far greater labors, far more imprisonments, with countless floggings, and often near death. (2 Cor. 11:21b-23)

Paul goes on to list all kinds of atrocities he suffered which he believes substantiate his claim to be a better minister of Christ. He says, "It is necessary to boast; nothing is to be gained by it, but I will go on to visions and revelations" (2 Cor. 12:1). He feels disgust for playing their game, but was driven to it: "I have been a fool! You forced me to it. Indeed you should have been the ones commending me, for I am not at all inferior to these super-apostles, even though I am nothing" (2 Cor. 12:11). Paul's irony is thick here as he boasts of his weaknesses in order to establish his credibility.

We see something similar in Philippians. There, he warns the church of the "dogs," the Judaizing element which was attempting to influence the

---

47. There is an analogy in pastoral counseling when the therapist uses the self narcissistically with clients in ways that hinder the healing process. See James F. Masterson's section entitled, "Portrait of the Narcissist," in *The Search for the Real Self: Unmasking the Personality Disorder of Our Age* (New York: Free Press, 1990), 90-106.

Philippian Christians to put their confidence "in the flesh." Paul says that those who worship in the Spirit of God boast in Christ Jesus and have no confidence *kata sarka*. But then Paul plays their game anyway and asserts,

> even though I, too, have reason for confidence in the flesh. If anyone has reason to be confident in the flesh, I have more: circumcised on the eighth day, a member of the people of Israel, of the tribe of Benjamin, a Hebrew born of Hebrews; as to the law, a Pharisee; as to zeal, a persecutor of the church; as to righteousness under the law, blameless. (Phil. 3:4-6)

If they wanted to argue on that level, Paul could. Paul knew, though, that such a use of polemical *ēthos* was only *kata sarka*, i.e., it was leverage for political positioning in structures this passing world values.

When viewed *kata stauron*, Paul's *kata sarka* credentials were less than worthless:

> Yet whatever gains I had, these I have come to regard as loss because of Christ. More than that, I regard everything as loss because of the surpassing value of knowing Christ Jesus my Lord. For his sake I have suffered the loss of all things, and I regard them as rubbish, in order that I may gain Christ and be found in him, not having a righteousness of my own that comes from the law, but one that comes through faith in Christ, the righteousness from God based on faith. I want to know Christ and the power of his resurrection and the sharing of his sufferings by becoming like him in his death, if somehow I might attain the resurrection of the dead. (Phil. 3:7-11)

We see, then, that Paul uses *kata sarka ēthos* appeals against antagonists, but subverts them in order that they might function for his proclamation of Christ. After subverting them, he returns to reverse-*ēthos* appeals, appeals which ironically credential him by the nature of their cruciform character as it connects to his cruciform message.

Two fundamental uses of polemical *ēthos* appeals exist: ones which operate *kata sarka* and ones which operate *kata stauron*. Polemical appeals used *kata sarka* are those which use cultural criteria of credibility to establish the preacher as trustworthy and believable because of his or her socially and culturally prized attributes. These function to fund the preacher's own personal goals of power, fame, wealth, acceptance by the many, or some other aspect of self-glorification. *Kata sarka ēthos* appeals are really self-promotion in the guise of service to Christ. Polemical appeals used *kata stauron* are those which the preacher deems necessary in particular instances where the hearers may be scandalized by the preacher in such a way that he or she has become a stumbling stone between the hearers and the gospel. The preacher uses such appeals, therefore only as they are necessary to remove the wrong stumbling block so that the preacher may faithfully signpost the gospel. Polemical *ēthos* appeals may do this by diverting attention away from the current criticism which is levied at the preacher and back to Christ and the gospel to which the preacher is bearing witness this week. If one finds it necessary to engage in extended polemical *ēthos* appeals, then those appeals should be refereed by the gospel itself. When *kata sarka* polemical *ēthos* appeals are used, the preacher must proceed to deconstruct them in view of the gospel, perhaps even returning to the kind of reverse-*ēthos* appeals which overturn cultural expectations for credibility but which, nevertheless, bear testimony to the gospel.

The description of polemical *ēthos* as a means to reposition the hearers for a hearing of the word, reminds us that we are speaking of polemical *ēthos* as a rhetorical phenomenon. Speaking with greater theological precision, whether or not the preacher ever repositions the hearers by skillful use of polemical *ēthos,* this does not imply that God is necessarily hampered in God's desire to act. If God chooses to still act for the hearers' salvation, God will do so. This reminds us, too, that the preacher's use of polemical *ēthos* has the purpose of orienting the hearers to the message first as the criteria for the hearers' assessment of the preacher. If they are still scandalized by the preacher after a right epistemic orientation, then they may have good reason, and it may be the preacher who is in the wrong.

It is possible, of course, that a new reversal may occur. An unscrupulous preacher may reverse reverse-*ēthos,* using it as a means of gaining pity or status in a church which prizes suffering. The counsel offered here suggests that self-deprecating stories that point away from the preacher, or stories in which the preacher's failure signposts God's redemptive activity in some way, are to be preferred in preaching and can function to serve the gospel. Because of that a whole new problem can arise: the professional sufferer. A classic sermon by William Muehl, "The Cult of the Publican," seems the right antidote to this potential problem. Muehl attacks the publican from Luke's gospel who refuses to move from judgment to grace, but lingers in between judgment and mercy a little too long. Somehow, the publican has realized his canonicity. He has heard the good press he received from Jesus for being so penitent, especially over against the proud Pharisee. The sin is that of the publican who has become self-aware:

> I mean to suggest that the publican's terrified humility has salutary power *only so long as he does not know that he is being observed and approved.* Only so long as his abject confession is a spontaneous reaction to the presence of God. The moment this fellow reads the book of Luke or even a good review of it and begins to realize that there is saving power in his sense of depravity, the well of his naive piety will have poisoned. Then his allegations of unworthiness become not an honest response to the holiness of the Almighty but mere liturgical exercises, more obnoxious than the self-congratulations of the Pharisee. For if there is anything worse than pride in one's righteousness, it must be pride in one's corruption.[48]

It is possible to imagine reverse-*ēthos* becoming a cold and calculating maneuver by contemporary homiletical sophists intent on self-gain. It is important to remember, nevertheless, that abuses of every system, no matter how theologically pure they might be, will happen. This does not render the right insight wrong, only the misuse of it. Such canonization and calculating use of reverse-*ēthos* by preachers for the purpose of advancing themselves is fundamentally a breach of their call to be servants of Christ and stewards of God's mysteries. They will have to answer to God for that; and even so, following Paul, we realize that God is not hampered by their failure:

> Others proclaim Christ out of selfish ambition, not sincerely. . . . What does it matter? Just this, that Christ is proclaimed in every way, whether out of false motives or true; and in that I rejoice. (Phil. 1:16-18)

## Apologetic *Ēthos*

If polemical *ēthos* is a defensive response to an attack, apologetic *ēthos* is an instance of self-portrayal on "offense." This is the use of self-portrayal as a means to bear witness to the gospel when no critical heat is on the preacher.

---

48. William Muehl, "The Cult of the Publican," in *A Chorus of Witnesses: Model Sermons for Today's Preacher,* ed. Thomas G. Long and Cornelius Plantinga, Jr. (Grand Rapids: William B. Eerdmans Publishing Company, 1994), 148.

In this use of *ēthos* appeal the preacher extends his or her function as a witness to the gospel by naming the gospel's interpreted occurrences within the temporal time frame of the preacher's own experience. Apologetic *ēthos* appeals are the preacher's personal testimony to God's redemptive activity in the world as the preacher has been privileged to see it or experience it.

In this sense, then, apologetic *ēthos* can usefully be labelled "temporal instantiation." An instantiation is a making concrete of what is abstract. In order for preaching to transcend the level of abstract talk about theological doctrines, or abstract talk of events from long ago, the preacher concretizes for the hearers, usually in narrative form, the way in which the gospel is both real and present.

It is important to remember in this regard that every redemptive event of God which is related in scripture, and which later became the source of dogmatic abstraction in the church's theological reflection, began as a concrete apocalyptic occurrence. The message of the cross itself is a concrete description of God's redemptive work at a specific point in time through specific people at a specific place. The apocalyptic character of the cross means, however, that the event is not confined to its original historical contingencies. God chooses to make the cross-event's concrete salvific benefits effective wherever and whenever the word of the cross is proclaimed anew. In this sense, the cross-event is not held hostage within any time-frame, but by God's grace becomes a new and efficacious act of God's salvific action in each new event of proclamation.

When preachers use *ēthos* appeals in the mode of "temporal instantiation," they relate concrete incidents as experienced events that they interpret as God's contemporaneous acts of redemption. This temporal instantiation is a fragile personal witness by the preacher that can function as a sign of God's work in the world. The fragility of the sign is such that faith can receive the life of the gospel in the narrated testimony, but unbelief may receive only death (2 Cor. 2:15-16).

Of course, just as the cross-event in its first manifestation was an event which was not accepted by all as a visible manifestation of God's working, but rather as merely the death of a revolutionary, so later manifestations of God's work can be dismissed. Simply saying that an event is redemptive does not make it so for hearers. Just as God's original act in Christ was often rejected as authentic, it still can be. When preachers name God's action in Christ anew in their own experiences, such naming can be rejected as well. The ever possible rejection of the preacher's witness accentuates the fragile and temporal character of such witness.

Ultimately, the goal in using *ēthos* appeals in preaching is to serve the *kata stauron* orientation that the gospel in its proclamation effects. Additionally, such uses must be of such a character that they do not perpetuate *kata sarka* orientations, unless those appeals are subverted and deconstructed by the preacher, as we saw in Paul. *Kata sarka* uses of *ēthos* appeals serve the preacher, the preacher's political agenda, the preacher's financial ends, the preacher's need for fame or affirmation, or some other selfish end. They serve self-promotion rather than Christ. *Kata stauron* uses of *ēthos* appeals serve Christ and God's continuing mysterious and redemptive activity in the world by showing concretely the ways in which God is still active today. The use of an apologetic *ēthos* appeal in a *kata stauron* orientation is an instance wherein one brokers one's personal experiences in view of how one might best be a steward of the mysterious ways in which God continues to break into the world redemptively.

Returning to the Steimle sermon, "Talk Is Not Always Cheap," one might argue that Steimle's use of his previous university chapel experience in this sermon was *kata sarka*. Its rhetorical function in the sermon established Steimle's wisdom and adeptness in deflecting the student's startling interruption. Such a critique may be feasible, but the real function of the story in the sermon itself was to illustrate that the gospel of God does not depend on the preacher. Steimle admits that he may indeed be a false prophet. Moreover, the conclusion to "Talk Is Not Always Cheap" consists of a prayer which is striking in its self-indictment of incompetence:

I spoke, Lord, and I am furious. I am furious because I worked so hard with gestures and with words. I threw my whole self into them and I'm afraid the essential didn't get across. For the essential is not mine, and words are too shallow to hold it. I spoke, Lord, and I am worried. I am afraid of speaking for speaking is serious. It's serious to disturb others, to bring them out, to keep them on their doorsteps. It's serious to keep them waiting with outstretched hands and longing hearts, seeking for light or some courage to live and act. Suppose, Lord, that I should send them away empty handed. Forgive me, Lord, for having spoken so badly. Forgive me for having spoken often to no purpose. Forgive me for the days when I have tarnished my lips with hollow words, false words, cowardly words, words through which you could not pass. Uphold me when I must speak in a meeting, intervene in a discussion, talk with a brother.

Grant above all, Lord, that my words may be like the sowing of seeds, that those who hear them may look to a fine harvest. Through Christ, our Lord, Amen.[49]

This prayer has a jarring effect on the listener. The sermon seemed to be complete, and well-spoken. It takes the hearers off guard as they are forced to overhear Steimle from his private prayer closet of confession. But when the hearers get over their initial shock, they realize that the prayer is actually an extension of the very message Steimle has been preaching. "Talk Is Not Always Cheap," but in Steimle's prayer of confession he is afraid that this sermon and, upon greater reflection, much of his preaching is precisely that: cheap, hollow, a failure. It is a self-humbling prayer. It is a prayer in which he admits his limitations, and, in so doing, the rhetorical effect is to cause the hearers to realize that it is indeed God who makes the babblings of preachers efficacious for God's redemptive ends.

One could still argue that Steimle perhaps crosses a line of protocol when he says, "Forgive me for having spoken so badly." That statement could easily be taken as an admission of rhetorical failure, when, in fact, Steimle is a clear master of articulation, having just proved it again in this sermon. I can imagine some hearers being moved to try to assure him that he did really speak well and shouldn't be so hard on himself. Others may think that his foray into self-deprecation here is actually a selfish ploy for affirmation from his hearers: "Please tell me I'm a good speaker, because I don't feel good about myself." In the context of the sermon I do not think that is Steimle's rhetorical intent by this confession. It is, however, ambiguous enough to be misunderstood.

Another good example of an apologetic *ēthos* appeal is in Thomas G. Long's sermon, "Just in Case." Long tackles the difficult text of 2 Samuel 6, where Uzzah is struck dead by God for reaching out and steadying the ark of the covenant as it was being carried into Jerusalem. After wrestling hard with the text and our sensitivities to it, Long suggests that the text may actually speak a word to us that we have missed. That word is a word of judgment against us when we reveal by our reflexive actions more of what is really going on inside of us than we would if we had time to gather our thoughts in a more orthodox manner. Uzzah becomes a paradigm of this

---

49. Steimle, *Talk Is Not Always Cheap.* Incidently, this prayer is one lifted verbatim and without citation from Michel Quoist, *Prayers*, trans. Agnes M. Forsyth and Anne Marie de Comaille (New York: Sheed and Ward, 1963), 69-71, a matter which raises other ethical questions about its use by the preacher.

kind of reflexive action which reveals what we really think, in spite of our confession. Uzzah revealed that he did not think that God could really make it into Jerusalem on his own; that he needed "a guy like Uzzah" to help him dodder down the road.

Long then relates stories which concretize for the hearer what this might look like in our world. In the process of these stories he bears personal witness by means of temporal instantiation. He tells of his summer internship at a church during his seminary schooling. He was assigned by the senior minister to care pastorally for several families in the church. One family seemed, as he describes, to have had a circle of light surrounding everyone in the family except for the youngest child who had cerebral palsy. This child always seemed excluded, off to the side. One day when Long was visiting the home, the mother told him of a recent incident. She was sitting in the living room reading or knitting. The youngest child was down the hall in the shadows, standing against the wall and staring at her. There was a shift of light in the room, and she looked down the hall and saw Jesus standing beside her son. He had his arms around him. She looked away and then back and the boy stood alone again. She told Long that for the first time she began to see her son as loved and healed in the power of God.

Long admits that he did not know what to make of the experience. But he does know what each of them, Long himself and the mother, did with it. She turned it into ethics and mission and established programs of education and care in her area for those who were afflicted like her son. Long admits, though, that he did something quite different. Having just completed a course in Clinical Pastoral Education, Long brought a predominately psychological frame of reference as hermeneutical guide in interpreting the woman's story. He thought to himself, "Guilt is being projected. Wish fulfillment is happening." Long continues:

> What I did was, I took an experience she needed theological language to describe [and] I reduced it to psychological language that I could manipulate around the chessboard of my own mentality because her experience caused the ark of my theology to totter and I, like Uzzah, reached out and steadied it, just in case.[50]

The event was both judging and redeeming for Long. Long was judged for reducing the woman's experience to psychological categories

---

50. Thomas G. Long, *Just in Case*, Denver Theological Seminary, cassette recording, January, 1990.

and for dismissing the theological import of her experience. But Long's telling of the story shows that he learned from the incident, and more, that he was reframed himself by the redemptive character of the woman's actions in her family and community. His telling of the incident in the sermon, though partly the telling of his own failure, witnesses to the gospel that the woman experienced, but also to the gospel that Long himself was given through it. Such reorientation through judgment and redemption is the work of the gospel. Long is able to communicate both through his telling of the story, while supporting the larger purposes of the sermon, namely to show how we often reveal our true convictions about reality by our spontaneous reflexive actions in certain situations.

Apologetic *ēthos* appeals, from a rhetorical frame of reference, are pragmatic efforts directed by humans to humans with the goal of persuasion. To function persuasively, such appeals must assume a commonly shared base of epistemic values between speaker and hearers. In order to safeguard their use in Christian proclamation from misuse either by intent or ignorance, one must first subject them to the core epistemic values of Christian community, namely those which proceed from the cross-event-proclaimed. Otherwise, the value-laden side of the pragmatic aspect of ministry may exert its own ideological force surreptitiously. Since rhetoric, and thus *ēthos* appeals, are not value-neutral, the test of the gospel message in their use is essential.

## Conclusion

Preaching can be analyzed according to two logically diverse frames of reference, rhetoric and theology. The primary difference in these frames of reference can be seen in how each treats the role of "God." Lack of differentiation between frames of rationality has resulted in a confusion over key concepts within each frame, i.e., efficacy and persuasion. Each of these concepts is descriptive within its own frame of reference, but becomes confusing and problematic when imported into the other frame: for example, when it is said that efficacy is "nothing but" persuasion. Such confusion has caused the theologically minded to attempt an embargo of rhetorical means of analysis in preaching, thereby dropping from homiletic discourses any talk of preacher-*ēthos*.

Paul helps us to avoid this either/or impasse by marking a path for using rhetoric with theological discretion. Paul's *ēthos* is guided primarily

175

by his *logos* of the cross rather than by hearer-driven phenomena. Such a move to the message of preaching first entails Paul's reframing of his own self by means of the apocalyptic word of the cross. It also involves his re-orienting the hearers' expectations for preacher credibility by that same apocalyptic word. Efficacy is thus dislodged from standard *ēthos* appeals and reassigned to the God of the gospel. What is annulled or put to death on the cross is not rhetoric as such but its *kata sarka* enslavement.

Reverse-*ēthos*, then, is a theologically-informed rhetorical category which describes the preacher's person in the rhetorical situation of Christian proclamation. It is designated "reverse" or "ironic" *ēthos* to differentiate it from an Aristotelian notion of *ēthos* which derives its meaning and function primarily from paying attention to audience expectations as to what makes a speaker credible.

This insistence on the lead role of preaching's *logos* heightens the need for clarity with regard to the content of the proclaimed *kērygma* or Christian message. The silence within the homiletical literature regarding preaching's message is striking. Moreover, this absence leads to weak theological guidance for *ēthos* appeals in the homiletical literature. In spite of the silence (or even confusion) in the homiletical literature as to preaching's message, I reaffirm the apocalyptic message of the cross as the core of the proclaimed *kērygma*. This is a controversial claim today, since some claim that this word heightens the oppression of already oppressed people. This misunderstanding, which reacts to the admitted misuse of the message of Christ's cross, cannot allow us to abandon the gospel that the New Testament and Christian witness through history clearly articulate as normative. To abandon the message of the cross because of unscrupulous or ignorant misuse of it is to magnify and extend these abusers' abuse, thereby allowing them to wrest the gospel from us. Rather than offering up our traditional message as a sacrifice in order to "speak to our time," what needs to be sacrificed are masochistic manifestations of a misinterpreted and mishandled cross.

The apocalyptic message of the cross makes claims on the "real" *ēthos* of the preacher, the person who is ultimately known only to God. The message also makes claims on the "perceived" *ēthos* of the preacher, that image that is projected by the preacher and interpreted and constructed by the hearers. The "real" person of the preacher is called to a life of discipleship, just as all disciples are called. This call may entail following a path which renders contemporary marks of Christ's stigmata, marks which attend to faithful following. The "real" person of the preacher is called through the apocalyptic message of the cross to shun temptations from the culture to sell out to its "bronze triumphalism." Shunning a cosmetic Christian persona which effectively rubber-stamps society's own denial of death, the preacher as disciple embraces Christ's call to embody the cruciform message as a means, not of self-glorification or advancement, and not of supplying needed validation for the gospel, but as a means of bearing witness in the flesh to Christ's efficacious and redemptive suffering.

The "perceived" *ēthos* of the preacher refers to that set of "character masks" which the preacher projects through word and deed and which hearers construct as their image of who the preacher is. The preacher concedes the role of "perceived" *ēthos* from a rhetorical point of view, but in the awareness at the juncture of the ages, does not give in to rhetoric's potential to reduce preaching to a set of predictable and manipulable processes. Rather, the preacher's role here is to appreciate rhetoric's insight into the power of "perceived" *ēthos* in the rhetorical situation of Christian proclamation and bring to bear on it the theological discrimination that the cross-event-proclaimed affords. Such discretion will entail the continuing orientation and reorientation of both the preacher and hearers alike to the fundamental epistemic values of the faith community as these are shaped by the apocalyptic message of the cross.

This theologically shaped understanding of rhetorical *ēthos* appeals has direct impact on the use of self-portrayal in sermons. While some have claimed that the preacher should never use the self in preaching, such a claim fails to recognize that one cannot fail to project *ēthos* in preaching. The issue is not "whether" such appeals ought to be used, but "how" and with what kind of theological discretion.

There are two concrete ways for projecting preacher *ēthos* verbally in sermons: polemical *ēthos* and apologetic *ēthos*. Both are to be understood within the purview of the gospel itself, i.e., within the context of critical dogmatic testing, with the gospel message serving as the primary criterion of the preacher's use of self-portrayal.

Polemical *ēthos* is the defensive use of self-portrayal in situations where one's person is under attack. Its purpose is to remove the current stumbling block of the preacher's person in order to reposition the hearers to hear again the true scandal of the message of the gospel. Polemical *ēthos* appeals can be carried out *kata sarka* by responding with a defense which uses the attacker's own non-gospel-shaped criteria of evaluation. Paul called this use "foolishness," yet dabbled in it anyway in defense of himself. He never conceded, however, to its validity in view of the cross of Christ, and would eventually deconstruct its use in view of the cross. The *kata stauron* orientation which the gospel gives enabled Paul to see the foolishness and shortsightedness of arguing in *kata sarka* ways.

It is conceivable that Paul's reverse-*ēthos* strategy for bearing witness to the gospel, one which he employed *kata stauron*, could be taken up by some as a *kata sarka* strategy for self-advancement. The "professional sufferer" can prey on the faith community's own *kata stauron* epistemic values in an attempt to use them for personal advantage. Such abuses are judged, of course, by the message itself, and though such (mis)uses may often be hard to judge at our current historical placement — "at the juncture of the ages" — Paul is confident that God will know what to do with such people.

Apologetic *ēthos* appeals are instances of self-portrayal in the service of witness-bearing to the gospel as it has been personally experienced by the preacher. An apologetic *ēthos* appeal is a temporal instantiation of the gospel in the sense that the abstract or historically distant claims of the gospel are given concrete, contemporary, and personal expression through the preacher's narrated lived experience.

As with polemical *ēthos* appeals, those of the apologetic variety can be carried out *kata sarka*. When they are, they function to elevate the human preacher and provide for his or her own ends. The preacher must subject all potential narrated personal testimony to the test of the gospel: does this instance of personal witness serve the greater purpose of God's redemptive work in Christ? Because the telling of stories which relate the preacher as hero run the risk of self-promotion, these should be avoided most of the time. Only when they can be told in such a way that God is held up as the power and provider of the preacher's success should they be considered. In the main, most instances of apologetic *ēthos* portray the preacher's own failure. They may point out the way the preacher's experience of the word-revealed-anew judged his or her preconceptions and "natural" reactions to the situation at hand. The telling of such failure within the context of the sermon functions, however, to witness to the reclamation of the preacher's own experience and perception of reality.

With the cross-event-proclaimed as the governing dogmatic test of every pragmatic principle of ministry, the preacher who uses *ēthos* appeals must be alert to the fact that the hearers' judgments of credible preacher character may conflict with those that the gospel demands, since their criteria may be culturally shaped in *kata sarka* ways. The preacher must be willing to name idolatrous conceptions of credible character that the hearers may have uncritically imported from the other social realms of which they are a part. In place of these, the preacher orients or reorients the hearers to the epistemic values that they share together in the cross of Christ, and in the community this word creates and sustains, namely, the church. This orientation gives preachers and hearers alike the substantive point of commonality they need to evaluate everything else amid the exigencies of preaching.

Remembering Paul's fundamental images for preacher, "servant of Christ" and "steward of God's mysteries," preachers will govern their use of self-portrayal in the pulpit based upon how such pulpit autobiography functions to serve Christ and to signpost faithfully God's mysteries. Fundamentally, to serve Christ means to render the epistemologically reorienting word of the cross known and intelligible to people in the true circumstances of their lives. Through the medium of personal witness, the preacher appeals to concrete moments in his or her life regarding the ways in which the gospel has been personally experienced as judging and redeeming, as disorienting and reorienting.

Thulin spoke of this aspect of witness in his discussion of the biblical text in relation to self-portrayal: "It is not [preachers'] experiences per se that I have encouraged them to share. It is their experiences of the good news."[51] As the preacher relates the apocalypse of the gospel in his or her own experience, the hearer may "see what the gospel looks like" in the present day precisely through the experience of the preacher. By using personal story as witness to God's redemptive activity through the cross in today's world, the preacher embodies the claim that God is still active in the world. Safeguards on the potential abuse of personal story through self-glorification are provided by the message itself. The gospel judges preachers when they take credit for any act of heroics. Preacher success is not the gospel. In fact, viewed from the perspective of the cross-event-proclaimed, most personal stories ought to point out the frailty and failure of the preacher even in the face of an action of God which turned the event around redemptively.

The gospel makes its claims on the preacher and congregation alike, leaving both with a decision to accept or reject those claims. For preachers, then, it boils down to whether or not they will be obedient in accepting their God-given role in preaching (the witness to the gospel as Christ's servant and God's steward), rather than turning preaching into an opportu-

---

51. Thulin, *The "I" of the Sermon*, 41.

nity for their own personal goals (power, fame, wealth, etc.). For the congregation which is oriented by the epistemic values of the cross-event-proclaimed, it is a matter of whether they are willing to be shaped by the apocalyptic orientation afforded by the cross. This orientation creates the kind of community discernment which enables the church to discern fraudulent uses of appeals in the pulpit, as well as fraudulent means of judging preacher. Moreover, this ongoing orientation provided by the gospel creates a commonality of epistemic value in Christian community which encourages authentic forms of instantiating the gospel in both word and deed by preacher and congregation alike. Such communal mutuality in the speaking, hearing, and living of the gospel creates the kind of witnessing community which itself becomes, by God's grace, an instrument of service for Christ and stewardship of God's ineffable mysteries.

# Conclusion

This study began with Richard Lischer's words: "The book on the preacher's holiness . . . has not been written."[1] Perhaps it is clearer now why that is so. For the topic of the "preacher's holiness" is problematic for either frame of rationality that pertains to preaching's analysis — theology or rhetoric — given each frame's assumptions and operating procedures.

The theological frame of reference recoils at the thought of "preacher holiness" for fear that it will obscure the claim that it is God alone who makes preaching efficacious. Because the theological frame of reference asserts that the gospel of Jesus Christ is God's word which God alone makes effective for salvation, any talk of human preachers causing the preached word to be more "effective" because of their "holiness" of character is idolatrous. The rhetorical frame of reference looks at "preacher holiness" from the hearer's perspective and deals pragmatically with the "perceived" preacher's effects on hearers with regard to persuasion. Because rhetoric brackets God out of its way of perceiving rhetorical situations, it cannot take into account "holiness" as a God-given or God-enacted character of being in a person. (I doubt that what Lischer laments is the lack of a pragmatics of preacher holiness in the preaching literature!) Moreover, an astounding lack of differentiation between the theological and rhetorical frames of reference in preaching's analysis has plagued homiletics so that issues of efficacy and persuasion typically have been

1. Richard Lischer, *Theories of Preaching: Selected Readings in the Homiletical Tradition* (Durham, NC: The Labyrinth Press, 1987), 3.

181

blended together, thus creating a virtual stalemate on the topic from both frames of reference.

In the history of homiletical theory on this topic I noted a clear divide, still to the present day, between theorists who are either predominately theological in their approach to the preacher's person or predominately rhetorical. As an arbitrator in the dispute, I retrieved the Apostle Paul's *ēthos* argument from 1 Cor. 1–4. For although Paul makes extensive use of classical rhetoric in his writing and preaching, his use of rhetoric (including his use of *ēthos* appeals) is tempered by his *logos* of the cross and not by the culturally conditioned prejudices of his hearers. Paul's *ēthos* appeals are thus ironic, or "reverse," in that they conflict with culturally prized standards for speaker credibility, but line up faithfully as signposts of Paul's message of Christ crucified.

Several implications for contemporary homiletical theory emerge. (1) Homiletical theory can be clarified (both in general and specifically on the topic of the preacher's person) by a more deliberate methodology which differentiates between the logically diverse frames of rationality — rhetoric and theology — that can be brought to bear on preaching's analysis. Because each frame of reference operates from radically different assumptions about "God," each deals with the nature of preaching, the goal of preaching, the nature of the hearer, and the role of the preacher quite differently. Moreover, each frame has key concepts indigenous to that frame's fundamental logic (i.e., for theology, "efficacy"; for rhetoric, "persuasion") that cannot be imported to the other frame of reference without ensuing significant confusion. "Persuasion" issues, from a rhetorical standpoint, force preachers to reevaluate the nature of their "implied" or "perceived" *ēthos* appeals, since they are making them whether they wish to or not. The preacher asks: What do the people see and perceive me to be? How does this perception relate to my responsibilities to serve Christ and be a steward of God's mysteries? How does this perception relate to who we are to be together as God's cruciform community of faith? "Efficacy" issues, from a theological perspective, remind the preacher that in spite of all that hearers may perceive, preaching the gospel is a situation that is ultimately in God's control. Salvation is something that only God can effect. Thus, speaking precisely, it is conceivable that a hearer may be persuaded by the preacher, yet remain unsaved; or, conversely, be unpersuaded by the preacher, yet be saved by the reconciling word of the gospel.

Since the preacher's message is the gospel and not just any message, preachers must be discriminating in their use of rhetoric. For the message sets the agenda for the preacher in the Christian rhetorical situation rather than the hearer. Contrary to the thinking of some, though, the cross of Christ annuls not rhetoric as such, but its *kata sarka* ("according to the flesh") enslavement. Without the insight that comes *kata stauron* ("according to the cross"), rhetoric cannot be used faithfully, i.e., in a way that accords with the message of preaching. Reverse-*ēthos*, then, is a theologically-informed rhetorical category which describes the nature and function of the preacher's person in the rhetorical situation of Christian proclamation. It is designated "reverse" or "ironic" to differentiate it from an Aristotelian notion of *ēthos* which derives its meaning and function primarily from paying attention to audience expectation for how a speaker is to be deemed credible. Reverse-*ēthos* highlights the turn first to the message of Christian proclamation and considers the demands that it exacts on the use of rhetoric.

(2) A second implication of this study for homiletics concerns the need for homileticians to be clearer about what preaching's message is. Clarity on this most important of matters for preaching is lacking in the homiletical literature, as is substantive discussion of the significance of preaching's message for all matters under consideration in the rhetorical situation of Christian proclamation. My claim that the theology of the cross undergirds our understanding of the gospel has significant implications for how one conceives the relationship of the preacher to preaching. For, understood this way, the message of preaching makes claims on both the "real" preacher as a person who stands before God's judgment, and on the "perceived" preacher as a person who stands before human judgment.

The "real" preacher, operating from a reverse-*ēthos* perspective, will stand over against a triumphalistic theology of glory which manifests itself in the present day through culturally deceived churches with numbers-driven, success-enamored criteria for judging the church's "effective" presence, and along with it the preacher's "effective" ministry. The "perceived" preacher is that hearer-construct that the preacher helps hearers build through the use of self in sermons. Though some have argued against the use of self-disclosure in preaching, this fails to take into account the fact that the preacher cannot hide in the pulpit. Even if one never references oneself in one's sermons, hearers construct *ēthos* construals of the preacher. Moreover, two kinds of pulpit autobiography, polemical and apologetic, can function in the preacher's task to serve Christ and be a steward of God's mysteries.

Polemical *ēthos* appeals are used for self-defense against antagonists. They attempt to remove the wrong stumbling block for hearers, in this case the preacher's person. Apologetic *ēthos* appeals are the preacher's personal testimony to God's redemptive activity in the world as the preacher has been privileged to see it or experience it. As acts of Christian witness, they can be usefully labelled "temporal instantiations" of the gospel. They concretize for the hearers instances of God's ongoing "gospel activity" in the world in which the hearers themselves live. Such testimony bears witness to a world wherein God continues redemptively to extend the gospel.

The critical dogmatic test for all uses of self-disclosure in preaching is the message of the gospel itself. For ultimately, the goal in using *ēthos* appeals in preaching is to serve the *kata stauron* orientation that the gospel in its proclamation effects. *Kata sarka* uses of *ēthos* selfishly serve the preacher; *kata stauron* uses of *ēthos* serve Christ and God's continuing mysterious and redemptive activity in the world by showing concretely the ways in which God is still active.

By the grace of God, the gospel creates a community of disciples, who exist partly to signpost faithfully God's ongoing redemptive work in Christ. Key to the disciples' faithfulness is their orientation and continuing reorientation to the epistemic values of the apocalyptic word of the cross. As a community oriented by the gospel, the church and its preachers bear witness to God's redemptive gospel with both words and actions. The world listens and watches. It constructs its own perception of who this people and its spokepersons are. It uses its own, often mixed, criteria for doing so. The church and its preachers care about this construct which the world imposes — sometimes well and sometimes poorly — as it should. The church is not, however, determined by the world's judgments, nor is it infallibly guided by the world's criteria of judgment. The decisions the church makes about how it will be perceived, and the measures and means it takes to shape the judgment of its observers are critical. And the questions press hardest, perhaps, upon the preacher, and demand a clear response: By what criteria will you be judged credible? By what criteria will you be judged "effective"? By what criteria will you be judged faithful?

Ronald Osborn is right: "No clear consensus prevails in America as to what a minister is or ought to be. The question lies deeper than frustration over priorities: It arises from perplexity as to essential identity." The constant temptation that confronts the minister is that of molding his or her identity to the wished-for shape in the popular culture. The church often becomes deceived by success-standards which are generated apart from the faith community's core epistemic values. The theological school, too, sometimes follows suit, formatting programs of ministerial development according to the rise of the cultural tide rather than based on the epistemic values which flow from the message of the gospel. Osborn's articulation of the disease is astute:

> Our crisis in ministry is conceptual, arising from our lack of a common understanding as to "goals, norms, and values." How can you and I agree to my effectiveness in ministry when we measure it by different standards based on different conceptions of what a minister is?[2]

The cross-event-proclaimed is the church's ongoing epistemological reorientation of value. Out of that center, the goals and norms for the community and its presence in the world radiate. By these standards a community of discernment is formed and grows, a community which judges its called and designated proclaimers in their service to this message, to this Christ, and ultimately as stewards who must give account to God. This orientation guides the preacher's use of self in bearing witness to the reconciling work of God in Christ — that work which alone holds hope for the redemption of all God's creation.

---

2. Ronald E. Osborn, *Creative Disarray: Models of Ministry in a Changing America* (St. Louis: Chalice Press, 1991), 5.

# Bibliography

Aristotle. *On Rhetoric.* Translated by George A. Kennedy. New York: Oxford University Press, 1991.

Arnold, William E. "Ethos — A View." *Pennsylvania Speech Review* 22 (1966).

Audi, Robert. "Responsible Action and Virtuous Character." *Ethics* 101 (1991).

Augustine. *On Christian Doctrine.* New York: Macmillan Publishers, 1958.

Aycock, Don M. *Preaching with Purpose and Power: Selected E. Y. Mullins Lectures on Preaching.* Macon, GA: Mercer University Press, 1982.

Bailey, Raymond. *Paul the Preacher.* Nashville: Broadman Publishing Company, 1991.

Barilli, Renato. *Rhetoric.* Translated by Giuliana Menozzi. Theory and History of Literature, vol. 63. Minneapolis: University of Minnesota Press, 1989.

Barr, James. *The Semantics of Biblical Language.* New York: Oxford University Press, 1961.

Barrett, C. K. *The First Epistle to the Corinthians.* New York: Harper and Row, 1967.

Barth, Karl. *Church Dogmatics.* Vol. I, Part I. Edinburgh: T. & T. Clark, 1936.

———. *Homiletics.* Translated by Geoffrey W. Bromiley and Donald E. Daniels. Louisville: Westminster/John Knox Press, 1991.

———. *The Preaching of the Gospel.* Translated by B. E. Hooke. Philadelphia: The Westminster Press, 1963.

Bassler, Jouette M., ed. *Pauline Theology I: Thessalonians, Philippians, Galatians, and Philemon.* Minneapolis: Fortress Press, 1991.

Baumann, Daniel J. *An Introduction to Contemporary Preaching.* Grand Rapids: Baker Book House, 1972, 1988.

Baxter, Batsall Barrett. *The Heart of the Yale Lectures.* New York: Macmillan Publishers, 1947.

Beardslee, William A., John B. Cobb, Jr., David J. Lull, Russell Pregeant, Theodore J. Weeden, Jr., and Barry A. Woodbridge. *Biblical Preaching on the Death of Jesus.* Nashville: Abingdon Press, 1989.

Beaudean, John William, Jr. *Paul's Theology of Preaching.* National Association of Baptist Professors of Religion Dissertation Series, No. 6. Macon, GA: Mercer University Press, 1988.

Beker, J. Christiaan. *Paul the Apostle.* Philadelphia: Fortress Press, 1980.

Betz, Hans Dieter. "The Problem of Rhetoric and Theology according to the Apostle Paul." In *L'Apôtre Paul: personnalité, style et conception du ministère.* Edited by A. VanHoye. Leuven: Leuven University Press, 1986.

Bjerkelund, C. J. *Parakaleō: Form, Funktion, und Sinn der parakalō Sätze in den paulinischen Briefen.* Bibliotheca theologica Norvegica 1. Oslo: Universitetsforlaget, 1967.

Bondi, Richard. "The Elements of Character." *The Journal of Religious Ethics* 12 (1984).

Bondi, Roberta. *Memories of God: Theological Reflections on a Life.* Nashville: Abingdon, 1995.

Booth, Wayne C. *The Rhetoric of Fiction.* Chicago: University of Chicago Press, 1961.

Bornkamm, Günther. *Paul.* New York: Harper and Row, 1969.

Brinton, Alan. "Ethotic Argument." *History of Philosophy Quarterly* 3 (1986).

———. "Quintilian, Plato, and the *Vir Bonus.*" *Philosophy and Rhetoric* 16 (1983).

Brooks, Phillips. *Lectures on Preaching. 1877.* New York: E. P. Dutton & Company, 1898.

Brown, Alexandra R. *The Cross and Human Transformation: Paul's Apocalyptic Word in 1 Corinthians.* Minneapolis: Fortress Press, 1995.

Brown, Peter. *Augustine of Hippo.* Berkeley: University of California Press, 1967.

Brueggemann, Walter. *Israel's Praise: Doxology Against Ideology.* Philadelphia: Fortress Press, 1988.

Bultmann, Rudolf. *Der Stil der paulinischen Predigt und die kynisch-stoische Diatribe.* Göttingen: Vandenhoeck & Ruprecht, 1910. Reprinted, 1984.

———. *Theology of the New Testament.* 2 vols. Translated by Kendrick Grobel. New York: Charles Scribner's Sons, 1954.

Buttrick, David. *Homiletic: Moves and Structures.* Philadelphia: Fortress Press, 1987.

Cameron, Averil. *Christianity and the Rhetoric of Empire: The Development of Christian Discourse.* Sather Classical Lectures. Vol. 55. Berkeley: University of California Press, 1991.

Chopp, Rebecca. "Practical Order and Liberation." In *Formation and Reflec-*

tion: *The Promise of Practical Theology.* Edited by Louis S. Mudge and James N. Poling. Philadelphia: Fortress Press, 1987.

Cicero. *De Oratore.* Translated by H. Rackham and E. W. Sutton. The Loeb Classical Library. Cambridge: Harvard University Press, 1992.

Clark, Donald Lemen. *Rhetoric in Greco-Roman Education.* New York: Columbia University Press, 1957.

Connors, Robert J., Lisa S. Ede, and Andrea A. Lunsford, eds. *Essays on Classical Rhetoric and Modern Discourse.* Carbondale, IL: Southern Illinois University Press, 1984.

Conzelmann, Hans. *1 Corinthians.* Philadelphia: Fortress Press, 1975.

Corts, Thomas E. "The Derivation of Ethos." *Speech Monographs* 35 (1968).

Cousar, Charles. *A Theology of the Cross: The Death of Jesus in the Pauline Letters.* Minneapolis: Fortress Press, 1990.

Craddock, Fred B. *As One Without Authority.* Nashville: Abingdon, 1978.

———. *Preaching.* Nashville: Abingdon, 1985.

Crafton, Jeffrey A. *The Agency of the Apostle: A Dramatist Analysis of Paul's Responses to Conflict in 2 Corinthians.* Journal for the Study of the New Testament, Supplement Series 51. Sheffield, England: Sheffield Academic Press, 1991.

Cunningham, David S. *Faithful Persuasion: In Aid of a Rhetoric of Christian Theology.* Notre Dame: University of Notre Dame Press, 1990.

Dahl, Nils. "Paul and the Church at Corinth According to 1 Corinthians 1:10–4:21." In *Christian History and Interpretation: Studies Presented to John Knox.* Edited by W. R. Farmer, C. F. D. Moule, and R. R. Niebuhr. Cambridge: Cambridge University Press, 1967.

DiCicco, Mario. *Paul's Use of Ethos, Pathos, and Logos in 2 Corinthians 10–13.* Lewiston, NY: Mellen Biblical Press, 1995.

Doyle, G. W. "Augustine's Sermonic Method." *Westminster Theological Journal* 39 (1976-77).

Eagleton, Terry. *Ideology: An Introduction.* New York: Verso, 1991.

Egan, Gerard. *The Skilled Helper.* 6th ed. Pacific Grove, CA: Brooks/Cole Publishing Company, 1998.

Ellis, E. Earle. "Paul and His Opponents: Trends in Research." In *Christianity, Judaism, and Other Greco-Roman Cults: Studies for Morton Smith at Sixty.* Leiden: Brill, 1975.

———. *Prophecy and Hermeneutic in Early Christianity: New Testament Essays.* Grand Rapids: Eerdmans Publishing Company, 1978.

Ellspermann, Gerard L. "The Attitude of the Early Christian Latin Writers Toward Pagan Literature and Learning." *The Catholic University of America Patristic Studies* 82 (1949).

Eskridge, James Burnette. *The Influence of Cicero upon Augustine in the De-*

*velopment of His Oratorical Training for the Training of the Ecclesiastical Orator.* Menasha, WI: The Collegiate Press, George Banta Publishing, 1912.

Fant, Clyde E. *Preaching for Today.* New York: Harper and Row, Publishers, 1975.

Fee, Gordon. *The First Epistle to the Corinthians.* Grand Rapids: William B. Eerdmans Publishing Company, 1987.

Fiore, Benjamin. "'Covert Allusion' in 1 Corinthians 1–4." *Catholic Biblical Quarterly* 47 (1985).

Fitzgerald, John T. *Cracks in an Earthen Vessel: An Examination of the Catalogues of Hardships in the Corinthian Correspondence.* SBL dissertation series, #99. Atlanta: Scholars Press, 1988.

Forsyth, P. T. *The Principle of Authority.* Hodder and Stoughton, 1913.

Foss, Sonja K., Karen A. Foss, and Robert Trapp. *Contemporary Perspectives on Rhetoric.* 2nd ed. Prospect Heights, IL: Waveland Press, Inc., 1991.

Fowl, Stephen E., and L. Gregory Jones. *Reading in Communion: Scripture and Ethics in Christian Life.* Grand Rapids: William B. Eerdmans Publishing Company, 1991.

Friedrich, Gerhard. "*Kēryx.*" In *Theological Dictionary of the New Testament.* Edited by Gerhard Kittel. Translated by Geoffrey W. Bromiley. Vol. 3. Grand Rapids: William B. Eerdmans Publishing Company, 1965.

Funk, Robert W. *Language, Hermeneutic, and Word of God.* New York: Harper and Row, 1966.

Gadamer, Hans-Georg. *Truth and Method.* Edited by Garrett Barden and John Cummings. New York: Seabury Press, 1975.

Geest, Hans van der. *Presence in the Pulpit: The Impact of Personality in Preaching.* Atlanta: John Knox Press, 1981.

Georgi, Dieter. *The Opponents of Paul in 2 Corinthians.* Philadelphia: Fortress Press, 1986.

Gill, Christopher. "The Ethos/Pathos Distinction in Rhetorical and Literary Criticism." *Classical Quarterly* 34 (1984).

Grayston, Kenneth. "A Problem of Translation: The Meaning of *parakaleō, paraclēsis* in the New Testament." *Scripture Bulletin* 11 (1980).

Grimaldi, William M. A. *Aristotle, Rhetoric, A Commentary.* New York: Fordham University Press, 1988.

Gunther, John J. *St. Paul's Opponents and Their Background.* Leiden: Brill, 1973.

Hart, J. H. A. "Apollos." *Journal of Theological Studies* 7 (1906).

Hart, Trevor A. "The Word, the Words, and the Witness: Proclamation as Divine and Human Reality in the Theology of Karl Barth." *Tyndale Bulletin* 46 (1995).

Hart, Trevor A., and Daniel P. Thimell, editors. *Christ in Our Place*. Exeter: The Paternoster Press, 1989.

Harvill, Jerry. *Aristotle's Concept of Ethos as Ground for a Modern Ethics of Communication*. Ph.D. dissertation. The University of Kentucky, 1990.

Hauerwas, Stanley. *Christian Existence Today: Essays on Church, World, and Living in Between*. Durham, NC: The Labyrinth Press, 1988.

————. *Vision and Virtue: Essays in Christian Ethical Reflection*. Notre Dame: Fides Publishers, Inc., 1974.

Hay, David M., ed. *Pauline Theology II: 1 & 2 Corinthians*. Minneapolis: Fortress Press, 1993.

Hedahl, Susan K. "Character." In *Concise Encylopedia of Preaching*. Edited by William H. Willimon and Richard Lischer. Louisville: Westminster/John Knox Press, 1995.

Hengel, Martin. *Crucifixion in the Ancient World and the Folly of the Message of the Cross*. Philadelphia: Fortress Press, 1977.

Hulse, Errol, R. C. Sproul, and Lester De Koster. *The Preacher and Preaching: Reviving the Art in the Twentieth Century*. Phillipsburg, NJ: Presbyterian and Reformed Publishing Company, 1986.

Hunsinger, Deborah van Deusen. *Theology and Pastoral Counseling: A New Interdisciplinary Approach*. Grand Rapids: William B. Eerdmans Publishing Co., 1995.

Ijsseling, Samuel. *Rhetoric and Philosophy in Conflict: An Historical Survey*. The Hague, Netherlands: Martinus Nijhoff, 1976.

Impson, Maribeth. *The Concept of Ethos in Classical and Modern Rhetoric*. Ph.D. dissertation. University of Kentucky, 1988.

Iser, Wolfgang. *From Reader Response to Literary Anthropology*. Baltimore: Johns Hopkins University Press, 1989.

Isocrates. *Antidosis*. Translated by George Norlin. The Loeb Classical Library. 3 vols. New York: G. P. Putnam's Sons, 1928-45.

————. *Institutia Oratoria*. Translated by George Norlin. The Loeb Classical Library. 3 vols. New York: G. P. Putnam's Sons, 1928-45.

Jabusch, Willard F. *The Person in the Pulpit: Preaching as Caring*. Nashville: Abingdon, 1980.

Jasper, David. *Rhetoric, Power and Community*. Louisville: Westminster/John Knox Press, 1993.

Jerome. *Selected Letters of Jerome*. Translated by F. A. Wright. The Loeb Classical Library. London: William Heinemann, Ltd., 1933.

Judge, E. A. "Paul's Boasting in Relation to Contemporary Professional Practice." *Australian Biblical Review* 16 (1968).

Käsemann, Ernst. *Perspectives on Paul*. Philadelphia: Fortress Press, 1971.

Kay, James F. *Christus Praesens: A Reconsideration of Rudolf Bultmann's Chris-*

*tology.* Grand Rapids: William B. Eerdmans Publishing Company, 1994.

Kennedy, George A. *A New History of Classical Rhetoric.* Princeton: Princeton University Press, 1994.

————. *Classical Rhetoric and Its Christian and Secular Tradition from Ancient to Modern Times.* Chapel Hill, NC: The University of North Carolina Press, 1980.

————. *New Testament Interpretation Through Rhetorical Criticism.* Chapel Hill, NC: University of North Carolina Press, 1984.

Kennedy, Rodney. *The Creative Power of Metaphor: A Rhetorical Homiletic.* New York: University Press of America, 1993.

Kenneson, Philip D. "Selling [Out] the Church in the Marketplace of Desire." *Modern Theology* 9 (1993).

Kettler, Christian D., and Todd H. Speidell, eds. *Incarnational Ministries: The Presence of Christ in Church, Society, and Family.* Colorado Springs: Helmers and Howard, 1990.

Kierkegaard, Søren. *Attack Upon "Christendom": 1854-1855.* Boston: Beacon Press, 1944, 1956.

Killinger, John. *The Centrality of Preaching in the Total Task of Ministry.* Waco, TX: Word Books, 1969.

Klein, Ralph W. *Israel in Exile.* Philadelphia: Fortress Press, 1979.

Kraftchick, Stephen J. *Ethos and Pathos Appeals in Galatians Five and Six: A Rhetorical Analysis.* Ph.D. dissertation. Emory University, 1985.

Kuhn, Thomas S. *The Structure of Scientific Revolutions.* 2nd rev. ed. Chicago: University of Chicago Press, 1962, 1970.

Lebacqz, Karen. *Professional Ethics: Power and Paradox.* Nashville: Abingdon Press, 1985.

Ladany, N., C. E. Hill, M. M. Corbett, and E. A. Nutt. "Nature, Extent, and Importance of What Psychotherapy Trainees Do Not Disclose to their Supervisors." *Journal of Counseling Psychology.* 43: 10-24.

Lewis, Ralph L. *Speech for Persuasive Preaching.* Berne, IN: Economy Printing Company, 1968.

Lewis, Sinclair. *Elmer Gantry.* New York: Signet Press, 1967.

Lischer, Richard. "Before Technique: Preaching and Personal Formation." *Dialog* 29 (1990).

————. *Theories of Preaching: Selected Readings in the Homiletical Tradition.* Durham, NC: The Labyrinth Press, 1987.

Litfin, Duane. *St. Paul's Theology of Proclamation: 1 Corinthians 1–4 and Greco-Roman Rhetoric.* Cambridge: Cambridge University Press, 1994.

Loder, James E. "Normativity and Context in Practical Theology: The

Interdiscipinary Issue." Unpublished paper presented to the annual conference on practical theology. November, 1995.

———. "Theology and Psychology." In *Dictionary of Pastoral Care and Counseling.* Edited by Rodney J. Hunter. Nashville: Abingdon, 1990.

Long, Thomas G. *The Witness of Preaching.* Louisville: Westminster/John Knox Press, 1989.

Long, Thomas G., and Gail O'Day, eds. *Listening to the Word: Studies in Honor of Fred B. Craddock.* Nashville: Abingdon, 1993.

Lowrie, Walter. *A Short Life of Kierkegaard.* Princeton: Princeton University Press, 1942, 1970.

MacIntyre, Alasdair. *After Virtue: A Study in Moral Theory.* Notre Dame: University of Notre Dame Press, 1981.

———. *Whose Justice? Whose Rationality?* Notre Dame: University of Notre Dame Press, 1988.

Malherbe, Abraham. *Paul and the Popular Philosophers.* Minneapolis: Fortress Press, 1989.

Marrou, Henry I. *A History of Education in Antiquity.* Translated by George Lamb. New York: Sheed & Ward, 1956.

Marshall, Peter. *Enmity at Corinth: Social Conventions in Paul's Relations with the Corinthians.* Tübingen: J. C. B. Mohr, 1987.

Martin, Dale. *Slavery as Salvation: The Metaphor of Slavery in Pauline Christianity.* New Haven: Yale University Press, 1990.

Martyn, J. Louis. "Epistemology at the Turn of the Ages: 2 Corinthians 5:16." In *Christian History and Interpretation: Studies Presented to John Knox.* Edited by W. R. Farmer, C. F. D. Moule, and R. R. Niebuhr. Cambridge: Cambridge University Press, 1967.

Martz, Louis L., ed. *George Herbert and Henry Vaughan.* London: Oxford University Press, 1986.

Masterson, James F. "Portrait of a Narcissist." In *The Search for the Real Self: Unmasking the Personality Disorder of Our Age.* New York: Free Press, 1990.

May, James M. *Trials of Character: The Eloquence of Ciceronian Ethos.* Chapel Hill, NC: The University of North Carolina Press, 1988.

McClendon, James W. *Biography as Theology.* Philadelphia: Trinity Press International, 1974, 1990.

McGrath, Alister. "Cross, Theology of the." In *Dictionary of Paul and His Letters.* Edited by Gerald F. Hawthorne and Ralph P. Martin. Downers Grove, IL: InterVarsity Press, 1993.

Meyers, Robin R. *With Ears to Hear: Preaching as Self-Persuasion.* Cleveland: The Pilgrim Press, 1993.

Middleton, J. Richard, and Brian J. Walsh. *Truth Is Stranger Than It Used to Be:*

*Biblical Faith in a Postmodern Age.* Downers Grove, IL: InterVarsity Press, 1995.

Mitchell, Margaret M. *Paul and the Rhetoric of Reconciliation: An Exegetical Investigation of the Language and Composition of 1 Corinthians.* Louisville: Westminster/John Knox Press, 1991.

Muehl, William. "The Cult of the Publican." In *A Chorus of Witnesses: Model Sermons for Today's Preacher.* Edited by Thomas G. Long and Cornelius Plantinga, Jr. Grand Rapids: William B. Eerdmans Publishing Company, 1994.

Murphy, James J. *Rhetoric in the Middle Ages: A History of Rhetorical Theory from St. Augustine to the Renaissance.* Berkeley: The University of California Press, 1974.

Murphy-O'Connor, Jerome. *Paul on Preaching.* New York: Sheed & Ward, 1963.

Nelson, Paul. *Narrative and Morality: A Theological Inquiry.* University Park, PA: The Pennsylvania State University Press, 1987.

Norden, Eduard. *Die antika Kunstprosa vom VI. Jahrhundert v. Chr. bis in die Zeit der Renaissance.* 2 vols. 3rd reprint. Stuttgart: Teubner, 1915.

O'Brien, P. T. *Introductory Thanksgivings in the Letters of Paul.* Supplements to Novum Testamentum no. 49. Leiden: Brill, 1977.

Osborn, Ronald E. *Creative Disarray: Models of Ministry in a Changing America.* St. Louis: Chalice Press, 1991.

Osmer, Richard Robert. "Practical Theology as Argument, Rhetoric, and Conversation." *The Princeton Seminary Bulletin* 18 (1997).

Oster, Richard E. *1 Corinthians.* Joplin, MO: College Press Publishing Company, 1995.

Outka, Gene. "Character, Vision, and Narrative." *Religious Studies Review* 6 (1980).

Patte, Daniel. *Preaching Paul.* Philadelphia: Fortress Press, 1984.

Plank, Karl A. *Paul and the Irony of Affliction.* Atlanta: Scholars Press, 1987.

Plato. *Apology.* Translated by W. Heinemann. The Loeb Classical Library. Cambridge: Harvard University Press, 1917.

———. *Gorgias.* Translated by W. Heinemann. The Loeb Classical Library. Cambridge: Harvard University Press, 1917.

Pogoloff, Stephen M. *Logos and Sophia: The Rhetorical Situation of 1 Corinthians.* Atlanta: Scholars Press, 1992.

Press, Gerald A. "The Subject and Structure of Augustine's De Doctrina Christiana." *Augustinian Studies* 11 (1980).

Purvis, Sally. *The Power of the Cross: Foundations for a Christian Feminist Ethic of Community.* Nashville: Abingdon, 1993.

Quintilian. *Institutes of Oratory.* London: Bell, 1875-76.

Randolph, David J. *The Renewal of Preaching.* Philadelphia: Fortress Press, 1969.

Reicke, Bo. "A Synopsis of Early Christian Preaching." In *The Fruit of the Vine*. Edited by A. Friedrichsen. Westminster: Dacre Press, 1953.

Reumann, John. "*Oikonomia*-Terms in Paul in Comparison with Lucan *Heilsgeschichte*." *New Testament Studies* 13 (1966/67).

———. "'Servants of God' — Pre-Christian Religious Application of the *oikonomos* in Greek." *Journal of Biblical Literature* 77 (1958).

Ritschl, Dietrich. *A Theology of Proclamation*. Richmond, VA: John Knox Press, 1960.

Rudin, John Jesse, II. *The Concept of Ethos in Late American Preaching*. Ph.D. dissertation. Northwestern University, 1950.

Sampley, Paul. *Walking Between the Times: Paul's Moral Reasoning*. Philadelphia: Fortress Press, 1991.

Schubert, P. *Form and Function of the Pauline Thanksgivings*. Berlin: Töpelmann, 1939.

Schütz, John H. *Paul and the Anatomy of Apostolic Authority*. Cambridge: Cambridge University Press, 1975.

Schweiker, William, ed. *Worldviews and Warrants: Plurality and Authority in Theology*. Lanham, MD: University Press of America, 1987.

Sleeth, Ronald L. *God's Word and Our Words: Basic Homiletics*. Atlanta: John Knox Press, 1986.

———. *Persuasive Preaching*. New York: Harper & Brothers, Publishers, 1956.

———. "Theology and Communication Theories." *Religion in Life* 32 (1964).

Smith, Lacey Baldwin. *Fools, Martyrs, Traitors: The Story of Martyrdom in the Western World*. New York: Alfred A. Knopf, 1997.

Stuhlmacher, Peter. *Reconciliation, Law, and Righteousness: Essays in Biblical Theology*. Philadelphia: Fortress Press, 1986.

Thulin, Richard L. *The "I" of the Sermon: Autobiography in the Sermon*. Minneapolis: Fortress Press, 1989.

Titelman, Peter, ed. *The Therapist's Own Family: Toward the Differentiation of the Self*. Northvale, NJ: Jason Aronson, Inc., 1992, 1987.

Tracy, David. *Blessed Rage for Order*. San Francisco: Harper and Row, Publishers, 1988.

Ward, Richard. *Paul and the Politics of Performance*. Ph.D. dissertation. Northwestern University, 1987.

Webber, Robert E., and Rodney Clapp. *People of the Truth: The Power of the Worshipping Community in the Modern World*. San Francisco: Harper and Row, 1988.

Weiss, Johannes. *Beiträge zur paulinischen Rhetorik*. Göttingen: Vandenhoeck & Ruprecht, 1897.

Wellborn, L. L. "On the Discord in Corinth: 1 Corinthians 1–4 and Ancient Politics." *Journal of Biblical Literature* 106 (1987).

Wilder, Amos N. "Story and Story-World." *Interpretation* 37 (1983).

Williams, Delores S. *Sisters in the Wilderness: The Challenge of Womanist God-Talk.* Maryknoll, NY: Orbis Books, 1993.

Willimon, William H. *Peculiar Speech: Preaching to the Baptized.* Grand Rapids: William B. Eerdmans Publishing Company, 1992.

————. "The Spiritual Formation of the Pastor: Call and Community." *Quarterly Review* 3 (1983).

Willis, Wendell. "The Mind of Christ in 1 Corinthians 2.16." *Biblica* 70 (1989).

Winterowd, W. Ross. *Rhetoric: A Synthesis.* New York: Holt, Rinehart, and Winston, Inc., 1968.

Wisse, Jakob. *Ethos and Pathos: From Aristotle to Cicero.* Amsterdam: Adolf M. Hakkert Publisher, 1989.

Witherington, Ben, III. *Conflict and Community in Corinth: A Socio-Rhetorical Commentary on 1 and 2 Corinthians.* Grand Rapids: William B. Eerdmans Publishing Company, 1995.

Wood, Charles. *Vision and Discernment.* Chico, CA: Scholars Press, 1985.

# Index of Subjects

# Index of Names

# Index of Names

# Index of Scripture References

# Index of Foreign Words